Hillbilly™

VOLUME TWO

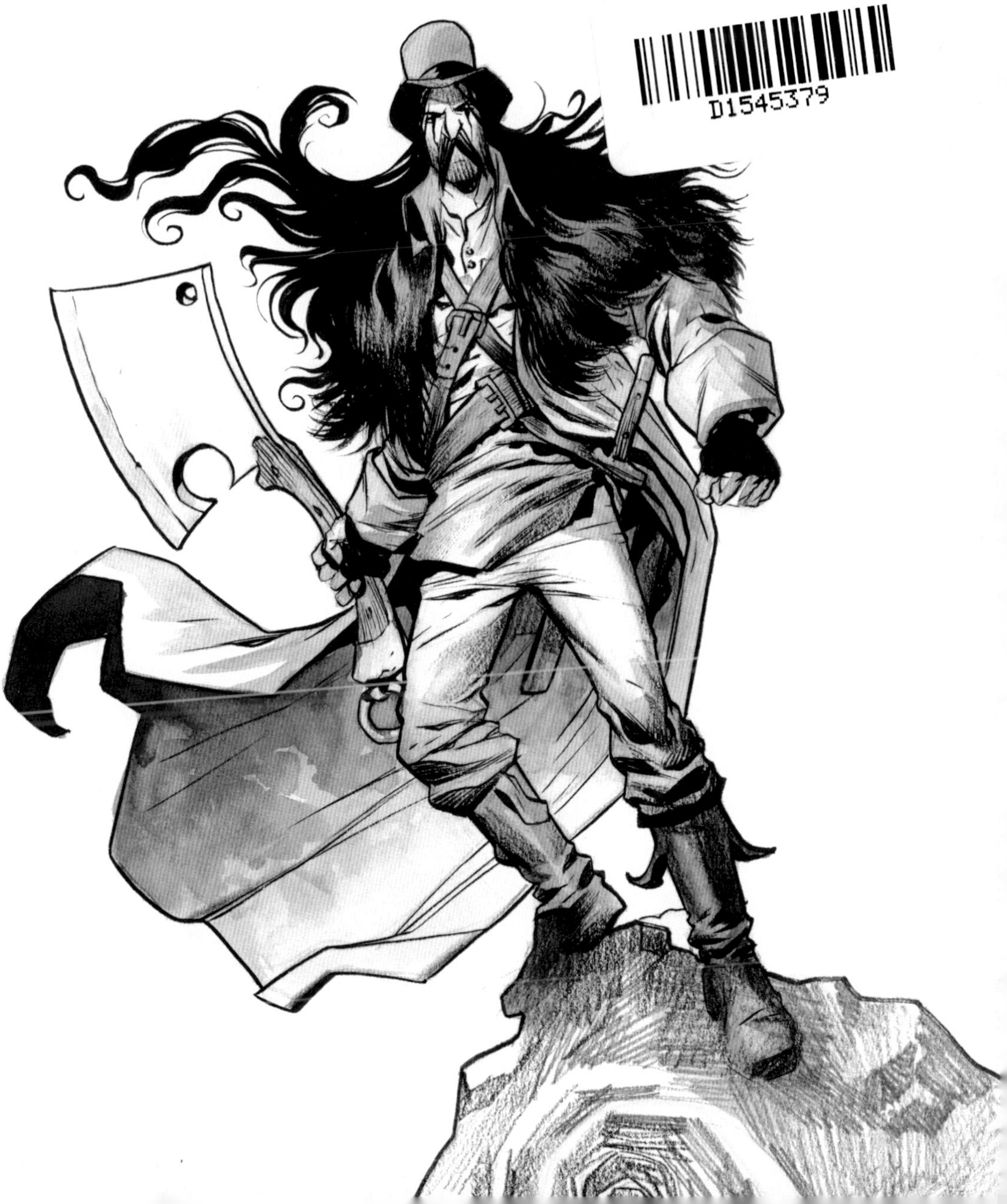

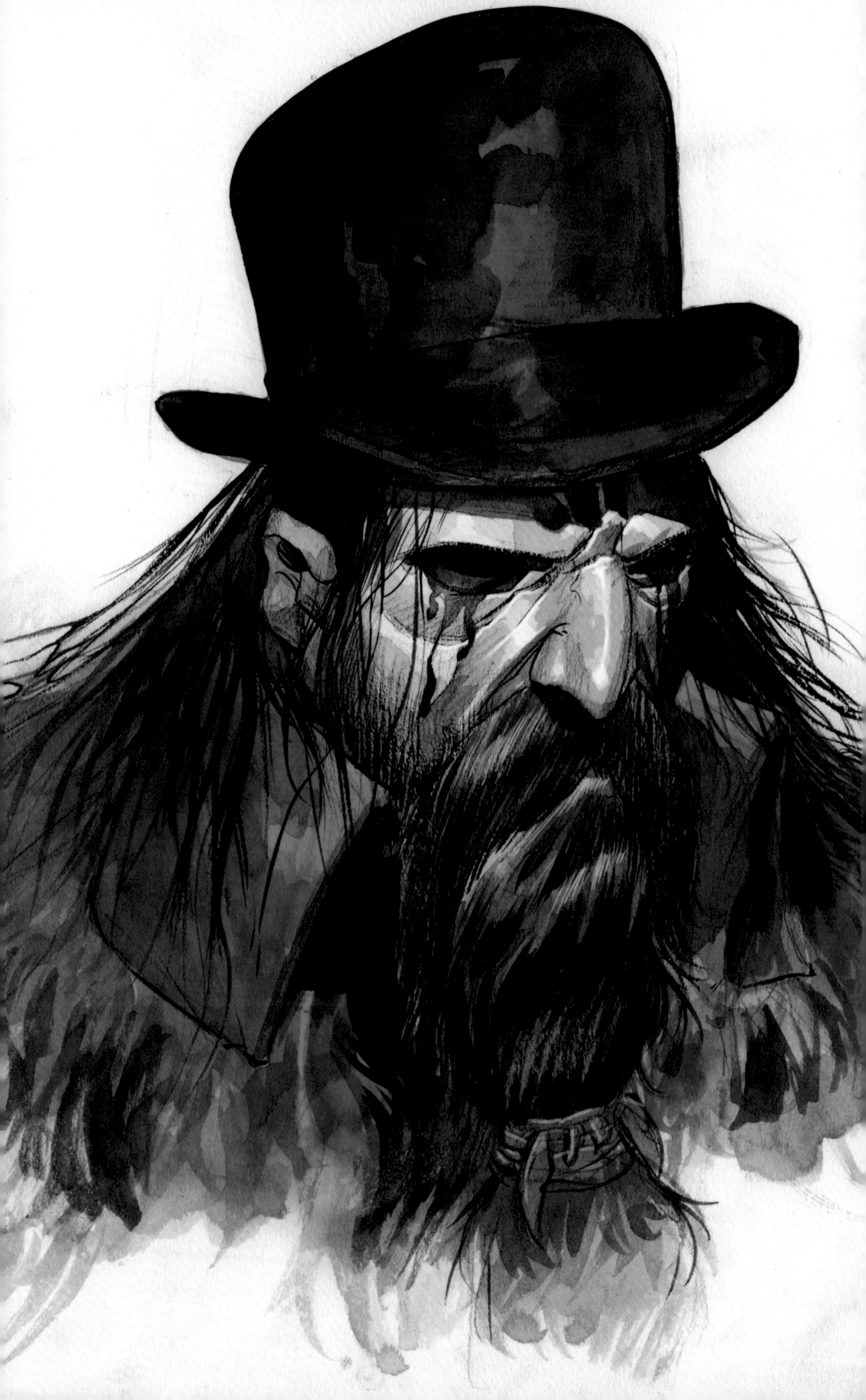

VOLUME TWO

BY

ERIC POWELL

with

STEVE MANNION
Art on TAILYPO AND THE IRON CHILD

SIMONE DI MEO
Art on THE OPPOSUM TRAMP WINS ALL

WARREN MONTGOMERY
Colors & lettering on THE OPPOSUM TRAMP WINS ALL

Edited by Tracy Marsh

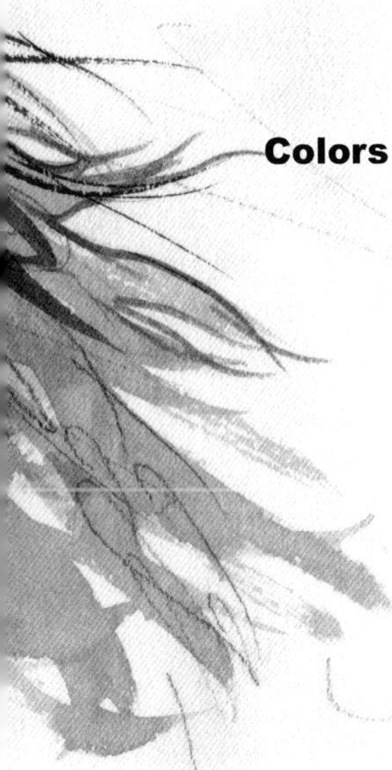

HILLBILLY™ Volume Two Published by Albatross Funnybooks, PO Box 60627, Nashville TN 37206, United States. HILLBILLY™ & © 2017 Eric Powell. All contents and related characters ™ & © 2017 Eric Powell. All rights reserved. No portion of this product may be reproduced or transmitted, by any form or by any means, without express written permission of Eric Powell. ALBATROSS FUNNYBOOKS™ and ALBATROSS FUNNYBOOKS Logo™ & © 2017 Eric Powell. Names, characters, places, and incidents featured in this publication are fictional. Any similarity to persons living or dead, places, and incidents is unintended or for satirical purposes.

This volume collects issues 5-8 of the Albatross Funnybooks series HILLBILLY.

ISBN- 978-0-9983792-3-4
(Printed in Canada)

www.albatrossfunnybooks.com

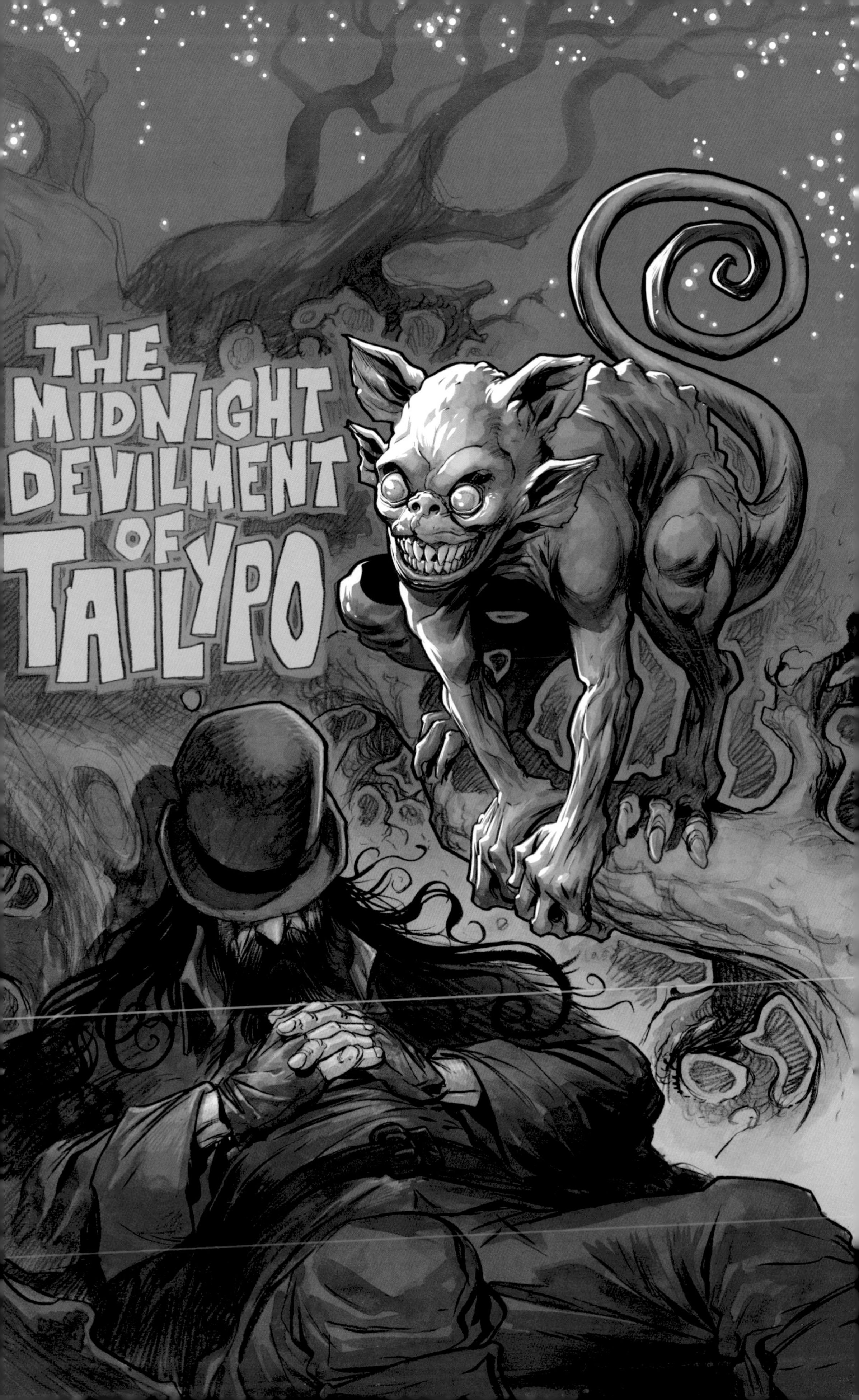
THE MIDNIGHT DEVILMENT OF TAILYPO

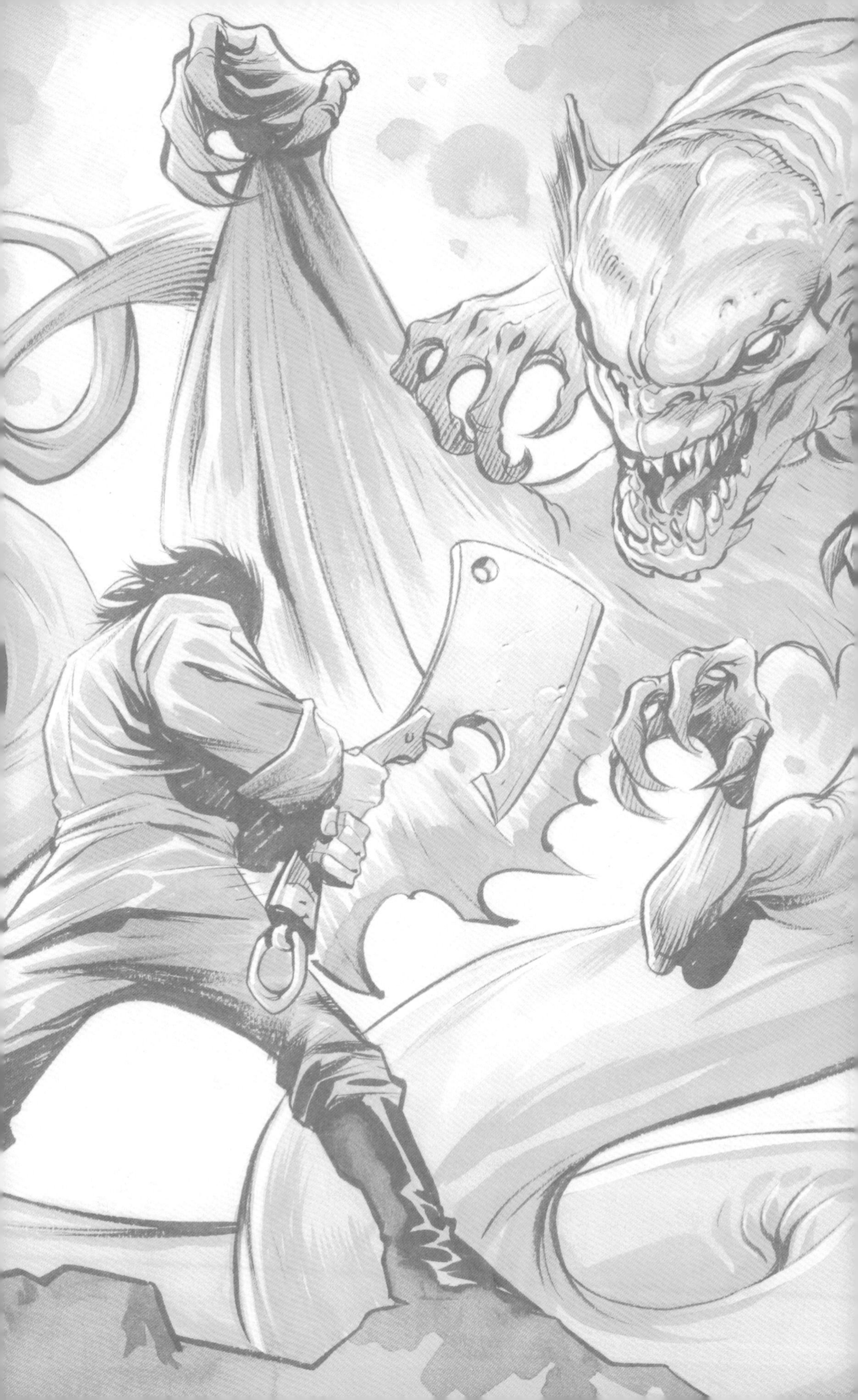

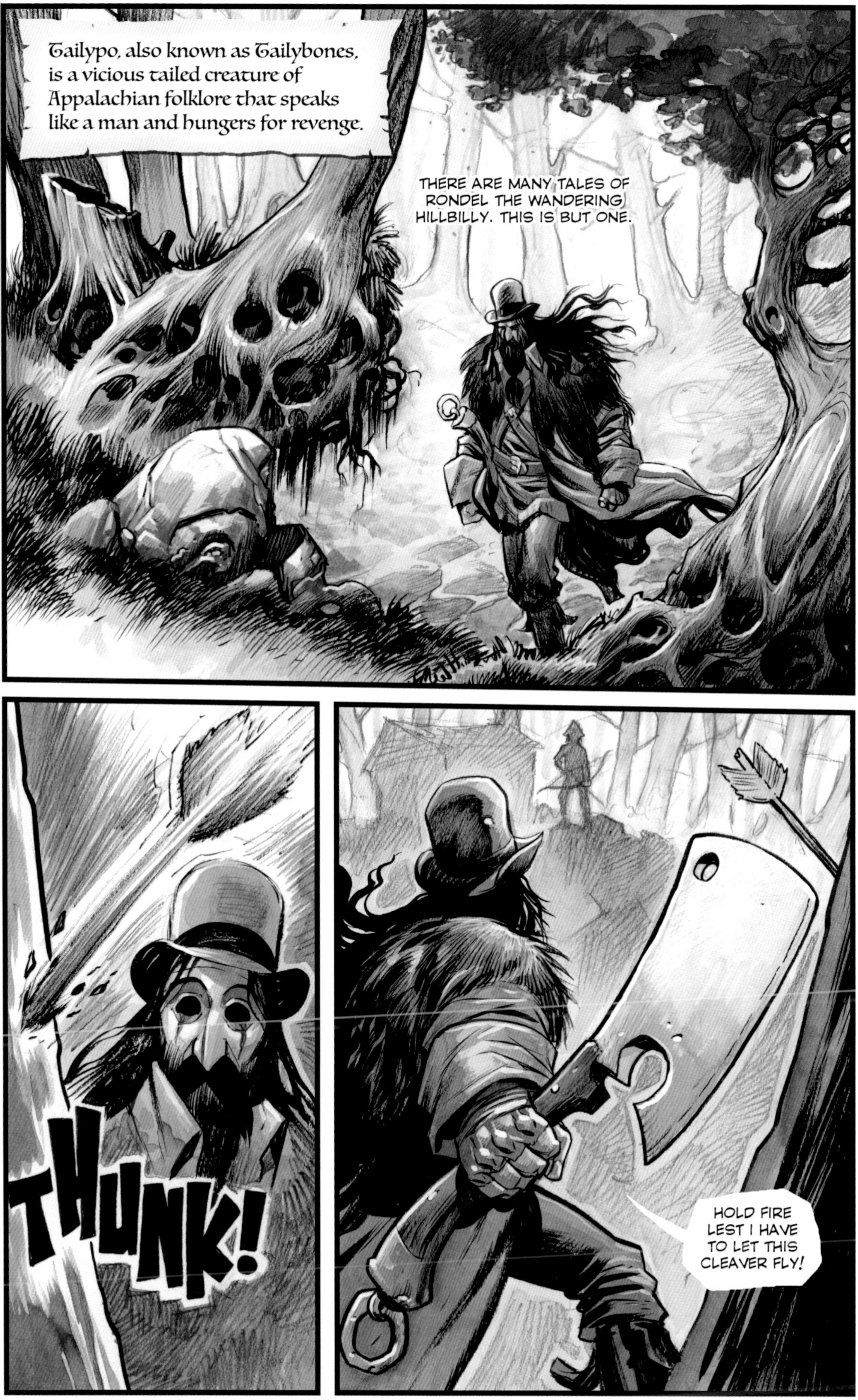
Ɓailypo, also known as Ɓailybones, is a vicious tailed creature of Appalachian folklore that speaks like a man and hungers for revenge.
THERE ARE MANY TALES OF RONDEL THE WANDERING HILLBILLY. THIS IS BUT ONE.
THUNK!
HOLD FIRE LEST I HAVE TO LET THIS CLEAVER FLY!

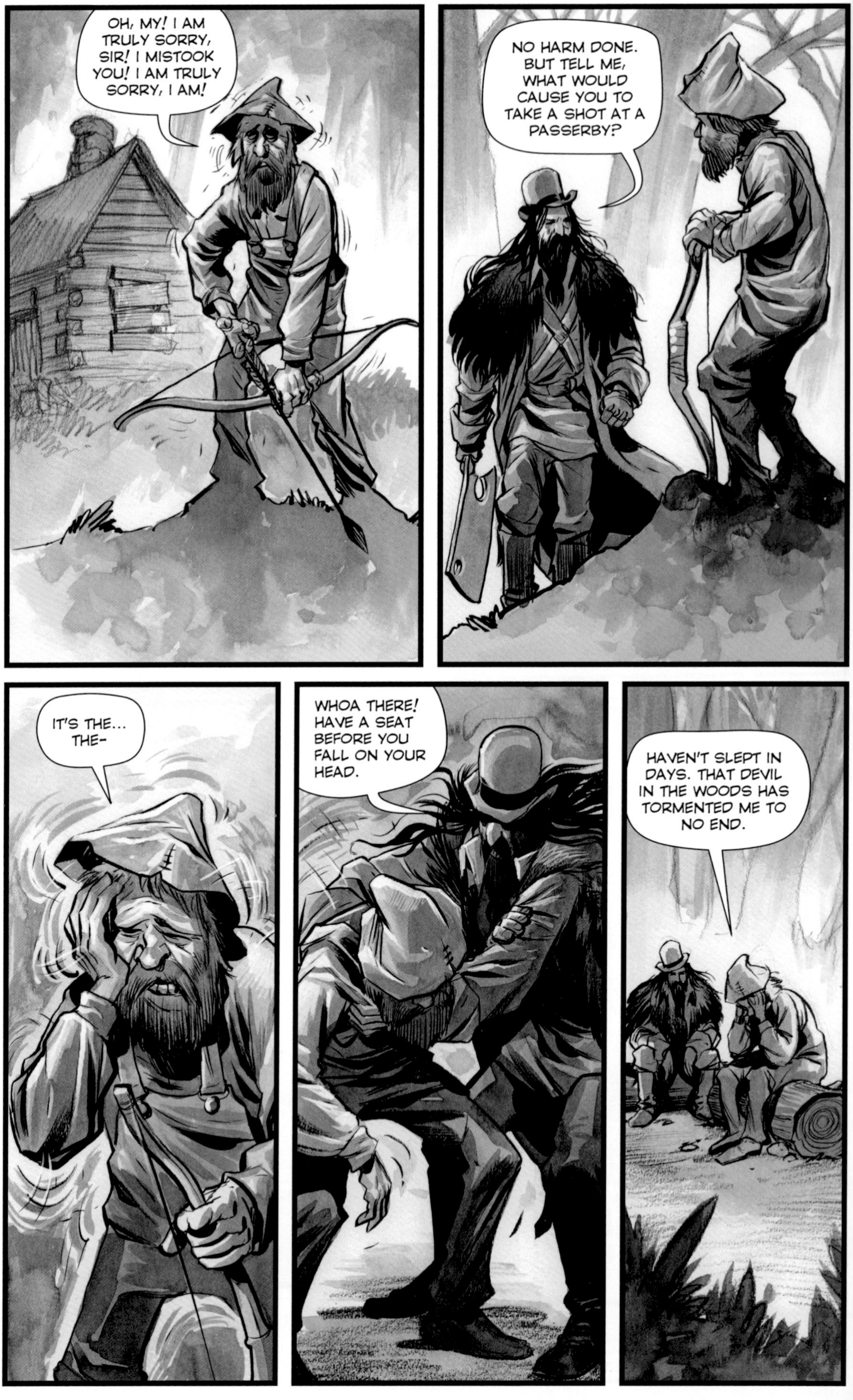
OH, MY! I AM TRULY SORRY, SIR! I MISTOOK YOU! I AM TRULY SORRY, I AM!
NO HARM DONE. BUT TELL ME, WHAT WOULD CAUSE YOU TO TAKE A SHOT AT A PASSERBY?
IT'S THE... THE-
WHOA THERE! HAVE A SEAT BEFORE YOU FALL ON YOUR HEAD.
HAVEN'T SLEPT IN DAYS. THAT DEVIL IN THE WOODS HAS TORMENTED ME TO NO END.

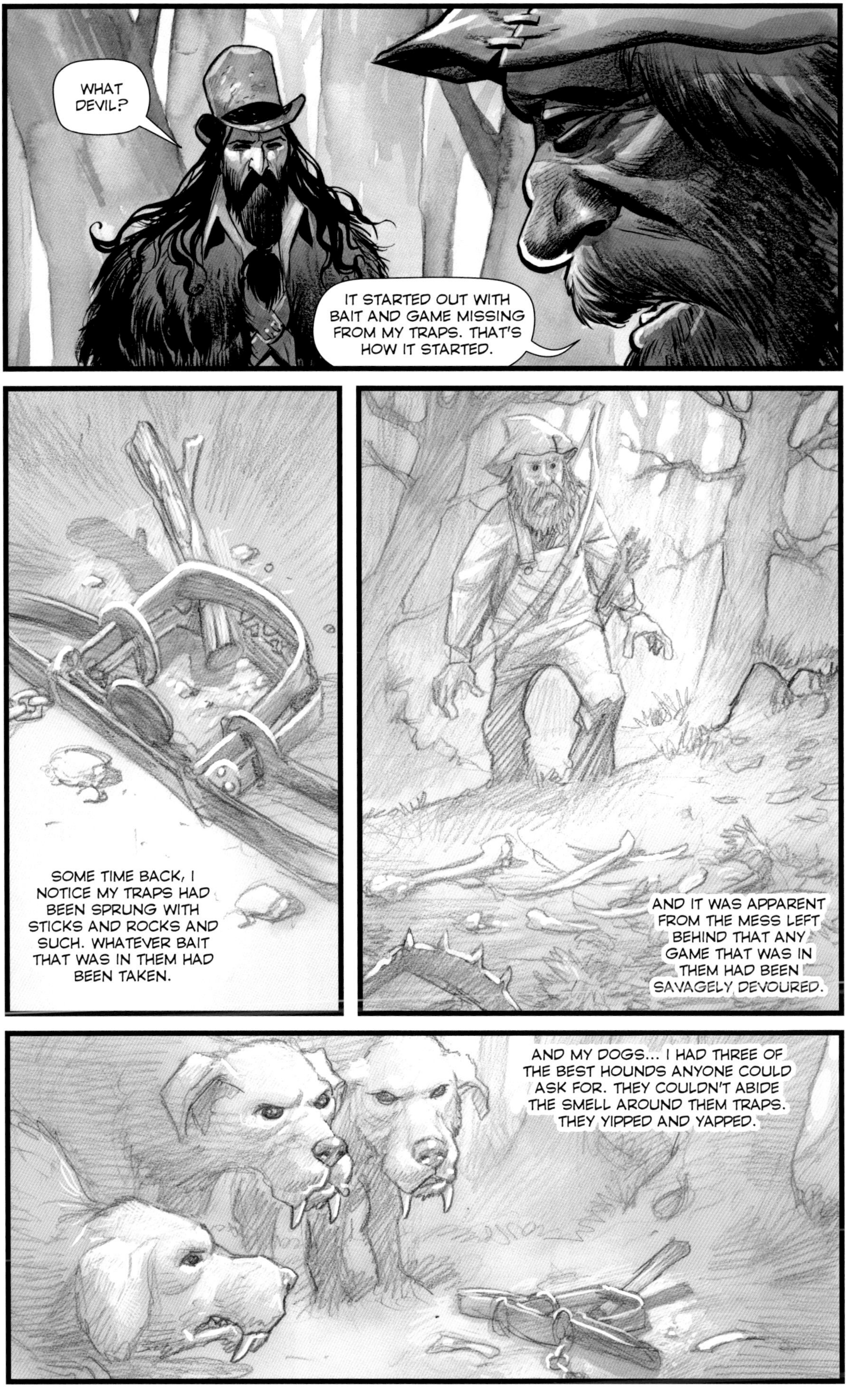
WHAT DEVIL?
IT STARTED OUT WITH BAIT AND GAME MISSING FROM MY TRAPS. THAT'S HOW IT STARTED.
SOME TIME BACK, I NOTICE MY TRAPS HAD BEEN SPRUNG WITH STICKS AND ROCKS AND SUCH. WHATEVER BAIT THAT WAS IN THEM HAD BEEN TAKEN.
AND IT WAS APPARENT FROM THE MESS LEFT BEHIND THAT ANY GAME THAT WAS IN THEM HAD BEEN SAVAGELY DEVOURED.
AND MY DOGS... I HAD THREE OF THE BEST HOUNDS ANYONE COULD ASK FOR. THEY COULDN'T ABIDE THE SMELL AROUND THEM TRAPS. THEY YIPPED AND YAPPED.

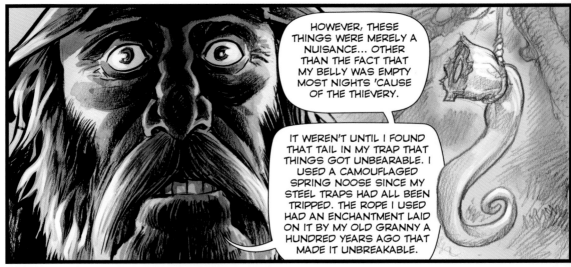

HOWEVER, THESE THINGS WERE MERELY A NUISANCE... OTHER THAN THE FACT THAT MY BELLY WAS EMPTY MOST NIGHTS 'CAUSE OF THE THIEVERY.

IT WEREN'T UNTIL I FOUND THAT TAIL IN MY TRAP THAT THINGS GOT UNBEARABLE. I USED A CAMOUFLAGED SPRING NOOSE SINCE MY STEEL TRAPS HAD ALL BEEN TRIPPED. THE ROPE I USED HAD AN ENCHANTMENT LAID ON IT BY MY OLD GRANNY A HUNDRED YEARS AGO THAT MADE IT UNBREAKABLE.

AND THAT TAIL WAS JUST HANGING THERE, CHEWED PLUM THROUGH. LOOKED LIKE I SNAGGED THE THING THAT HAD BEEN STEALING FROM ME AND IT CHEWED ITS OWN TAIL OFF TO GET AWAY.

WELL, BEING MIGHTY HUNGRY, AND MORE THAN ANNOYED BY THE THING RAIDING MY TRAPS, MY NEXT ACT WAS OUT OF SHEER SPITE.

I TOOK THAT TAIL AND ROASTED IT.

I ATE EVERY BIT OF THAT FOUL MEAT, CHOKING DOWN EVERY BITE OUT OF ANGER.

AND TOSSING THE TAIL BONES IN THE ASH BUCKET.

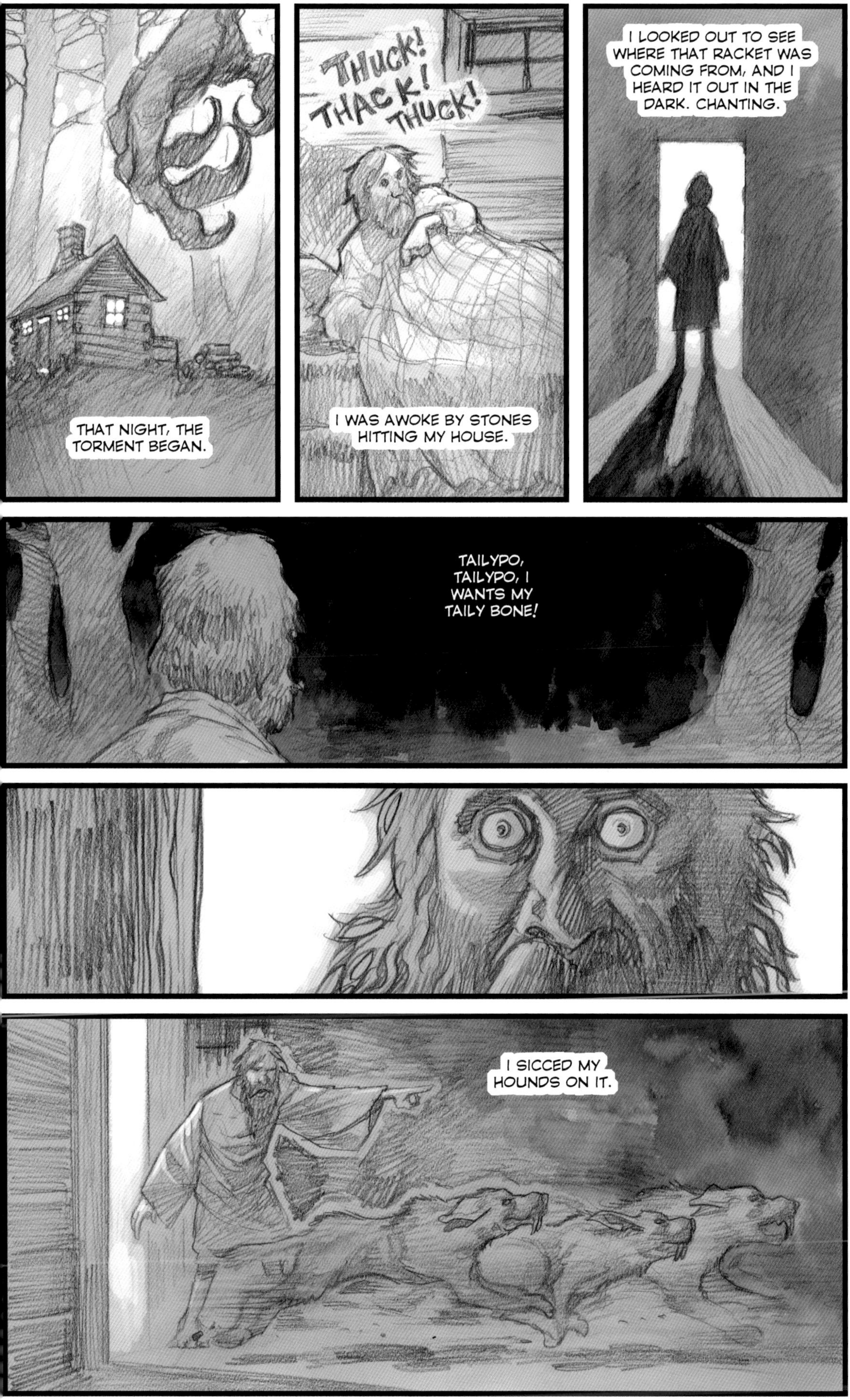
THAT NIGHT, THE TORMENT BEGAN.
THUCK! THACK! THUCK!
I WAS AWOKE BY STONES HITTING MY HOUSE.
I LOOKED OUT TO SEE WHERE THAT RACKET WAS COMING FROM, AND I HEARD IT OUT IN THE DARK. CHANTING.
TAILYPO, TAILYPO, I WANTS MY TAILY BONE!
I SICCED MY HOUNDS ON IT.

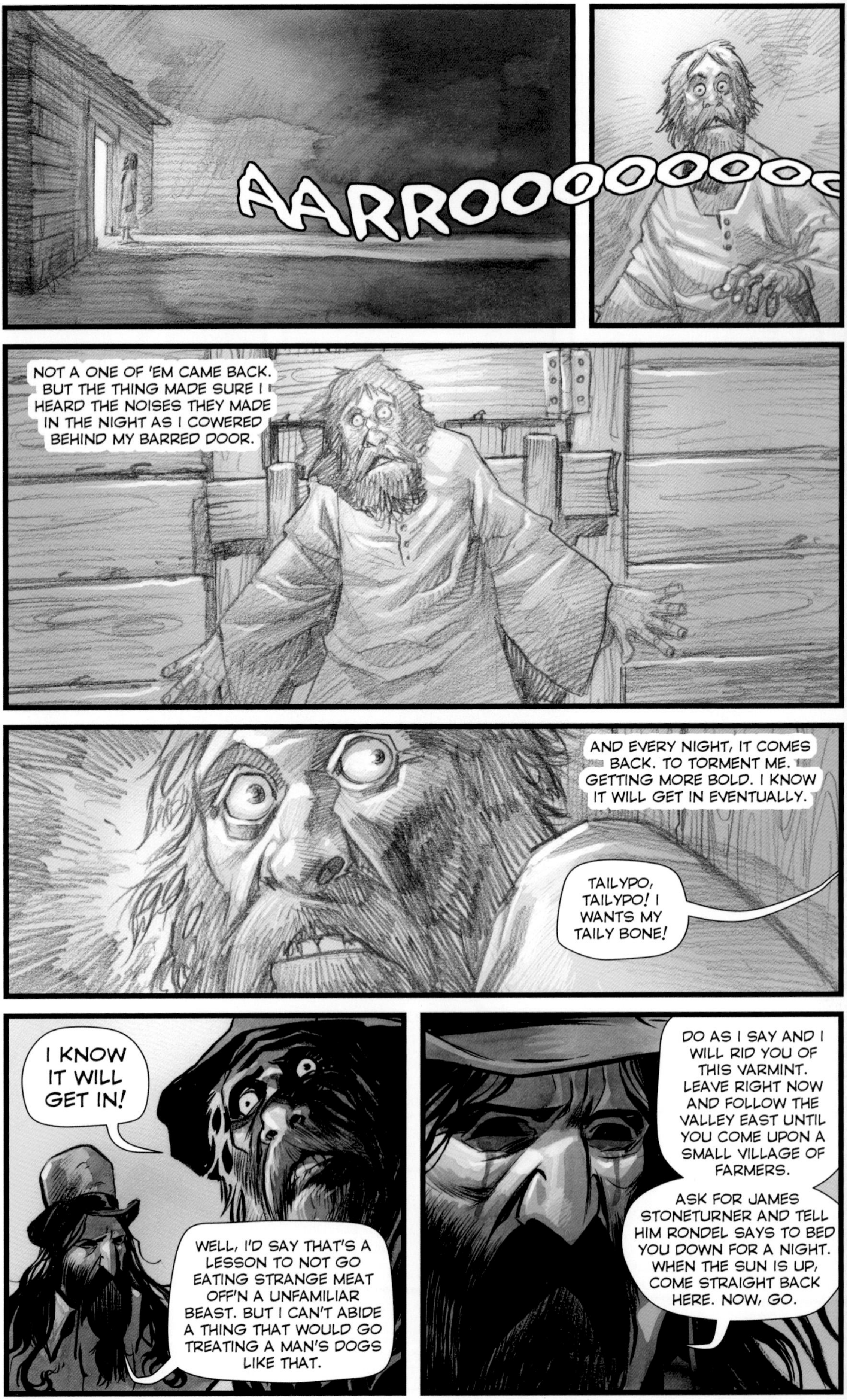
AARROOOOOOOOO
NOT A ONE OF 'EM CAME BACK. BUT THE THING MADE SURE I HEARD THE NOISES THEY MADE IN THE NIGHT AS I COWERED BEHIND MY BARRED DOOR.
AND EVERY NIGHT, IT COMES BACK. TO TORMENT ME. GETTING MORE BOLD. I KNOW IT WILL GET IN EVENTUALLY.
TAILYPO, TAILYPO! I WANTS MY TAILY BONE!
I KNOW IT WILL GET IN!
WELL, I'D SAY THAT'S A LESSON TO NOT GO EATING STRANGE MEAT OFF'N A UNFAMILIAR BEAST. BUT I CAN'T ABIDE A THING THAT WOULD GO TREATING A MAN'S DOGS LIKE THAT.
DO AS I SAY AND I WILL RID YOU OF THIS VARMINT. LEAVE RIGHT NOW AND FOLLOW THE VALLEY EAST UNTIL YOU COME UPON A SMALL VILLAGE OF FARMERS.
ASK FOR JAMES STONETURNER AND TELL HIM RONDEL SAYS TO BED YOU DOWN FOR A NIGHT. WHEN THE SUN IS UP, COME STRAIGHT BACK HERE. NOW, GO.

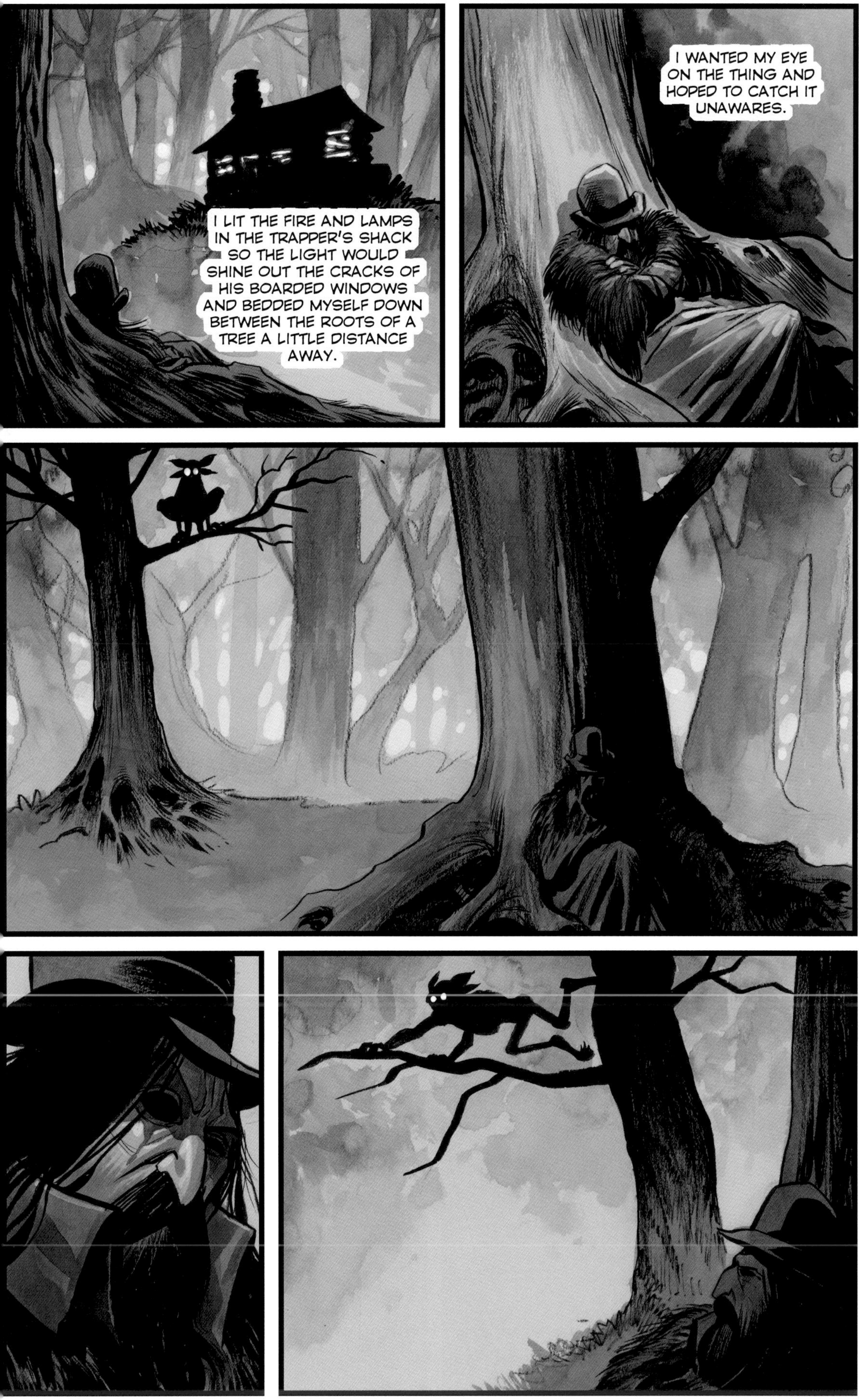
I LIT THE FIRE AND LAMPS IN THE TRAPPER'S SHACK SO THE LIGHT WOULD SHINE OUT THE CRACKS OF HIS BOARDED WINDOWS AND BEDDED MYSELF DOWN BETWEEN THE ROOTS OF A TREE A LITTLE DISTANCE AWAY.
I WANTED MY EYE ON THE THING AND HOPED TO CATCH IT UNAWARES.

TAILYPO... TAILYPO.

I WANTS MY TAILY BONE!

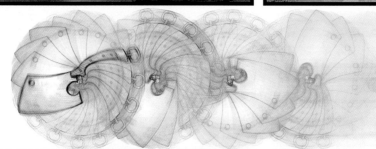

KA-CHUNK!

YOU'LL BE MISSING MORE THAN YOUR TAILBONE WHEN I GET DONE WITH YOU, YOU DOG-KILLING VARMINT YOU!

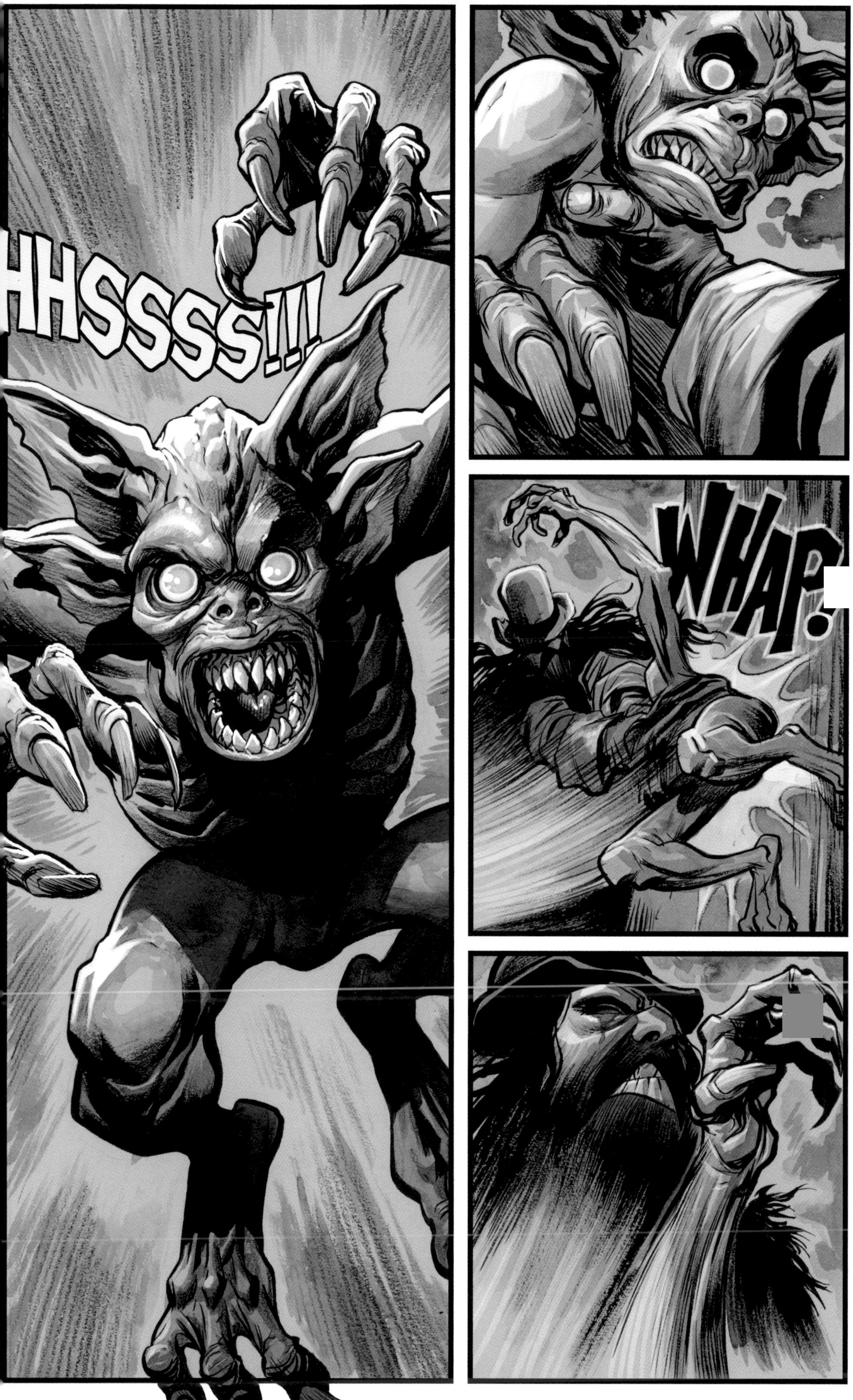
HHSSSSS!!!
WHAP!

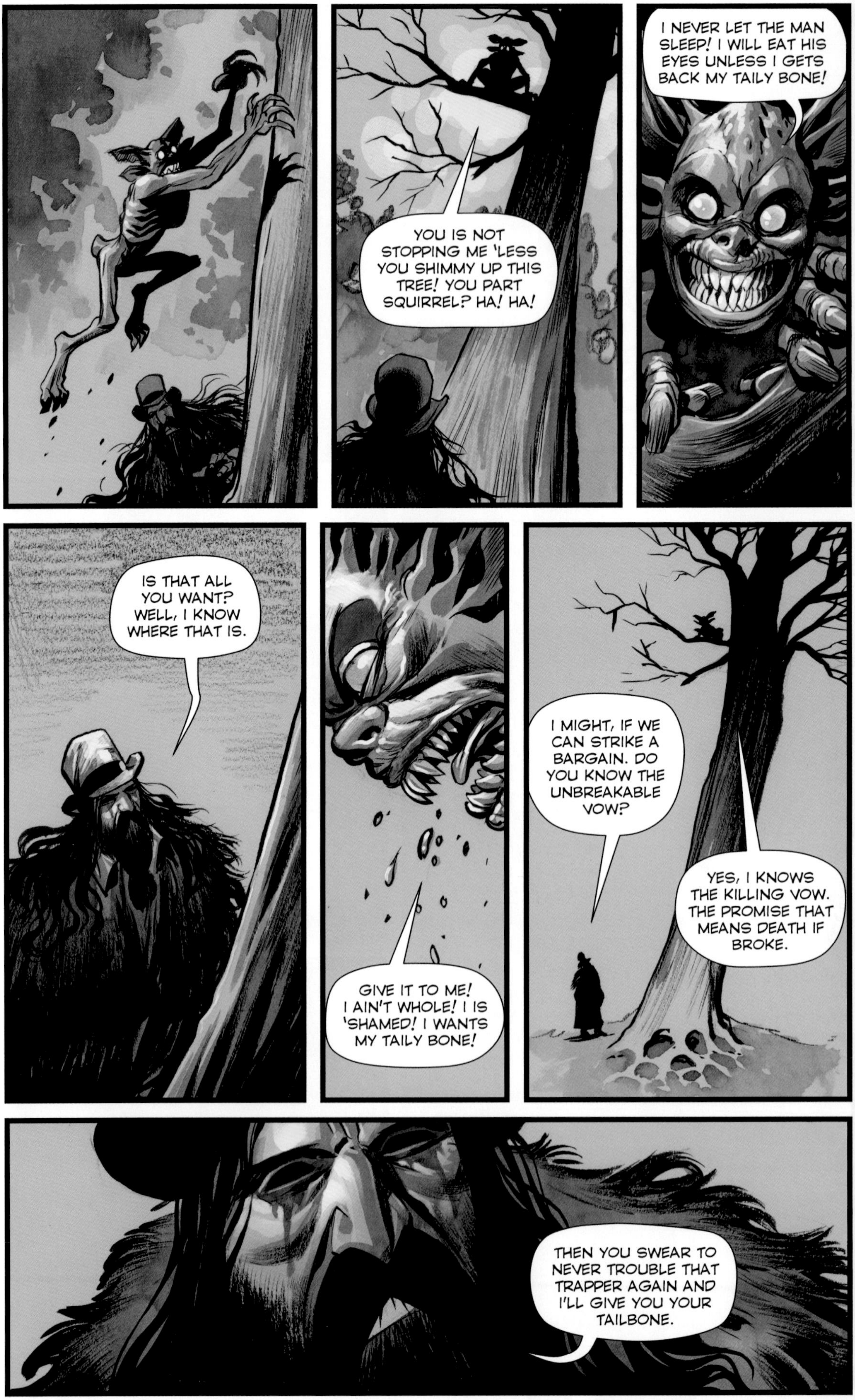
YOU IS NOT STOPPING ME 'LESS YOU SHIMMY UP THIS TREE! YOU PART SQUIRREL? HA! HA!
I NEVER LET THE MAN SLEEP! I WILL EAT HIS EYES UNLESS I GETS BACK MY TAILY BONE!
IS THAT ALL YOU WANT? WELL, I KNOW WHERE THAT IS.
GIVE IT TO ME! I AIN'T WHOLE! I IS 'SHAMED! I WANTS MY TAILY BONE!
I MIGHT, IF WE CAN STRIKE A BARGAIN. DO YOU KNOW THE UNBREAKABLE VOW?
YES, I KNOWS THE KILLING VOW. THE PROMISE THAT MEANS DEATH IF BROKE.
THEN YOU SWEAR TO NEVER TROUBLE THAT TRAPPER AGAIN AND I'LL GIVE YOU YOUR TAILBONE.

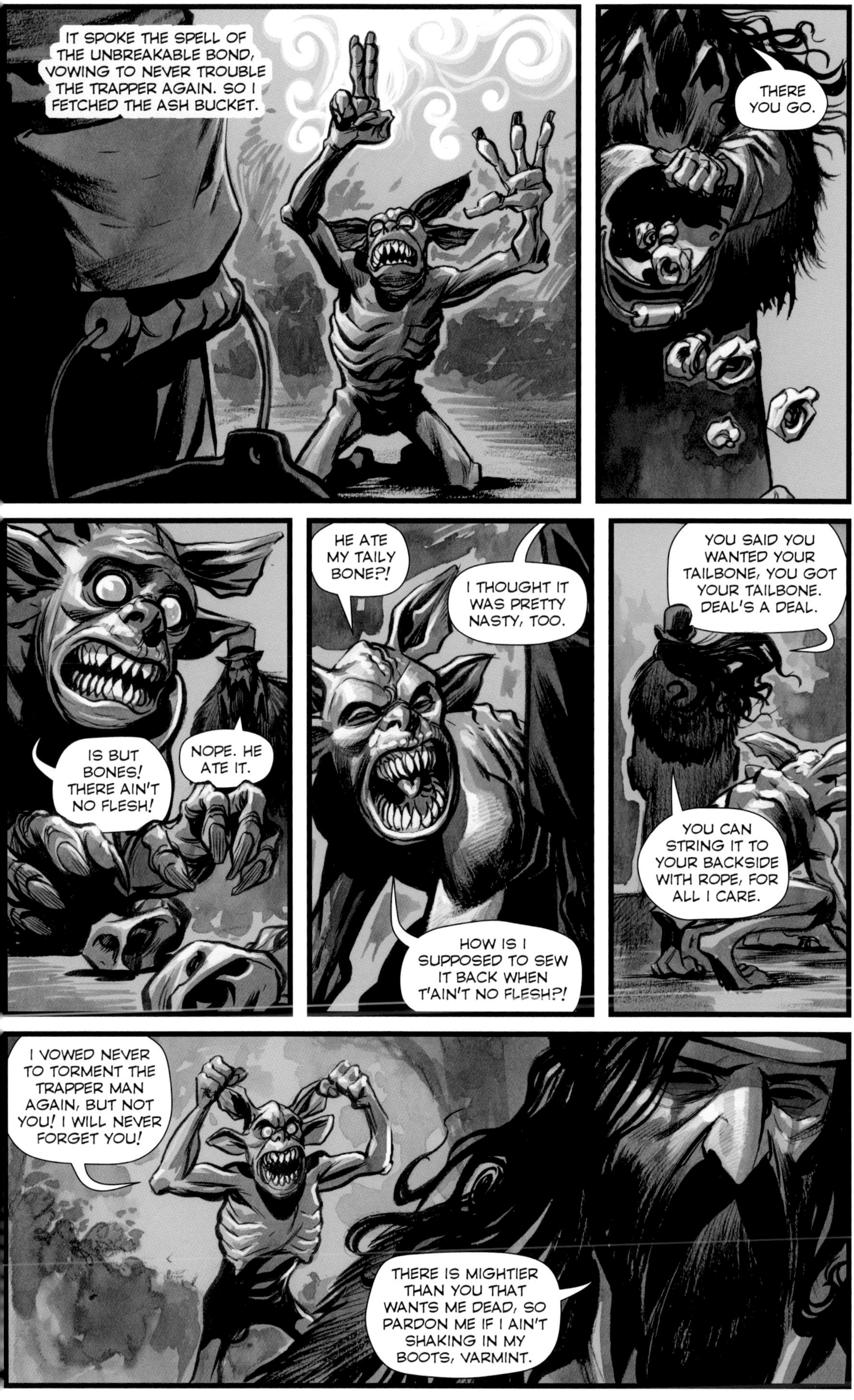
IT SPOKE THE SPELL OF THE UNBREAKABLE BOND, VOWING TO NEVER TROUBLE THE TRAPPER AGAIN. SO I FETCHED THE ASH BUCKET.
THERE YOU GO.
IS BUT BONES! THERE AIN'T NO FLESH!
NOPE. HE ATE IT.
HE ATE MY TAILY BONE?!
I THOUGHT IT WAS PRETTY NASTY, TOO.
HOW IS I SUPPOSED TO SEW IT BACK WHEN T'AIN'T NO FLESH?!
YOU SAID YOU WANTED YOUR TAILBONE, YOU GOT YOUR TAILBONE. DEAL'S A DEAL.
YOU CAN STRING IT TO YOUR BACKSIDE WITH ROPE, FOR ALL I CARE.
I VOWED NEVER TO TORMENT THE TRAPPER MAN AGAIN, BUT NOT YOU! I WILL NEVER FORGET YOU!
THERE IS MIGHTIER THAN YOU THAT WANTS ME DEAD, SO PARDON ME IF I AIN'T SHAKING IN MY BOOTS, VARMINT.

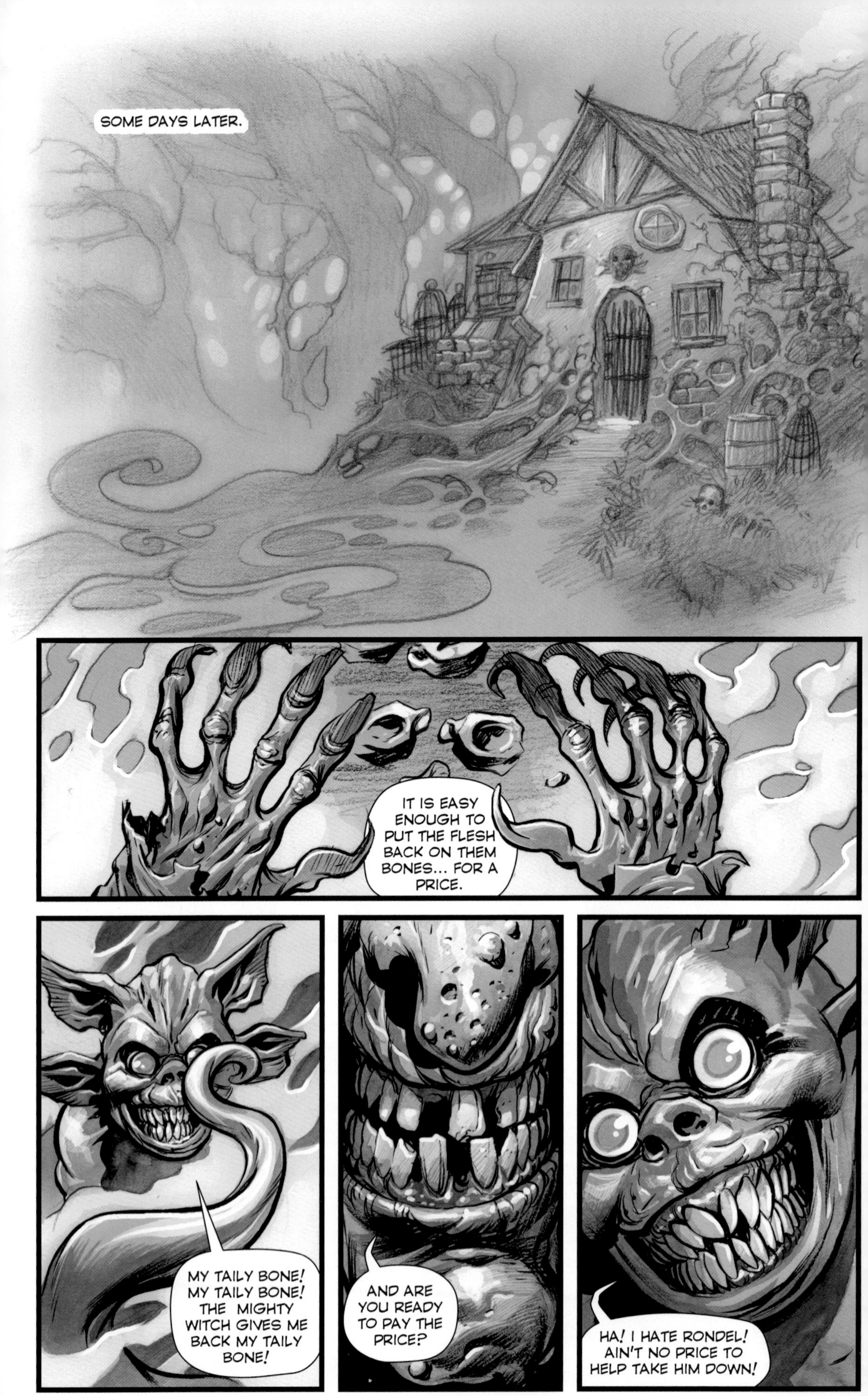
SOME DAYS LATER.
IT IS EASY ENOUGH TO PUT THE FLESH BACK ON THEM BONES... FOR A PRICE.
MY TAILY BONE! MY TAILY BONE! THE MIGHTY WITCH GIVES ME BACK MY TAILY BONE!
AND ARE YOU READY TO PAY THE PRICE?
HA! I HATE RONDEL! AIN'T NO PRICE TO HELP TAKE HIM DOWN!

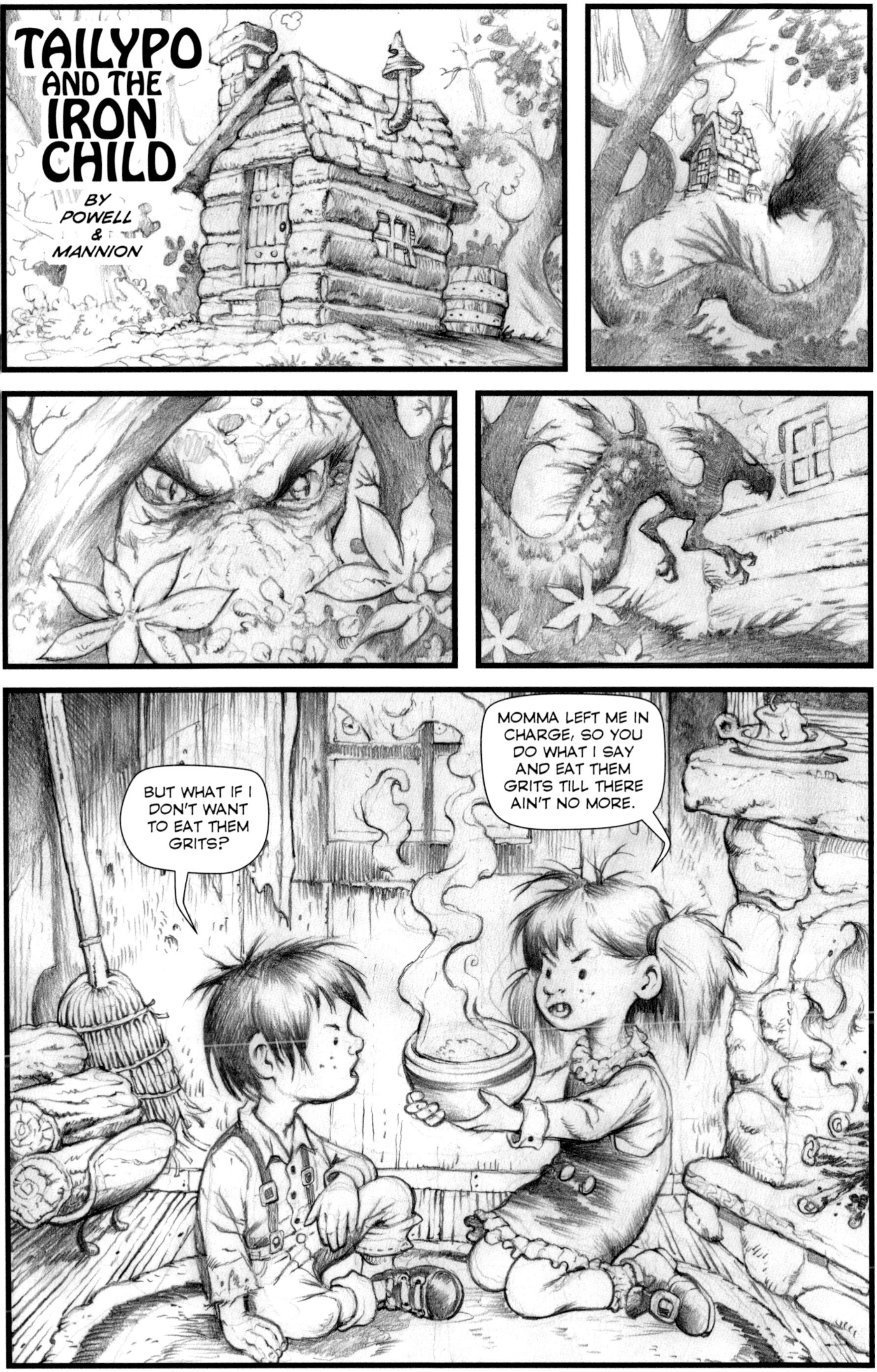
TAILYPO AND THE IRON CHILD
BY POWELL & MANNION
BUT WHAT IF I DON'T WANT TO EAT THEM GRITS?
MOMMA LEFT ME IN CHARGE, SO YOU DO WHAT I SAY AND EAT THEM GRITS TILL THERE AIN'T NO MORE.

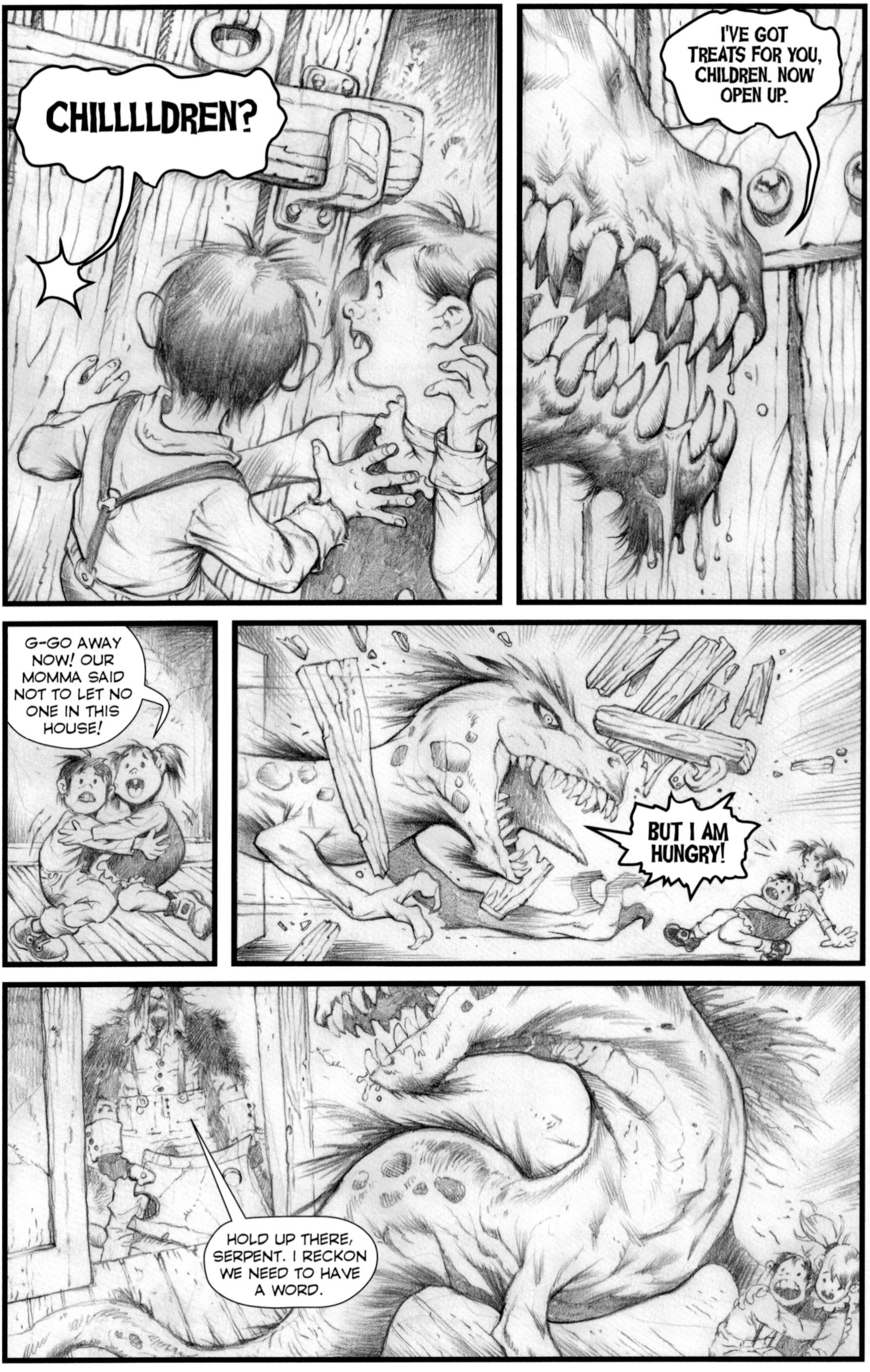
CHILLLLDREN?
I'VE GOT TREATS FOR YOU, CHILDREN. NOW OPEN UP.
G-GO AWAY NOW! OUR MOMMA SAID NOT TO LET NO ONE IN THIS HOUSE!
BUT I AM HUNGRY!
HOLD UP THERE, SERPENT. I RECKON WE NEED TO HAVE A WORD.

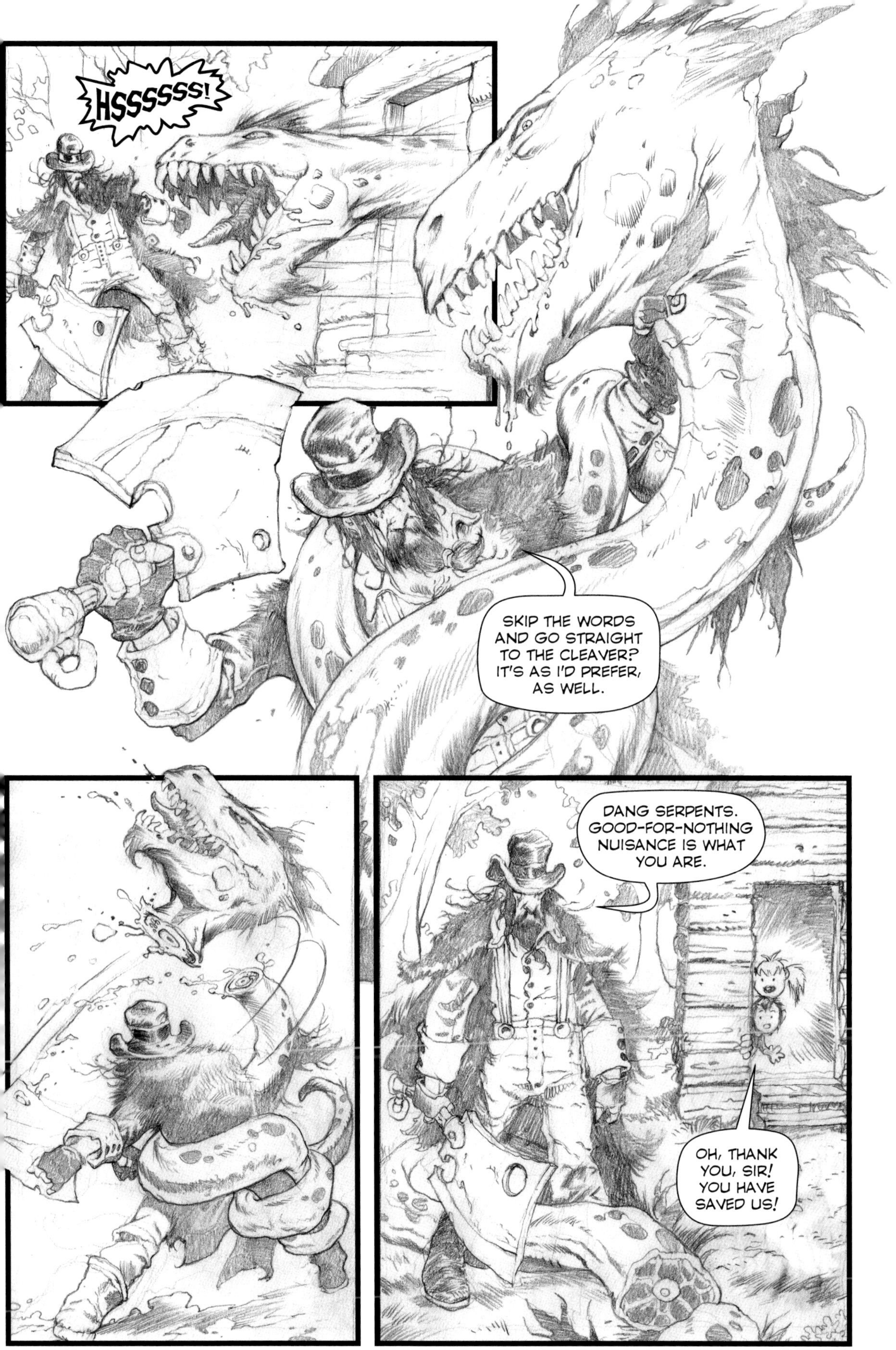
HSSSSSS!
SKIP THE WORDS AND GO STRAIGHT TO THE CLEAVER? IT'S AS I'D PREFER, AS WELL.
DANG SERPENTS. GOOD-FOR-NOTHING NUISANCE IS WHAT YOU ARE.
OH, THANK YOU, SIR! YOU HAVE SAVED US!

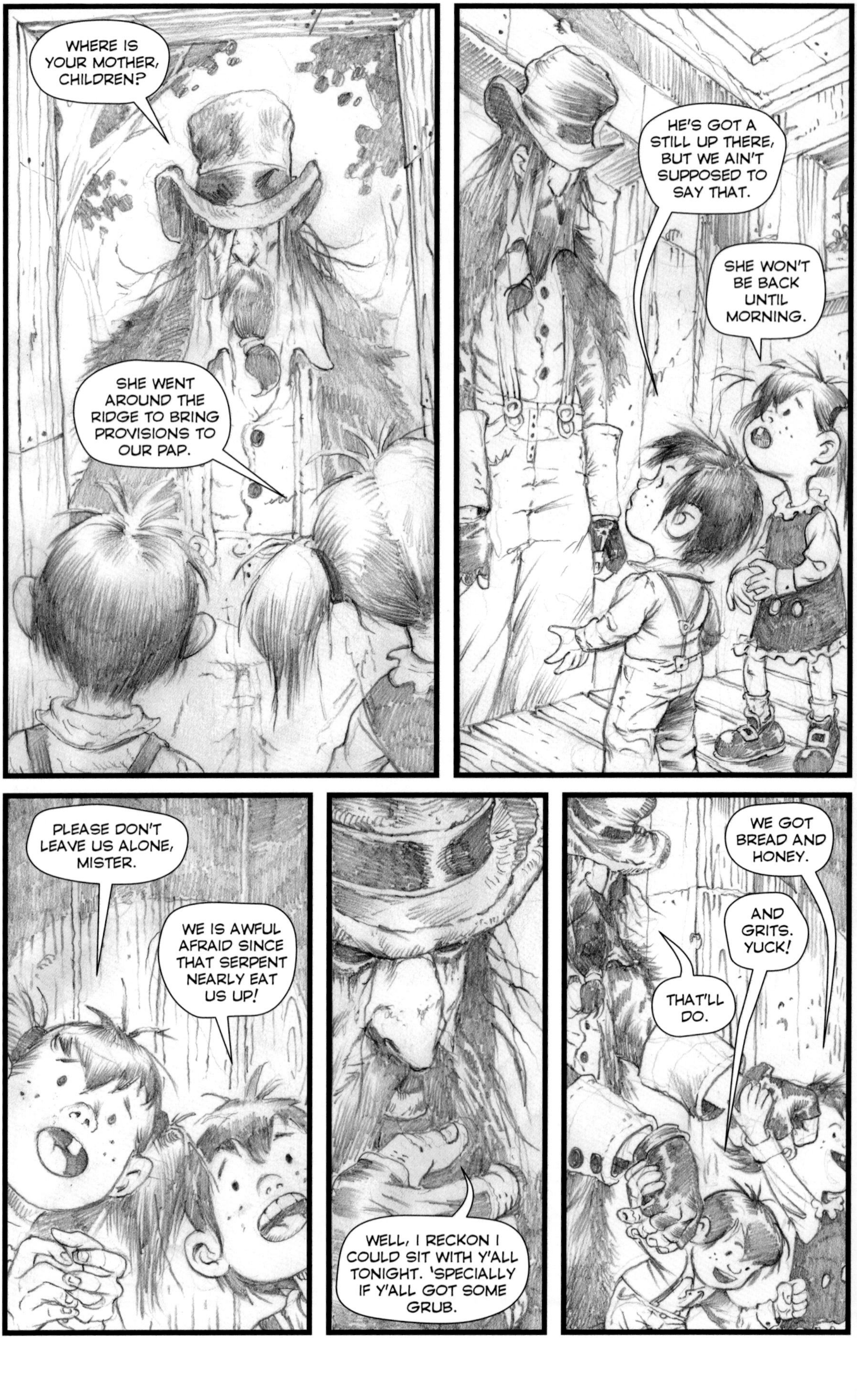
WHERE IS YOUR MOTHER, CHILDREN?
SHE WENT AROUND THE RIDGE TO BRING PROVISIONS TO OUR PAP.
HE'S GOT A STILL UP THERE, BUT WE AIN'T SUPPOSED TO SAY THAT.
SHE WON'T BE BACK UNTIL MORNING.
PLEASE DON'T LEAVE US ALONE, MISTER.
WE IS AWFUL AFRAID SINCE THAT SERPENT NEARLY EAT US UP!
WELL, I RECKON I COULD SIT WITH Y'ALL TONIGHT. 'SPECIALLY IF Y'ALL GOT SOME GRUB.
WE GOT BREAD AND HONEY.
AND GRITS. YUCK!
THAT'LL DO.

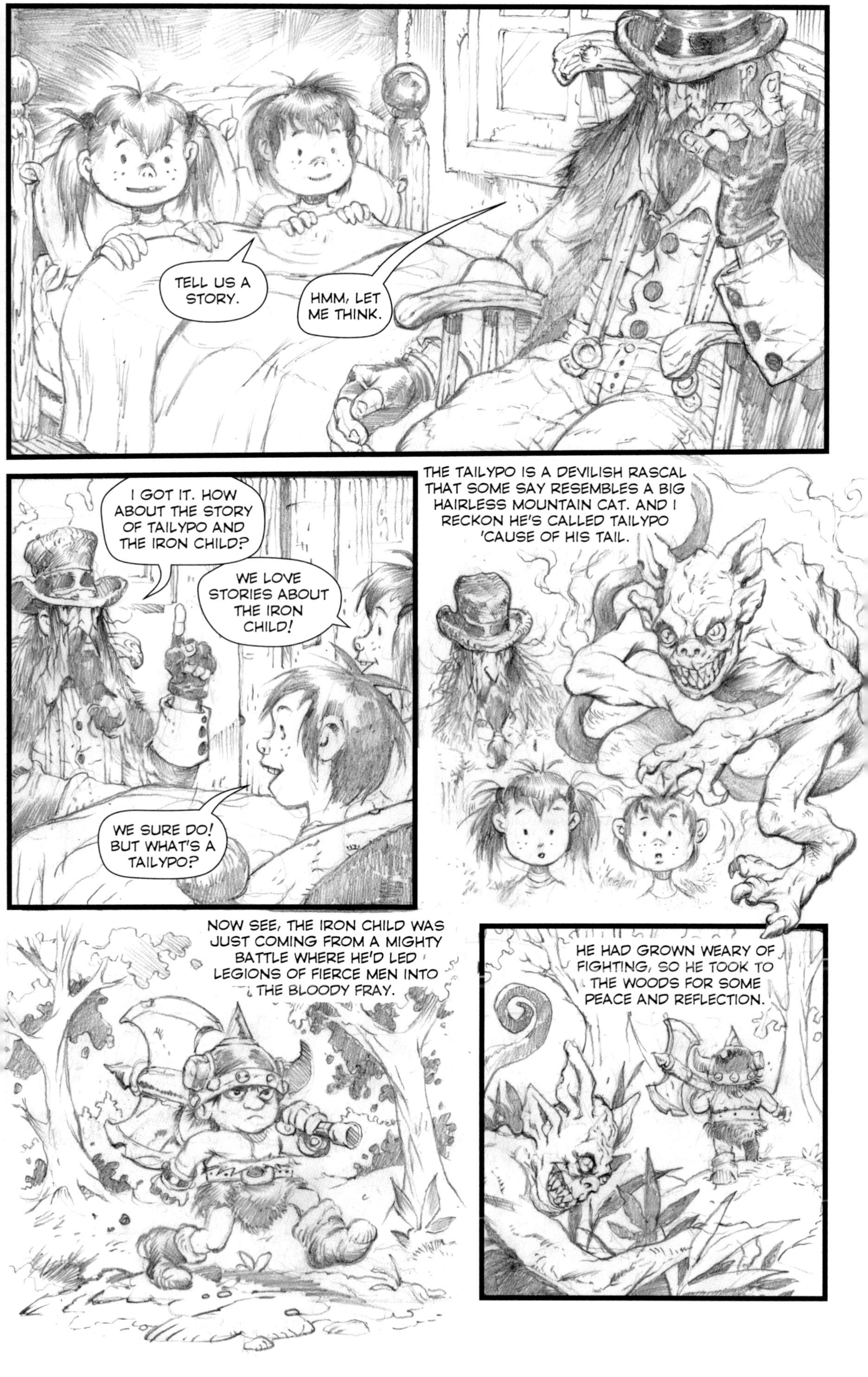

TELL US A STORY.
HMM, LET ME THINK.
I GOT IT. HOW ABOUT THE STORY OF TAILYPO AND THE IRON CHILD?
WE LOVE STORIES ABOUT THE IRON CHILD!
WE SURE DO! BUT WHAT'S A TAILYPO?
THE TAILYPO IS A DEVILISH RASCAL THAT SOME SAY RESEMBLES A BIG HAIRLESS MOUNTAIN CAT. AND I RECKON HE'S CALLED TAILYPO 'CAUSE OF HIS TAIL.
NOW SEE, THE IRON CHILD WAS JUST COMING FROM A MIGHTY BATTLE WHERE HE'D LED LEGIONS OF FIERCE MEN INTO THE BLOODY FRAY.
HE HAD GROWN WEARY OF FIGHTING, SO HE TOOK TO THE WOODS FOR SOME PEACE AND REFLECTION.

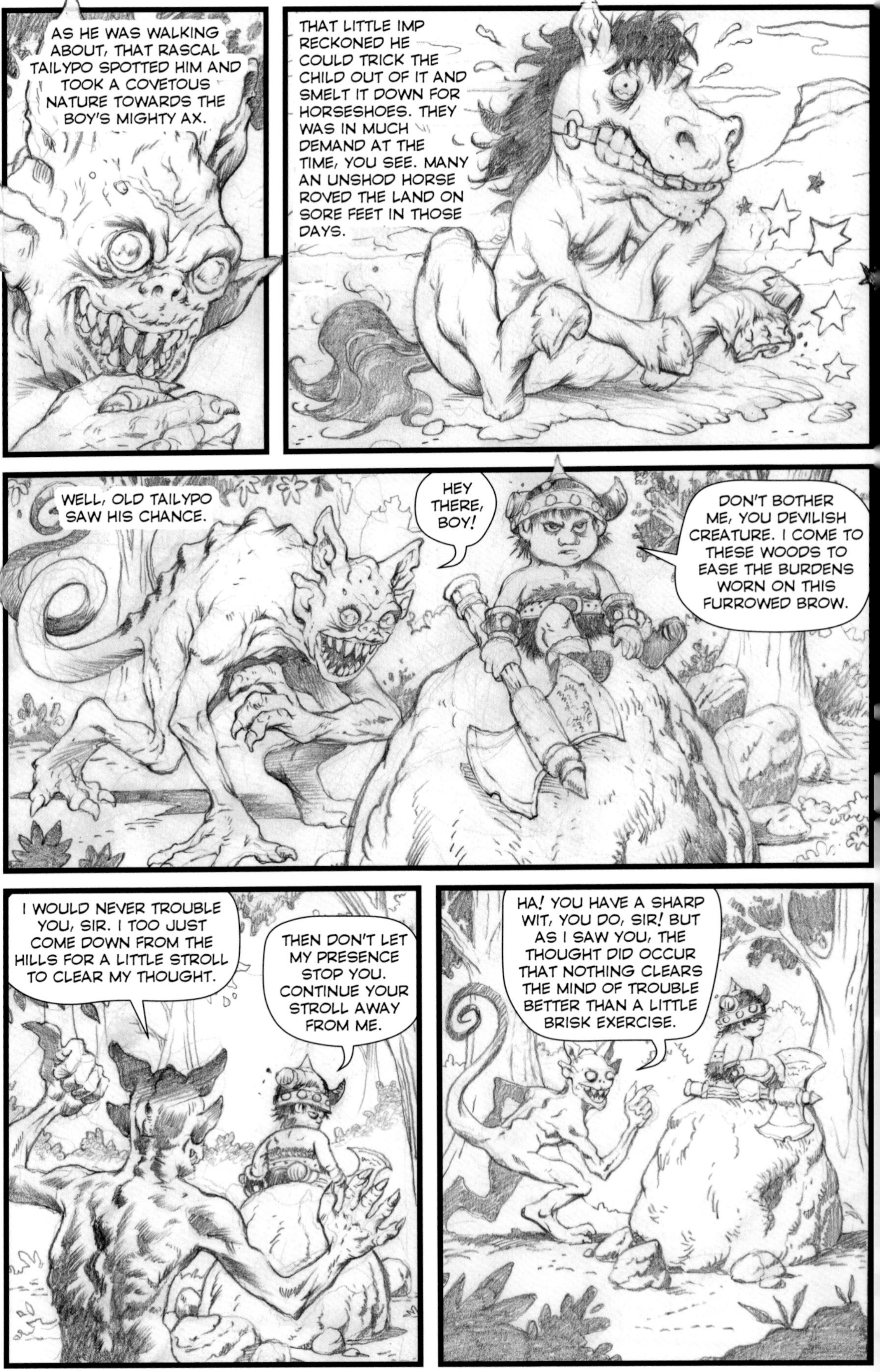

AS HE WAS WALKING ABOUT, THAT RASCAL TAILYPO SPOTTED HIM AND TOOK A COVETOUS NATURE TOWARDS THE BOY'S MIGHTY AX.
THAT LITTLE IMP RECKONED HE COULD TRICK THE CHILD OUT OF IT AND SMELT IT DOWN FOR HORSESHOES. THEY WAS IN MUCH DEMAND AT THE TIME, YOU SEE. MANY AN UNSHOD HORSE ROVED THE LAND ON SORE FEET IN THOSE DAYS.
WELL, OLD TAILYPO SAW HIS CHANCE.
HEY THERE, BOY!
DON'T BOTHER ME, YOU DEVILISH CREATURE. I COME TO THESE WOODS TO EASE THE BURDENS WORN ON THIS FURROWED BROW.
I WOULD NEVER TROUBLE YOU, SIR. I TOO JUST COME DOWN FROM THE HILLS FOR A LITTLE STROLL TO CLEAR MY THOUGHT.
THEN DON'T LET MY PRESENCE STOP YOU. CONTINUE YOUR STROLL AWAY FROM ME.
HA! YOU HAVE A SHARP WIT, YOU DO, SIR! BUT AS I SAW YOU, THE THOUGHT DID OCCUR THAT NOTHING CLEARS THE MIND OF TROUBLE BETTER THAN A LITTLE BRISK EXERCISE.

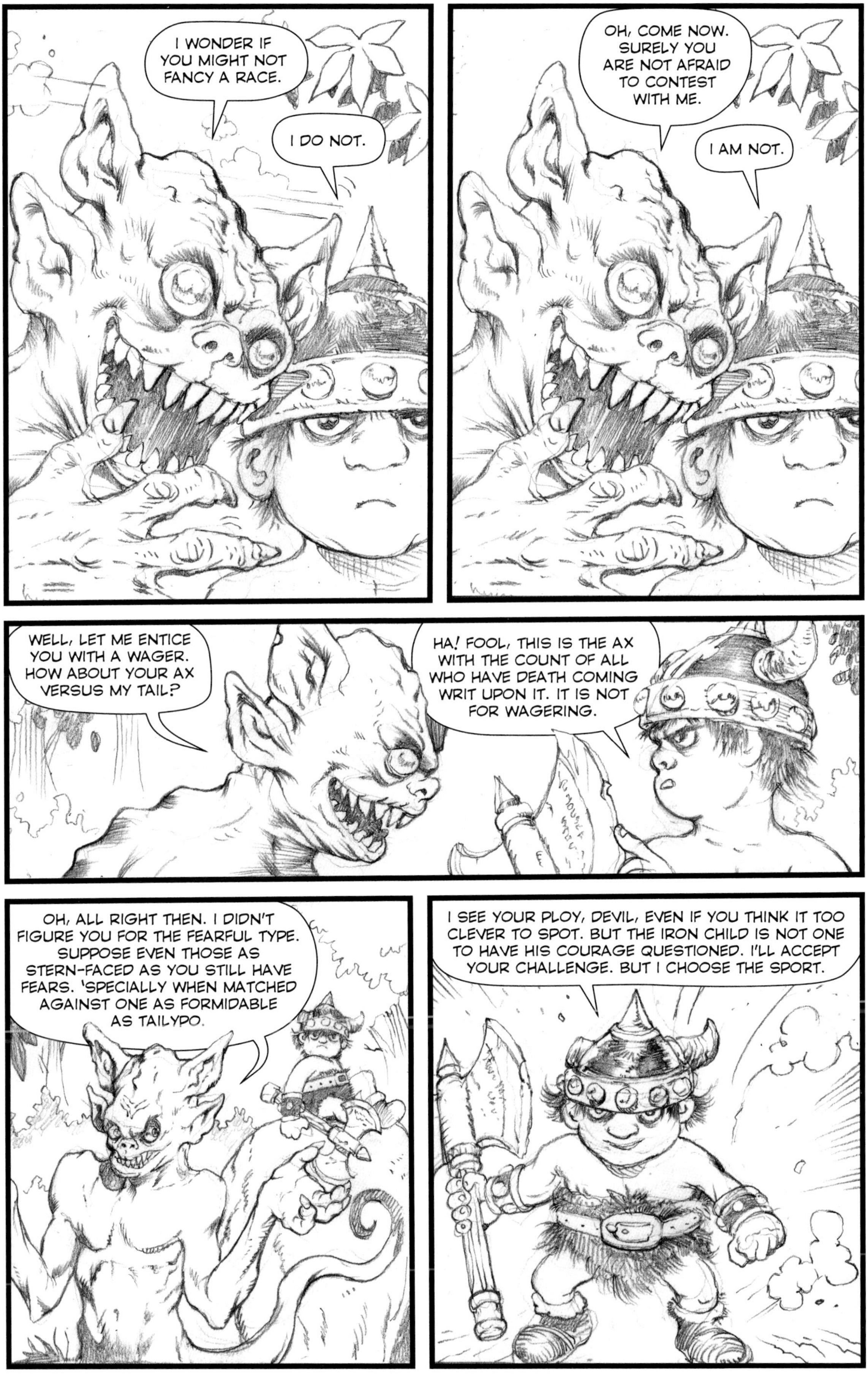
I WONDER IF YOU MIGHT NOT FANCY A RACE.
I DO NOT.
OH, COME NOW. SURELY YOU ARE NOT AFRAID TO CONTEST WITH ME.
I AM NOT.
WELL, LET ME ENTICE YOU WITH A WAGER. HOW ABOUT YOUR AX VERSUS MY TAIL?
HA! FOOL, THIS IS THE AX WITH THE COUNT OF ALL WHO HAVE DEATH COMING WRIT UPON IT. IT IS NOT FOR WAGERING.
OH, ALL RIGHT THEN. I DIDN'T FIGURE YOU FOR THE FEARFUL TYPE. SUPPOSE EVEN THOSE AS STERN-FACED AS YOU STILL HAVE FEARS. 'SPECIALLY WHEN MATCHED AGAINST ONE AS FORMIDABLE AS TAILYPO.
I SEE YOUR PLOY, DEVIL, EVEN IF YOU THINK IT TOO CLEVER TO SPOT. BUT THE IRON CHILD IS NOT ONE TO HAVE HIS COURAGE QUESTIONED. I'LL ACCEPT YOUR CHALLENGE. BUT I CHOOSE THE SPORT.

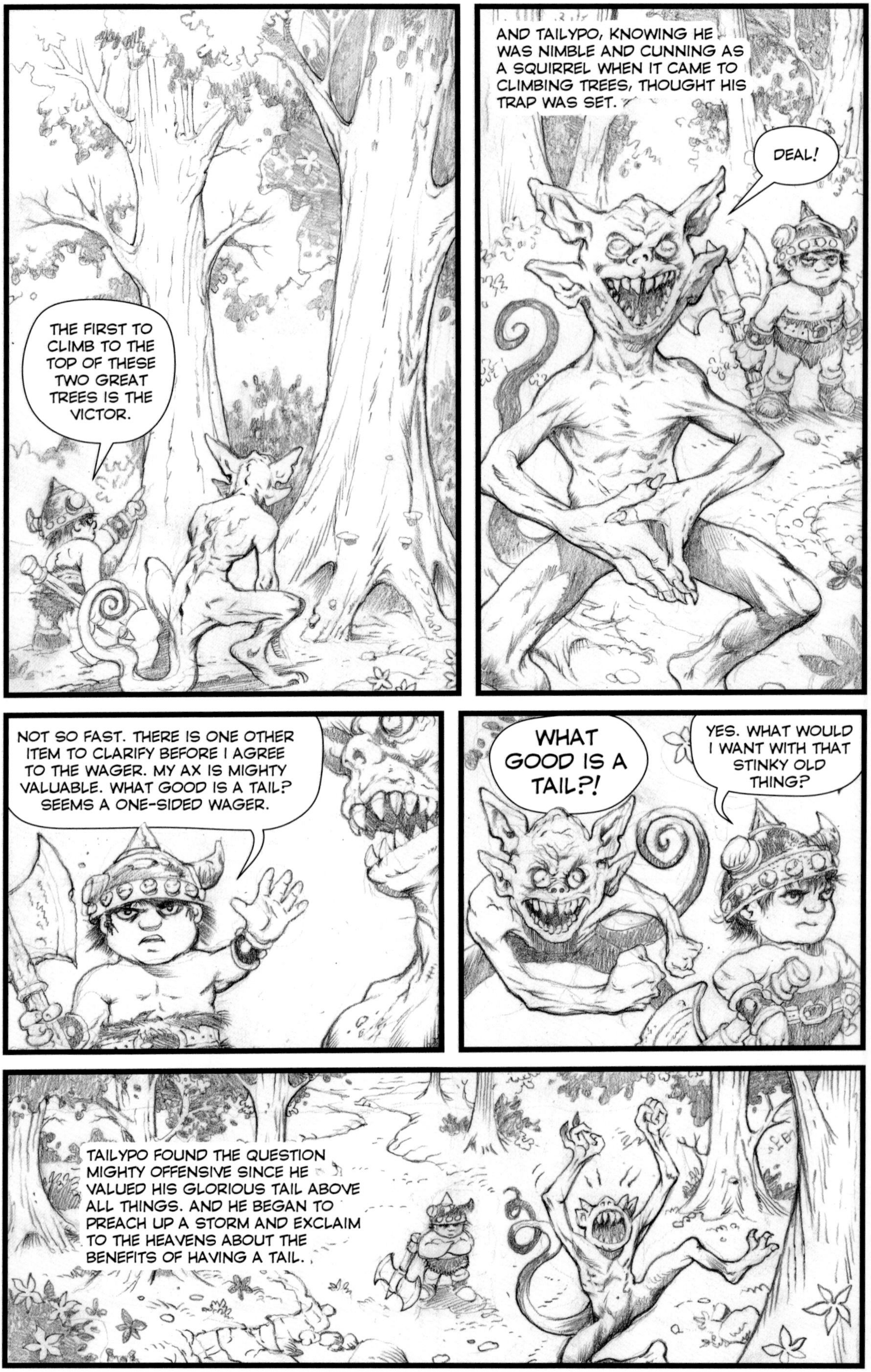
THE FIRST TO CLIMB TO THE TOP OF THESE TWO GREAT TREES IS THE VICTOR.
AND TAILYPO, KNOWING HE WAS NIMBLE AND CUNNING AS A SQUIRREL WHEN IT CAME TO CLIMBING TREES, THOUGHT HIS TRAP WAS SET.
DEAL!
NOT SO FAST. THERE IS ONE OTHER ITEM TO CLARIFY BEFORE I AGREE TO THE WAGER. MY AX IS MIGHTY VALUABLE. WHAT GOOD IS A TAIL? SEEMS A ONE-SIDED WAGER.
WHAT GOOD IS A TAIL?!
YES. WHAT WOULD I WANT WITH THAT STINKY OLD THING?
TAILYPO FOUND THE QUESTION MIGHTY OFFENSIVE SINCE HE VALUED HIS GLORIOUS TAIL ABOVE ALL THINGS. AND HE BEGAN TO PREACH UP A STORM AND EXCLAIM TO THE HEAVENS ABOUT THE BENEFITS OF HAVING A TAIL.

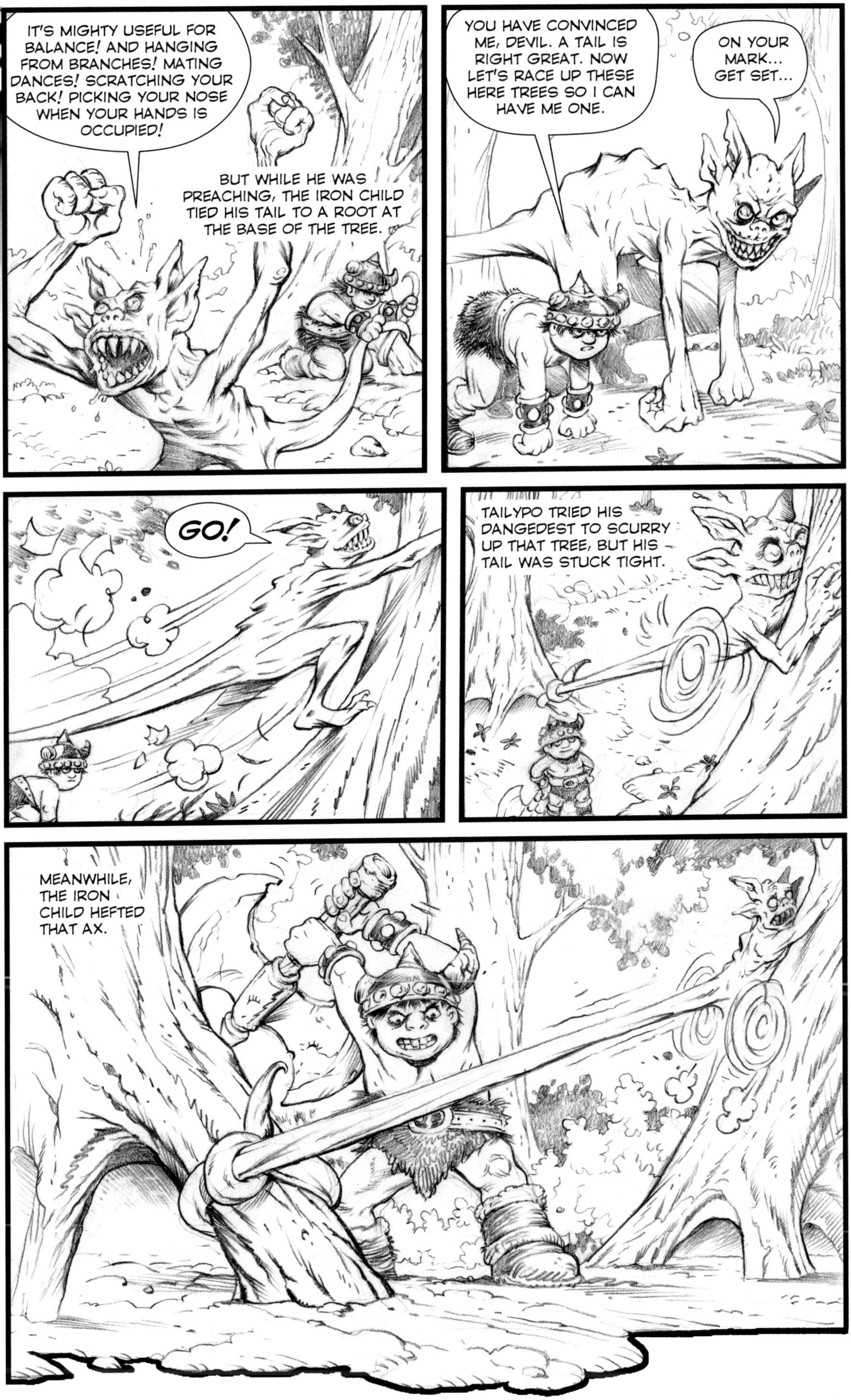
IT'S MIGHTY USEFUL FOR BALANCE! AND HANGING FROM BRANCHES! MATING DANCES! SCRATCHING YOUR BACK! PICKING YOUR NOSE WHEN YOUR HANDS IS OCCUPIED!
BUT WHILE HE WAS PREACHING, THE IRON CHILD TIED HIS TAIL TO A ROOT AT THE BASE OF THE TREE.
YOU HAVE CONVINCED ME, DEVIL. A TAIL IS RIGHT GREAT. NOW LET'S RACE UP THESE HERE TREES SO I CAN HAVE ME ONE.
ON YOUR MARK... GET SET...
GO!
TAILYPO TRIED HIS DANGEDEST TO SCURRY UP THAT TREE, BUT HIS TAIL WAS STUCK TIGHT.
MEANWHILE, THE IRON CHILD HEFTED THAT AX.

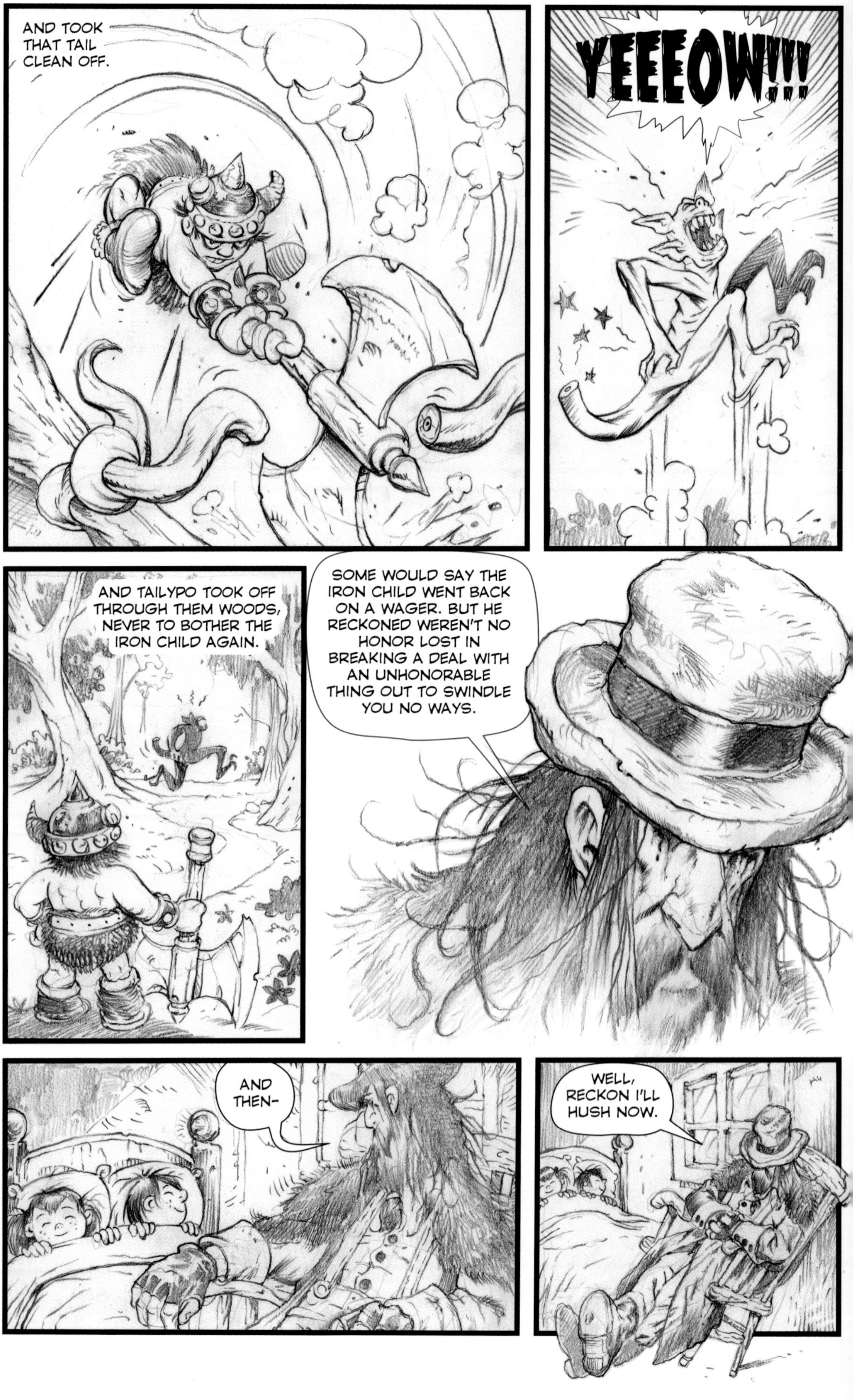
AND TOOK THAT TAIL CLEAN OFF.
YEEEOW!!!
AND TAILYPO TOOK OFF THROUGH THEM WOODS, NEVER TO BOTHER THE IRON CHILD AGAIN.
SOME WOULD SAY THE IRON CHILD WENT BACK ON A WAGER. BUT HE RECKONED WEREN'T NO HONOR LOST IN BREAKING A DEAL WITH AN UNHONORABLE THING OUT TO SWINDLE YOU NO WAYS.
AND THEN-
WELL, RECKON I'LL HUSH NOW.

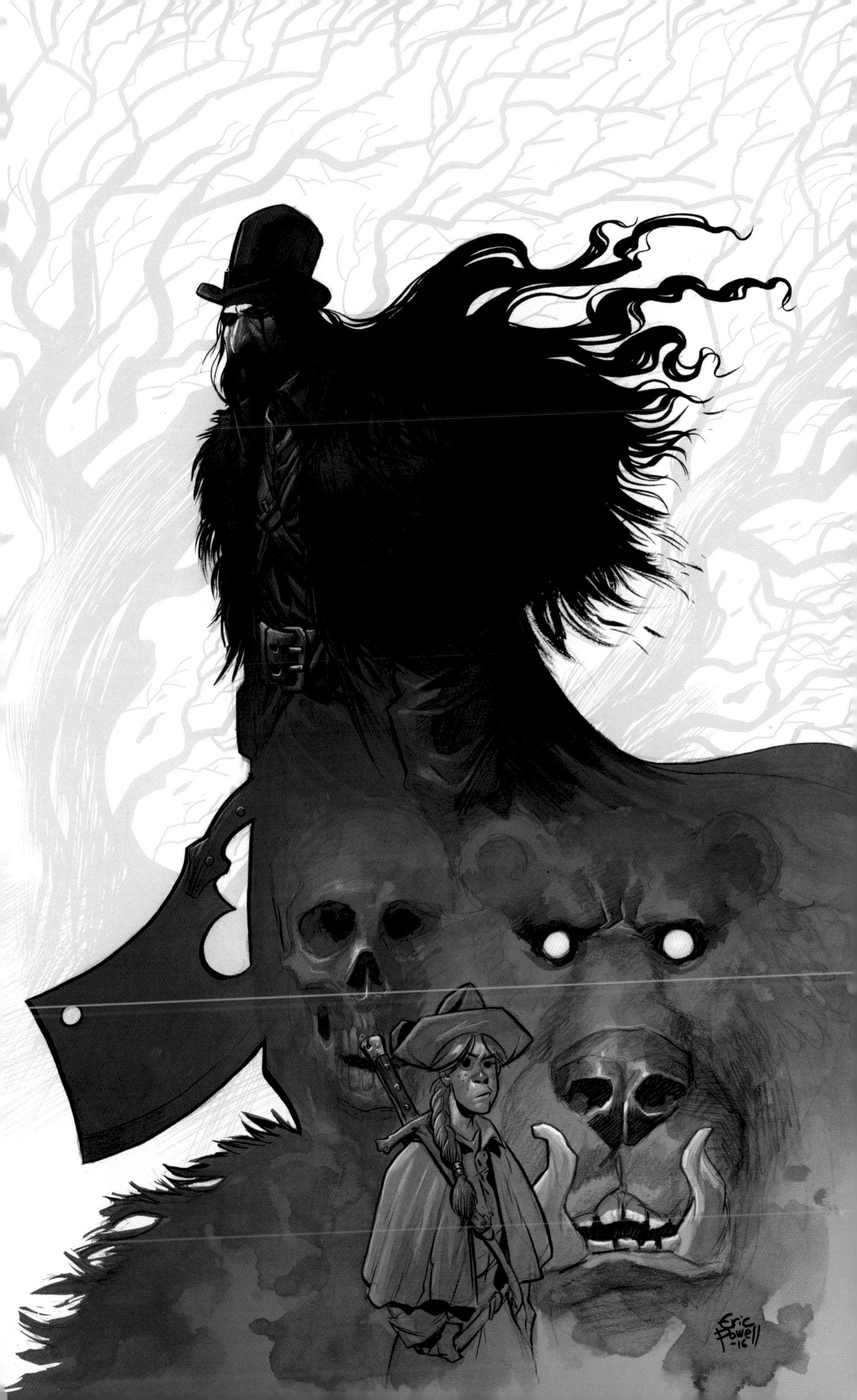
Eric Powell -16

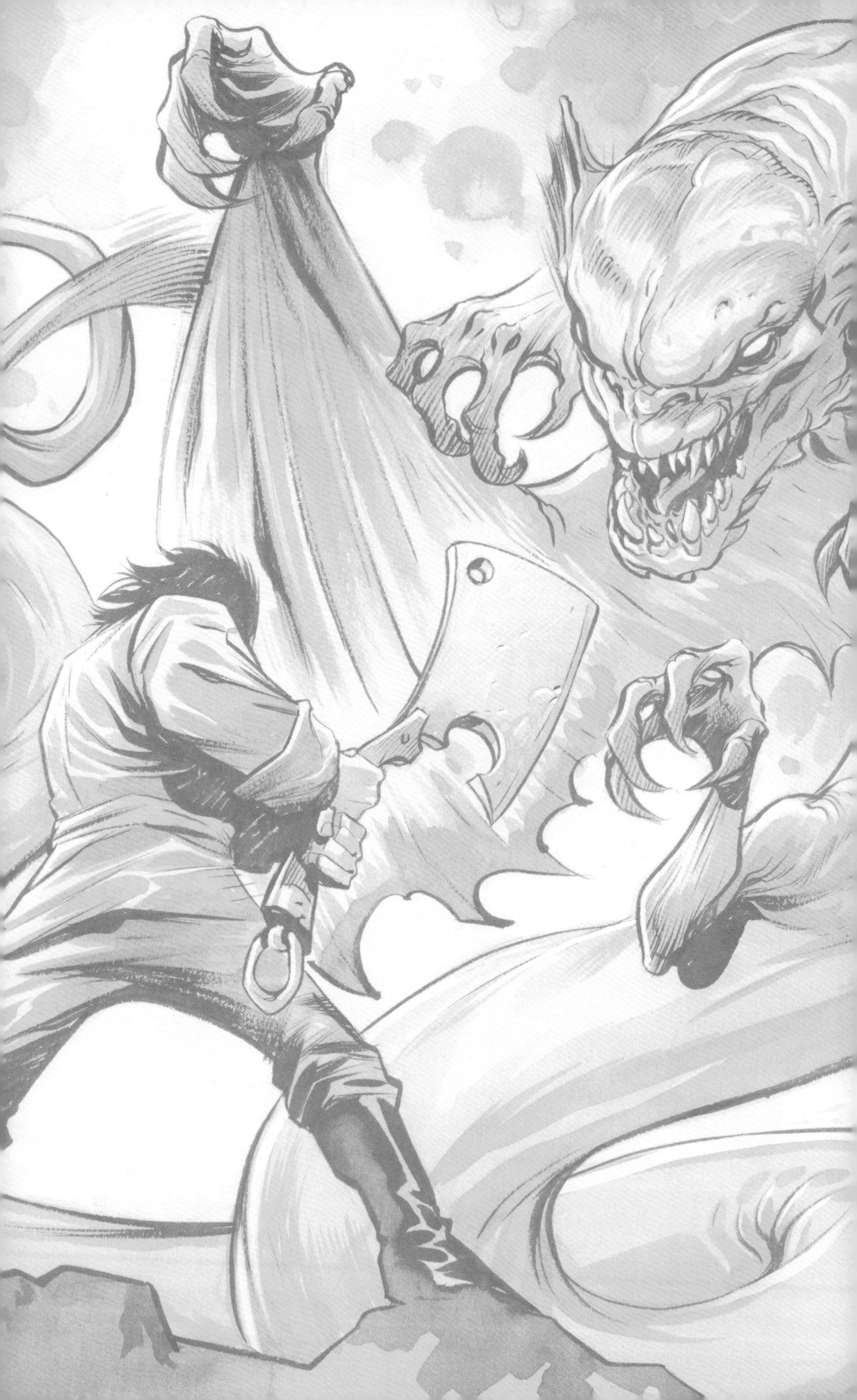

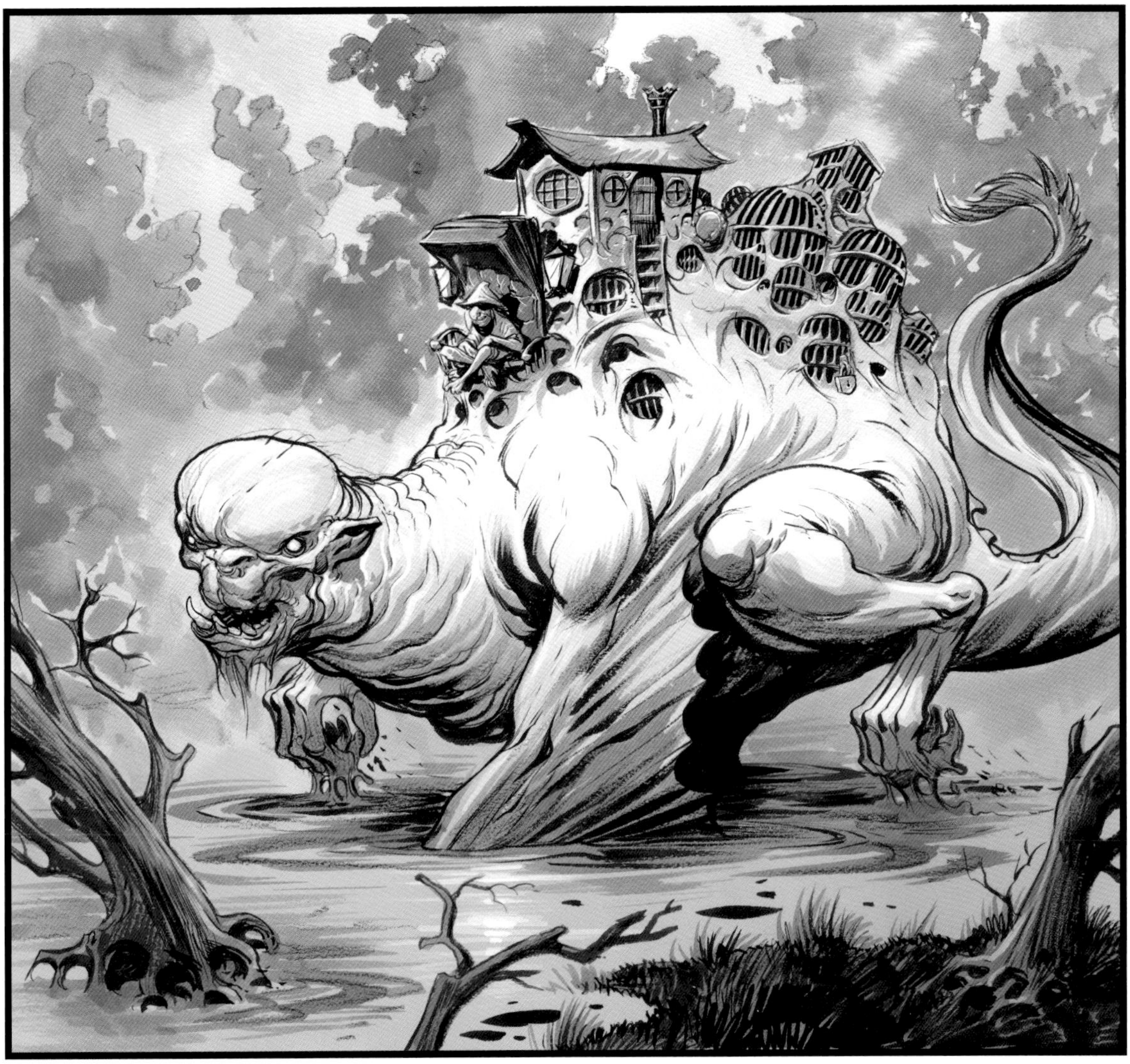

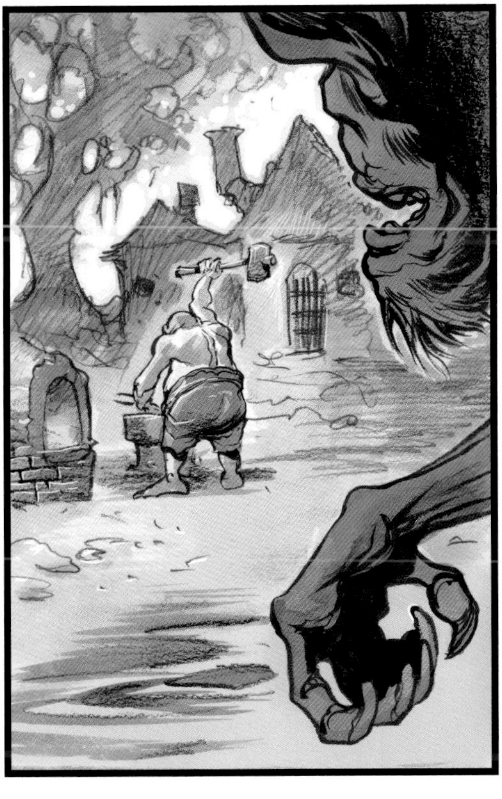

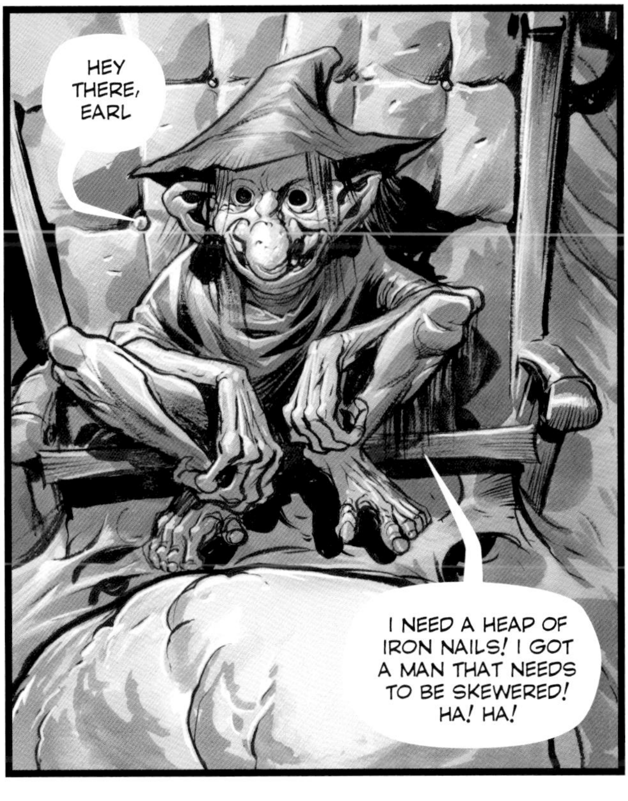
HEY THERE, EARL
I NEED A HEAP OF IRON NAILS! I GOT A MAN THAT NEEDS TO BE SKEWERED! HA! HA!

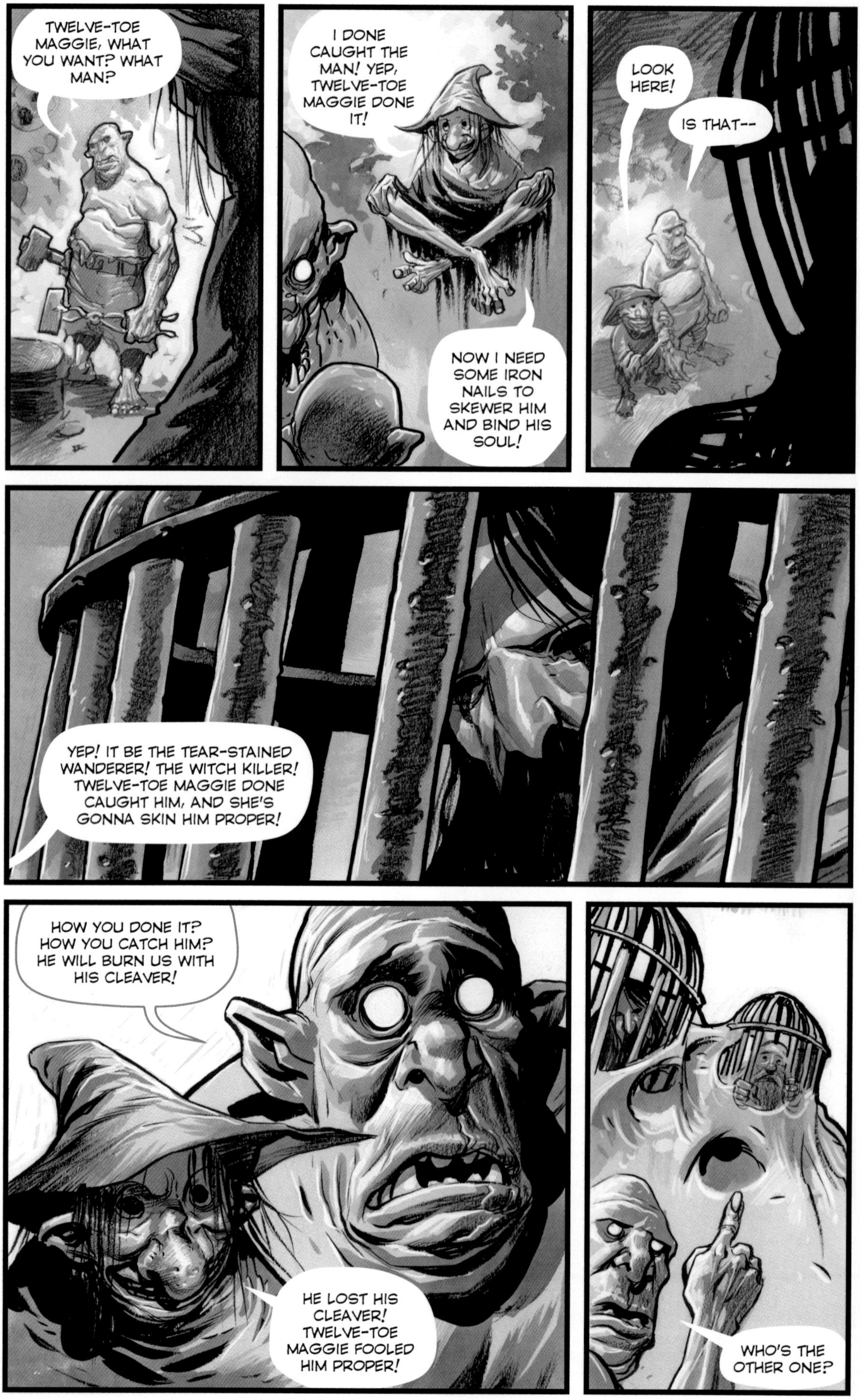
TWELVE-TOE MAGGIE, WHAT YOU WANT? WHAT MAN?
I DONE CAUGHT THE MAN! YEP, TWELVE-TOE MAGGIE DONE IT!
NOW I NEED SOME IRON NAILS TO SKEWER HIM AND BIND HIS SOUL!
LOOK HERE!
IS THAT--
YEP! IT BE THE TEAR-STAINED WANDERER! THE WITCH KILLER! TWELVE-TOE MAGGIE DONE CAUGHT HIM, AND SHE'S GONNA SKIN HIM PROPER!
HOW YOU DONE IT? HOW YOU CATCH HIM? HE WILL BURN US WITH HIS CLEAVER!
HE LOST HIS CLEAVER! TWELVE-TOE MAGGIE FOOLED HIM PROPER!
WHO'S THE OTHER ONE?

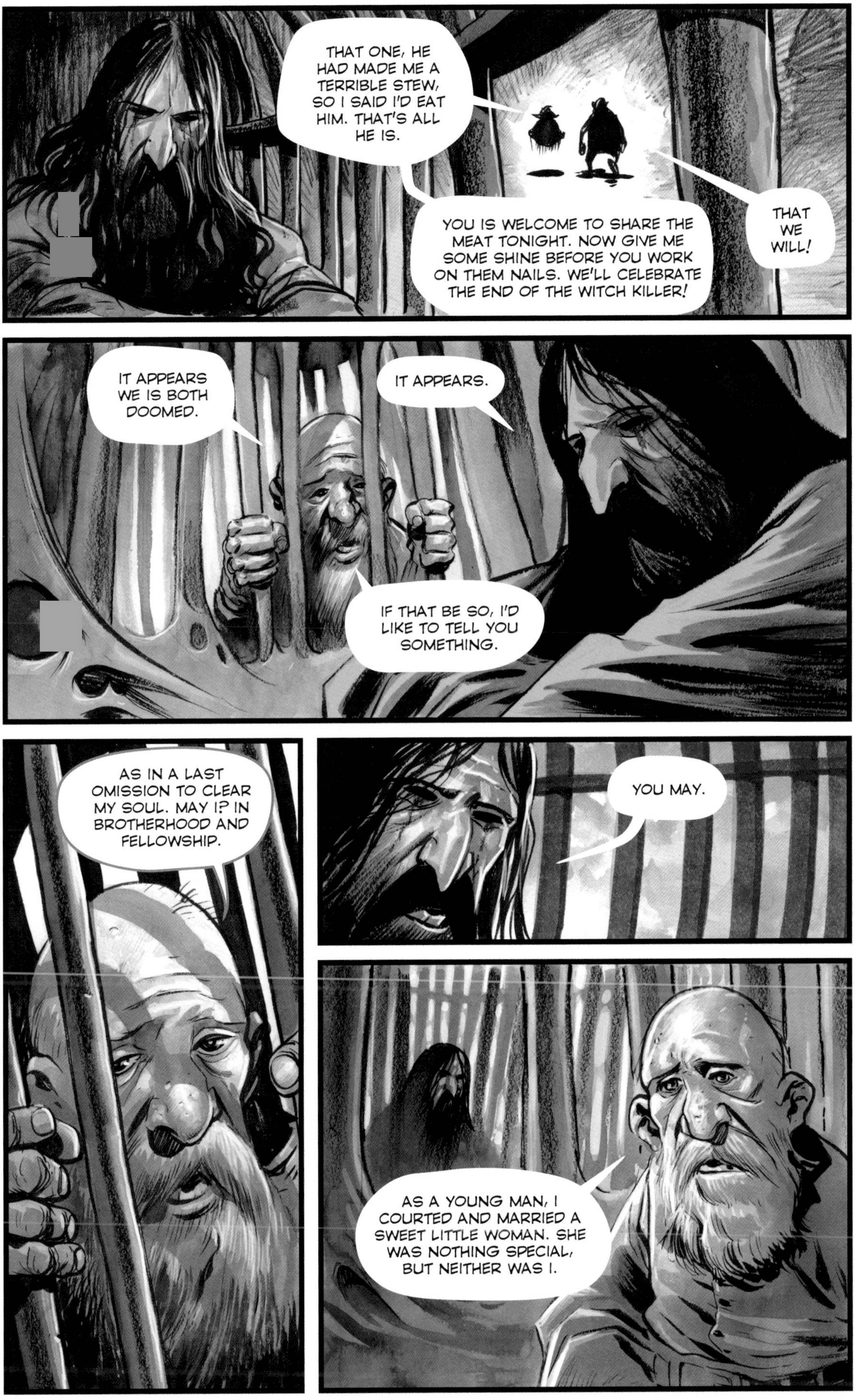
THAT ONE, HE HAD MADE ME A TERRIBLE STEW, SO I SAID I'D EAT HIM. THAT'S ALL HE IS.
YOU IS WELCOME TO SHARE THE MEAT TONIGHT. NOW GIVE ME SOME SHINE BEFORE YOU WORK ON THEM NAILS. WE'LL CELEBRATE THE END OF THE WITCH KILLER!
THAT WE WILL!
IT APPEARS WE IS BOTH DOOMED.
IT APPEARS.
IF THAT BE SO, I'D LIKE TO TELL YOU SOMETHING.
AS IN A LAST OMISSION TO CLEAR MY SOUL. MAY I? IN BROTHERHOOD AND FELLOWSHIP.
YOU MAY.
AS A YOUNG MAN, I COURTED AND MARRIED A SWEET LITTLE WOMAN. SHE WAS NOTHING SPECIAL, BUT NEITHER WAS I.

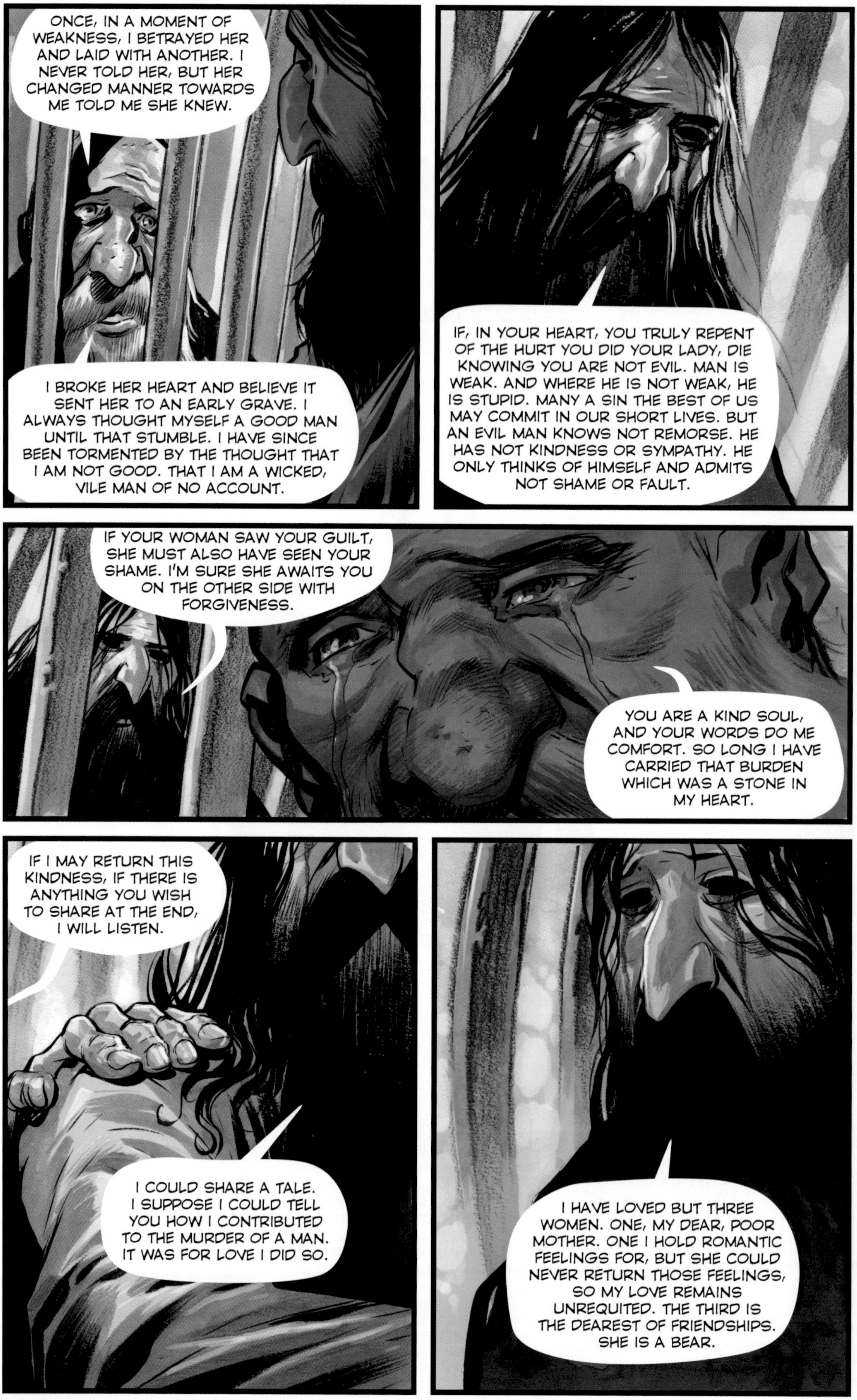
ONCE, IN A MOMENT OF WEAKNESS, I BETRAYED HER AND LAID WITH ANOTHER. I NEVER TOLD HER, BUT HER CHANGED MANNER TOWARDS ME TOLD ME SHE KNEW.
I BROKE HER HEART AND BELIEVE IT SENT HER TO AN EARLY GRAVE. I ALWAYS THOUGHT MYSELF A GOOD MAN UNTIL THAT STUMBLE. I HAVE SINCE BEEN TORMENTED BY THE THOUGHT THAT I AM NOT GOOD. THAT I AM A WICKED, VILE MAN OF NO ACCOUNT.
IF, IN YOUR HEART, YOU TRULY REPENT OF THE HURT YOU DID YOUR LADY, DIE KNOWING YOU ARE NOT EVIL. MAN IS WEAK. AND WHERE HE IS NOT WEAK, HE IS STUPID. MANY A SIN THE BEST OF US MAY COMMIT IN OUR SHORT LIVES. BUT AN EVIL MAN KNOWS NOT REMORSE. HE HAS NOT KINDNESS OR SYMPATHY. HE ONLY THINKS OF HIMSELF AND ADMITS NOT SHAME OR FAULT.
IF YOUR WOMAN SAW YOUR GUILT, SHE MUST ALSO HAVE SEEN YOUR SHAME. I'M SURE SHE AWAITS YOU ON THE OTHER SIDE WITH FORGIVENESS.
YOU ARE A KIND SOUL, AND YOUR WORDS DO ME COMFORT. SO LONG I HAVE CARRIED THAT BURDEN WHICH WAS A STONE IN MY HEART.
IF I MAY RETURN THIS KINDNESS, IF THERE IS ANYTHING YOU WISH TO SHARE AT THE END, I WILL LISTEN.
I COULD SHARE A TALE. I SUPPOSE I COULD TELL YOU HOW I CONTRIBUTED TO THE MURDER OF A MAN. IT WAS FOR LOVE I DID SO.
I HAVE LOVED BUT THREE WOMEN. ONE, MY DEAR, POOR MOTHER. ONE I HOLD ROMANTIC FEELINGS FOR, BUT SHE COULD NEVER RETURN THOSE FEELINGS, SO MY LOVE REMAINS UNREQUITED. THE THIRD IS THE DEAREST OF FRIENDSHIPS. SHE IS A BEAR.

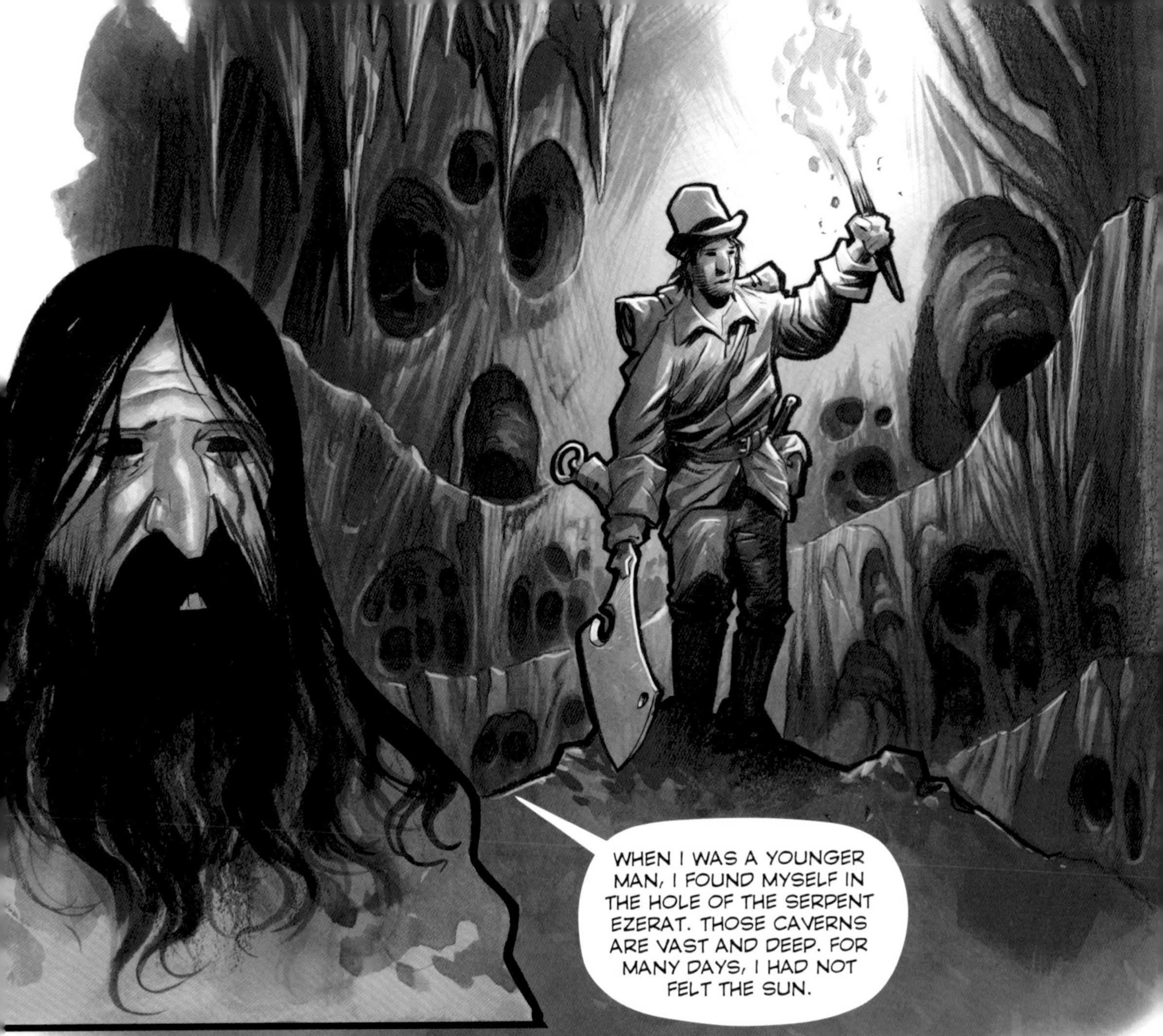
WHEN I WAS A YOUNGER MAN, I FOUND MYSELF IN THE HOLE OF THE SERPENT EZERAT. THOSE CAVERNS ARE VAST AND DEEP. FOR MANY DAYS, I HAD NOT FELT THE SUN.

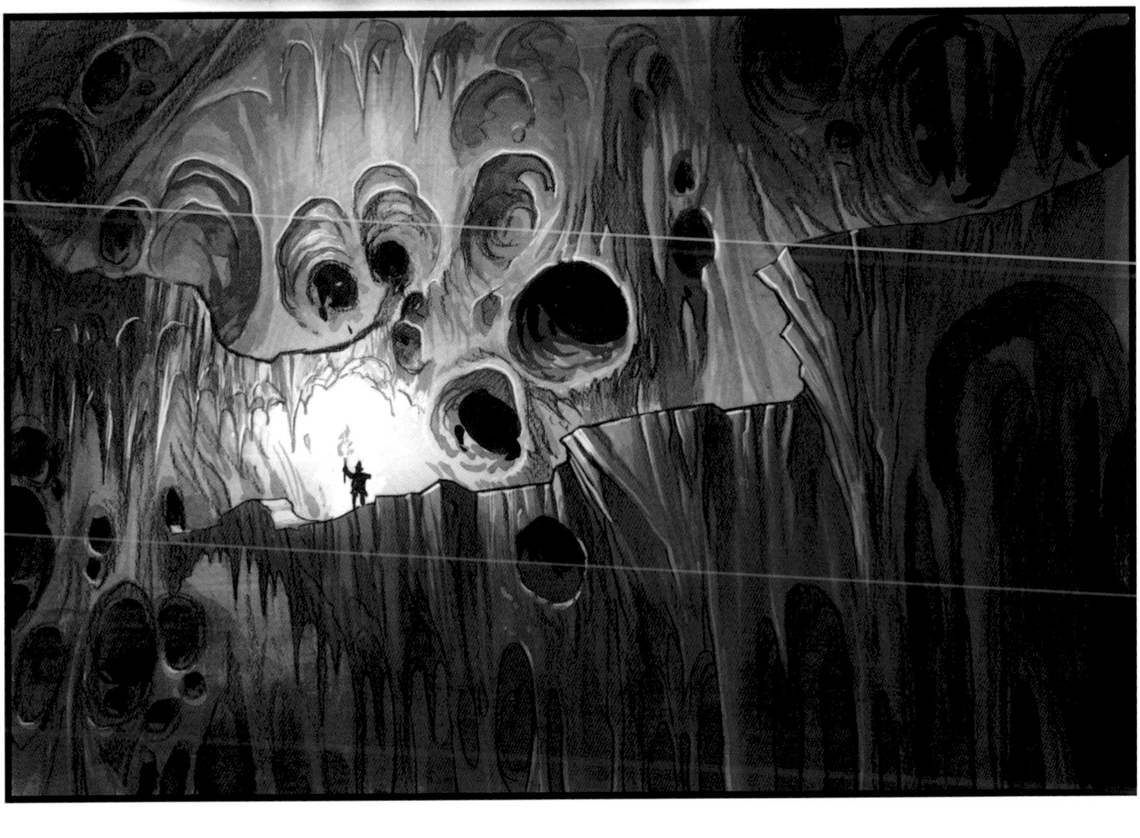

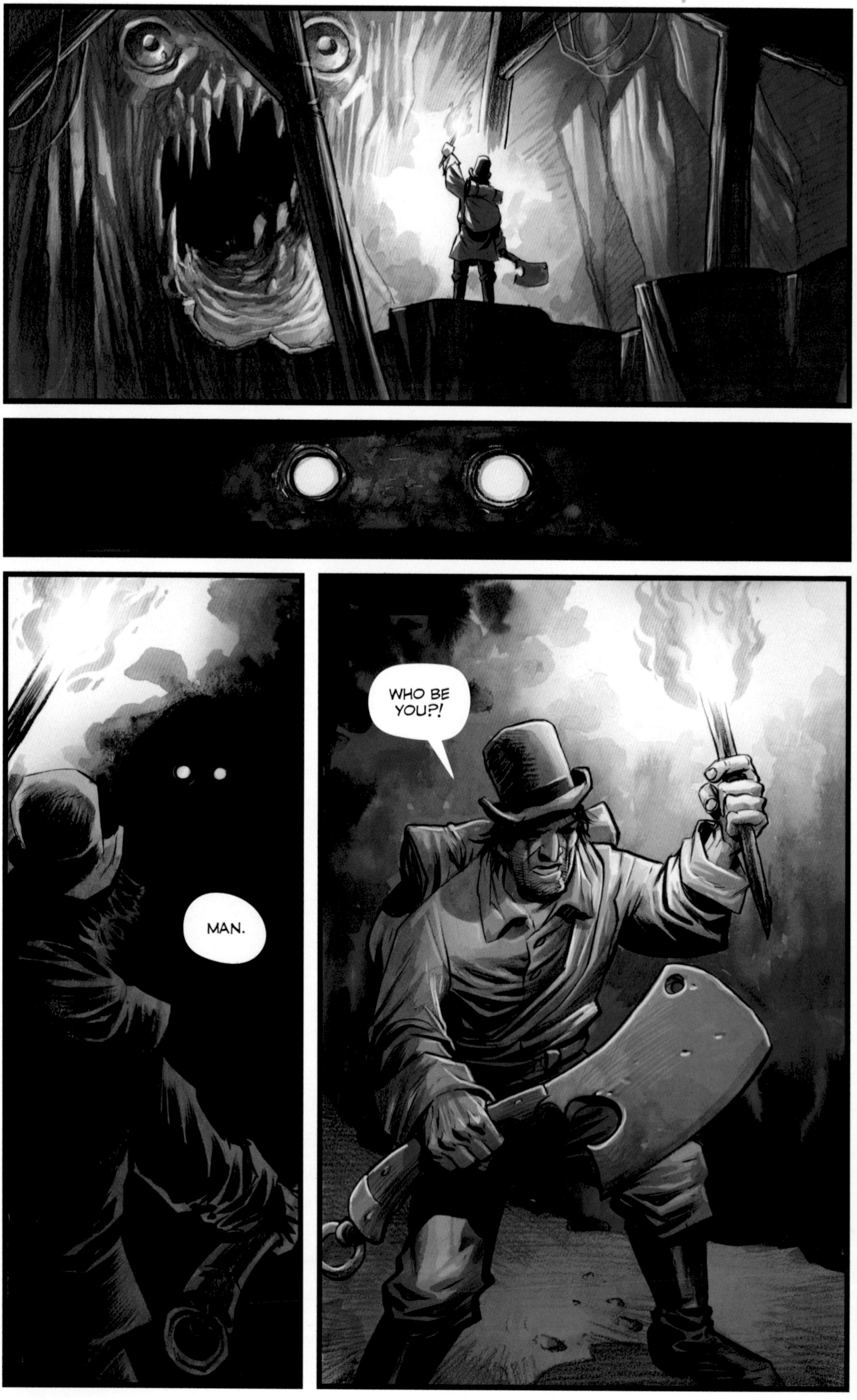
MAN.
WHO BE YOU?!

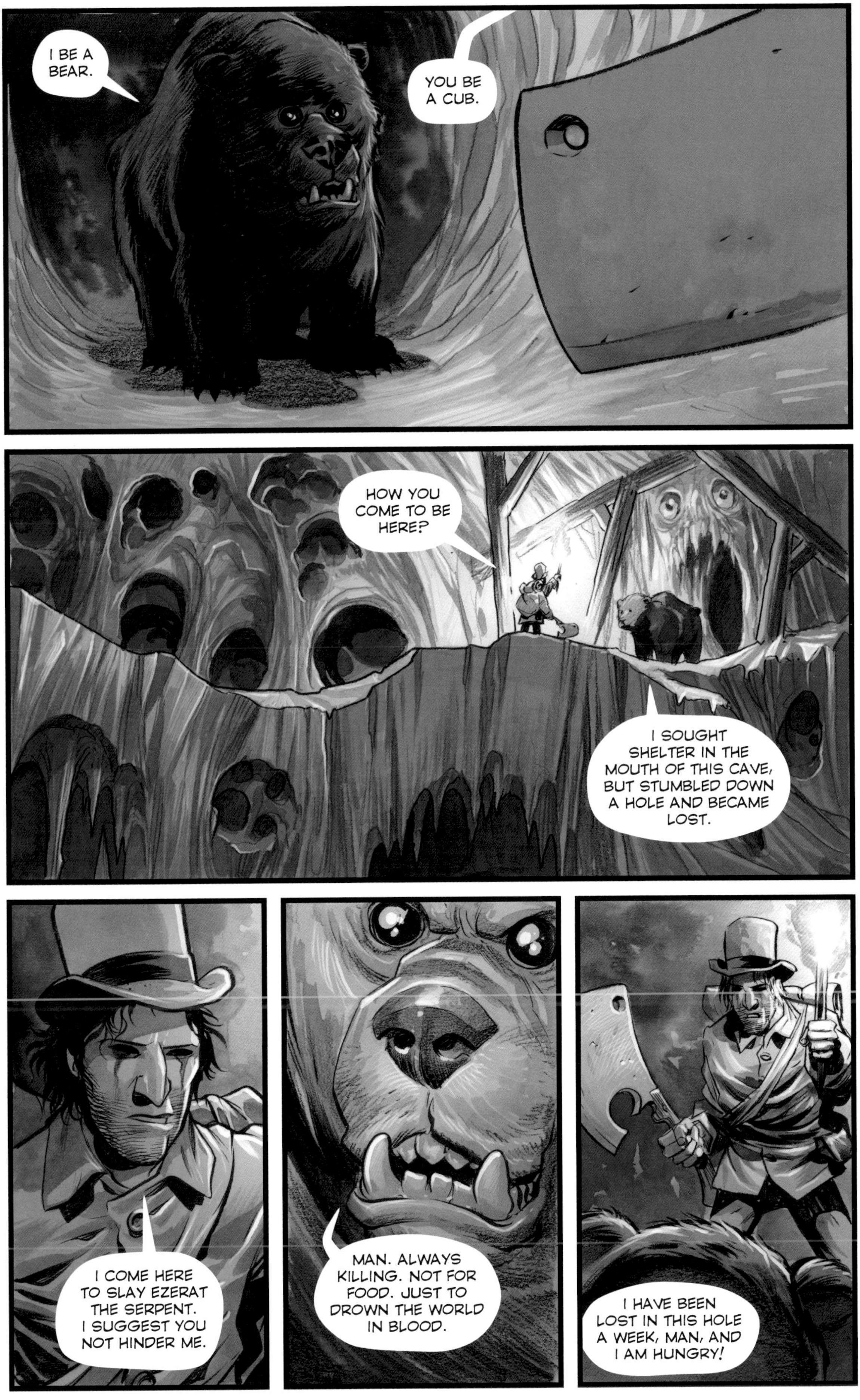
I BE A BEAR.
YOU BE A CUB.
HOW YOU COME TO BE HERE?
I SOUGHT SHELTER IN THE MOUTH OF THIS CAVE, BUT STUMBLED DOWN A HOLE AND BECAME LOST.
I COME HERE TO SLAY EZERAT THE SERPENT. I SUGGEST YOU NOT HINDER ME.
MAN. ALWAYS KILLING. NOT FOR FOOD. JUST TO DROWN THE WORLD IN BLOOD.
I HAVE BEEN LOST IN THIS HOLE A WEEK, MAN, AND I AM HUNGRY!

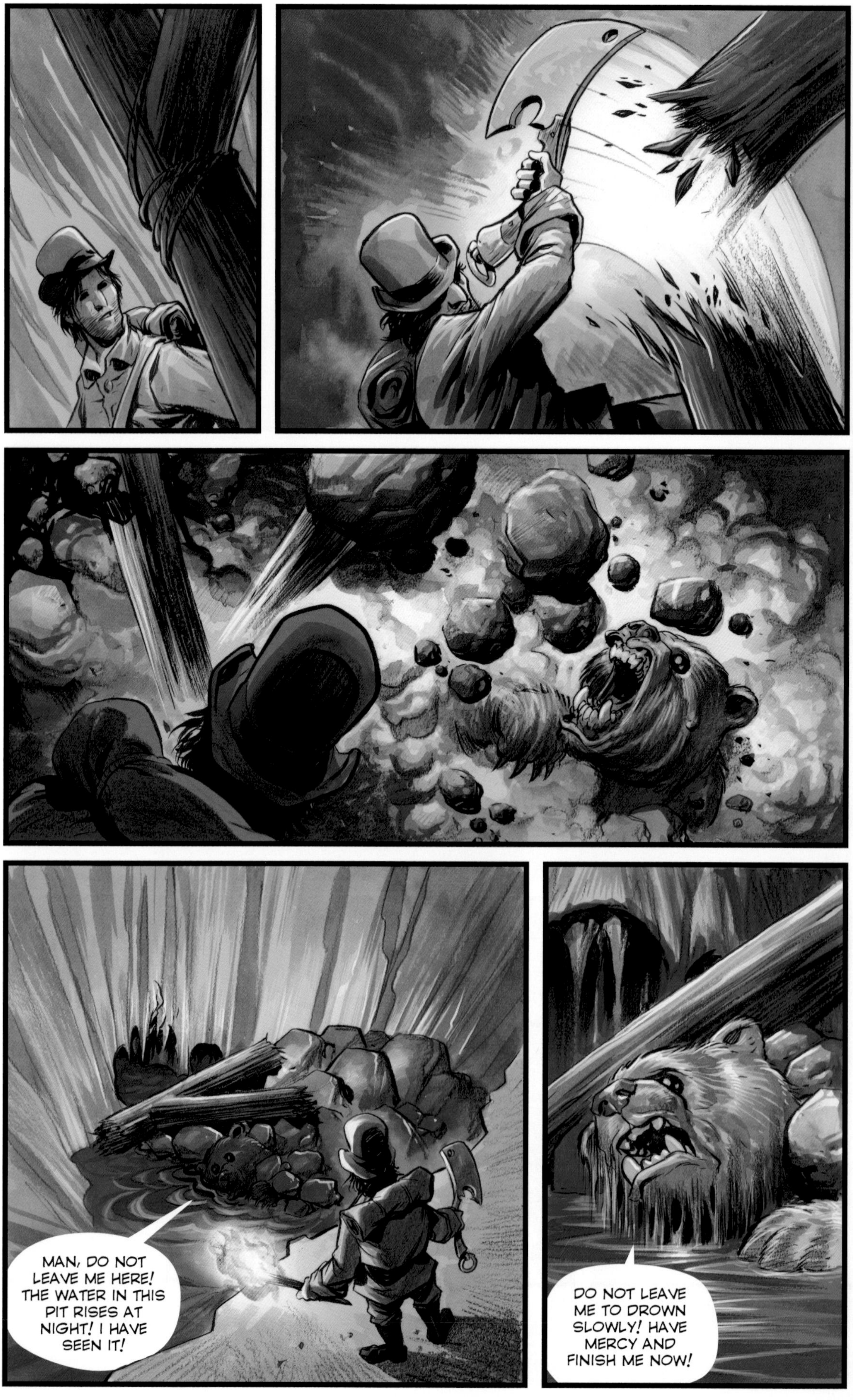
MAN, DO NOT LEAVE ME HERE! THE WATER IN THIS PIT RISES AT NIGHT! I HAVE SEEN IT!
DO NOT LEAVE ME TO DROWN SLOWLY! HAVE MERCY AND FINISH ME NOW!

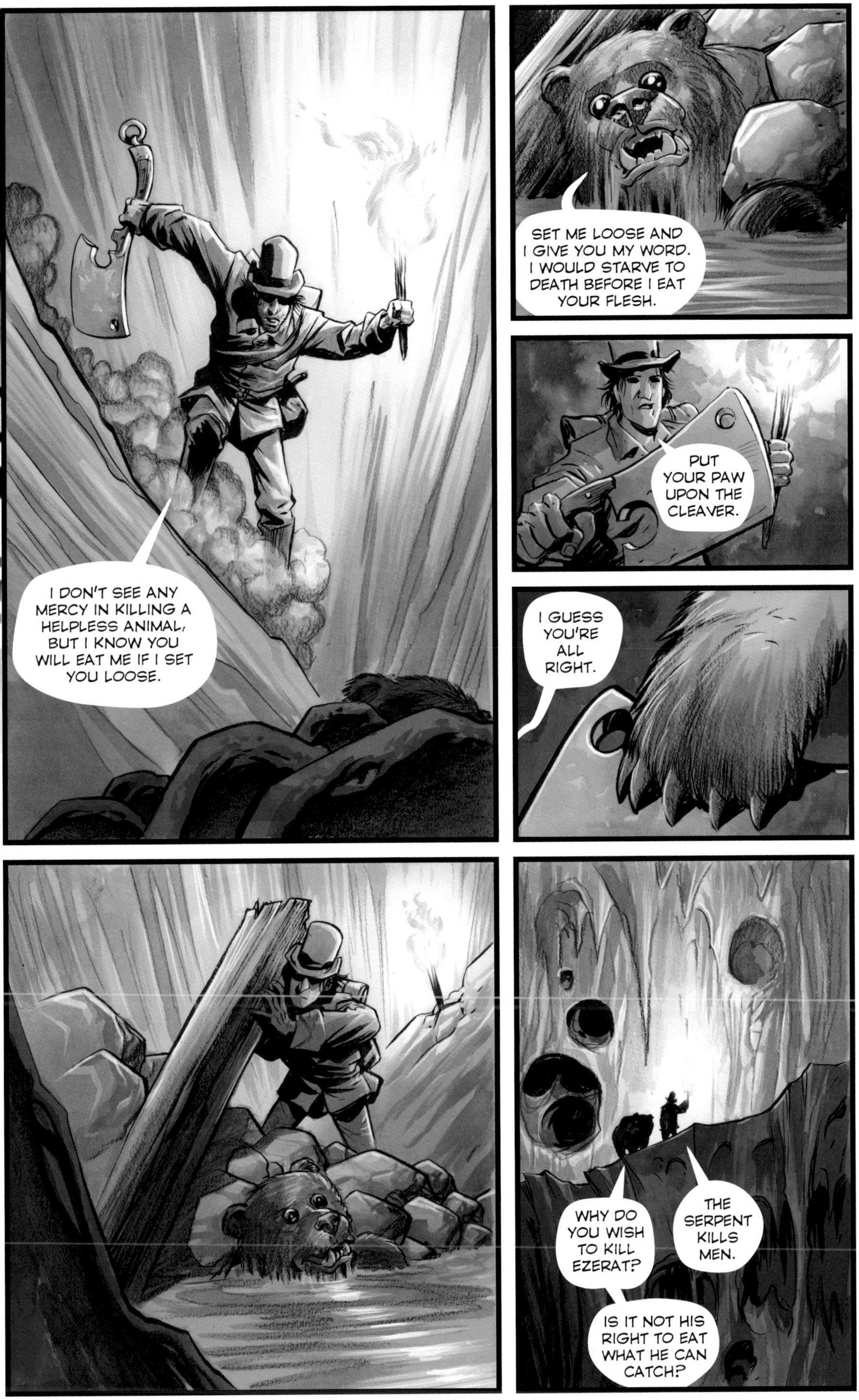
I DON'T SEE ANY MERCY IN KILLING A HELPLESS ANIMAL, BUT I KNOW YOU WILL EAT ME IF I SET YOU LOOSE.
SET ME LOOSE AND I GIVE YOU MY WORD. I WOULD STARVE TO DEATH BEFORE I EAT YOUR FLESH.
PUT YOUR PAW UPON THE CLEAVER.
I GUESS YOU'RE ALL RIGHT.
WHY DO YOU WISH TO KILL EZERAT?
THE SERPENT KILLS MEN.
IS IT NOT HIS RIGHT TO EAT WHAT HE CAN CATCH?

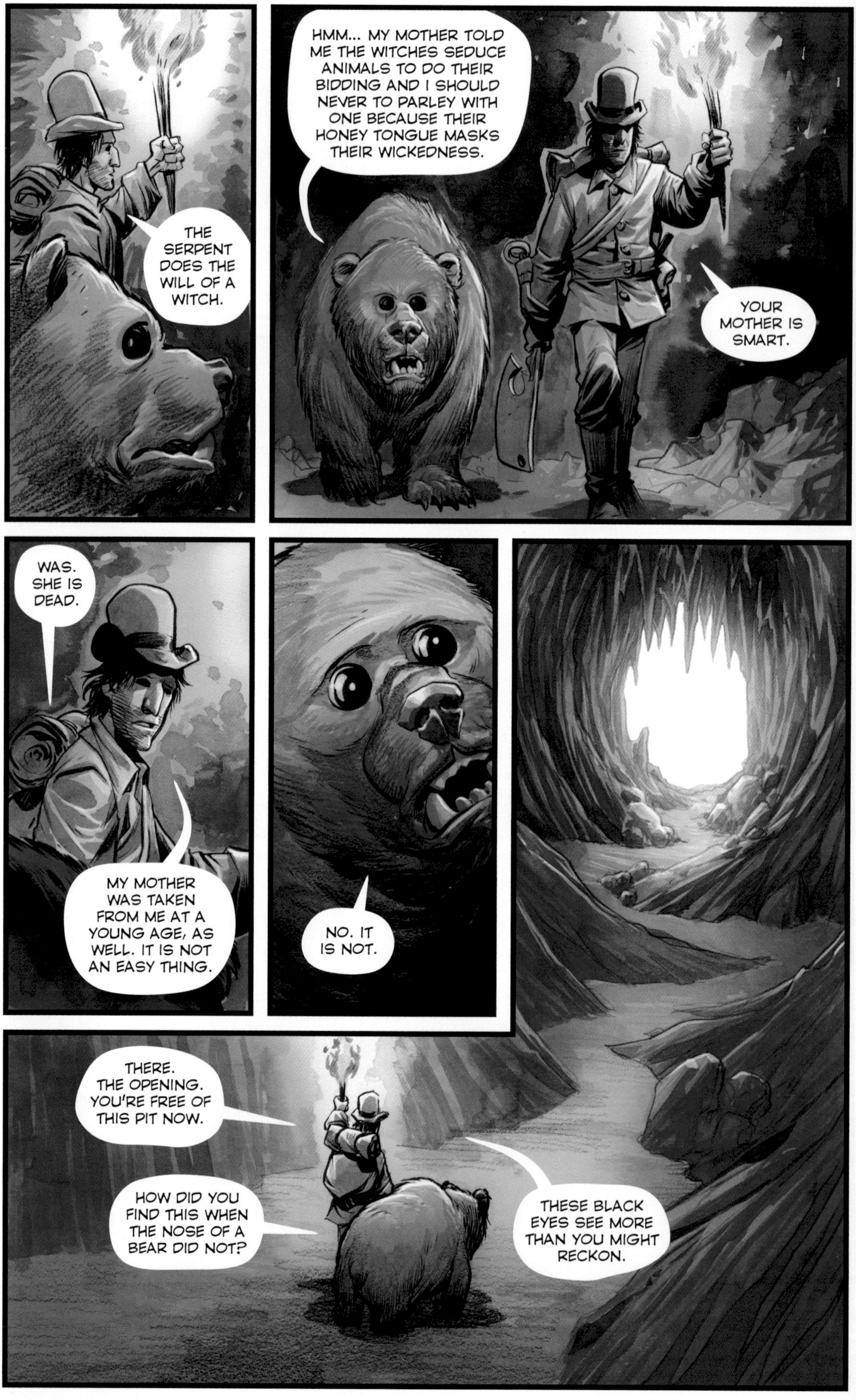
THE SERPENT DOES THE WILL OF A WITCH.
HMM... MY MOTHER TOLD ME THE WITCHES SEDUCE ANIMALS TO DO THEIR BIDDING AND I SHOULD NEVER TO PARLEY WITH ONE BECAUSE THEIR HONEY TONGUE MASKS THEIR WICKEDNESS.
YOUR MOTHER IS SMART.
WAS. SHE IS DEAD.
MY MOTHER WAS TAKEN FROM ME AT A YOUNG AGE, AS WELL. IT IS NOT AN EASY THING.
NO. IT IS NOT.
THERE. THE OPENING. YOU'RE FREE OF THIS PIT NOW.
HOW DID YOU FIND THIS WHEN THE NOSE OF A BEAR DID NOT?
THESE BLACK EYES SEE MORE THAN YOU MIGHT RECKON.

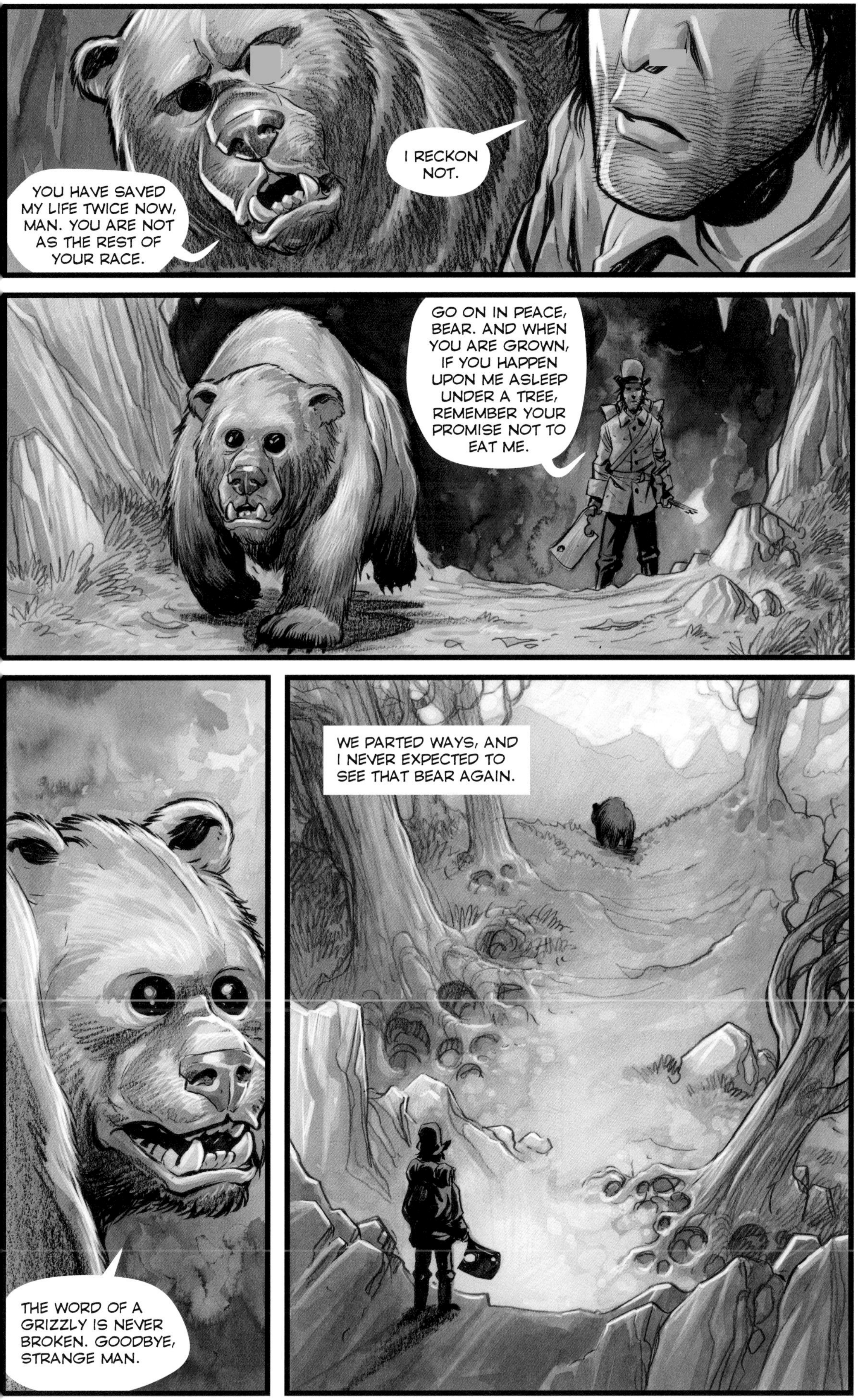
YOU HAVE SAVED MY LIFE TWICE NOW, MAN. YOU ARE NOT AS THE REST OF YOUR RACE.
I RECKON NOT.
GO ON IN PEACE, BEAR. AND WHEN YOU ARE GROWN, IF YOU HAPPEN UPON ME ASLEEP UNDER A TREE, REMEMBER YOUR PROMISE NOT TO EAT ME.
THE WORD OF A GRIZZLY IS NEVER BROKEN. GOODBYE, STRANGE MAN.
WE PARTED WAYS, AND I NEVER EXPECTED TO SEE THAT BEAR AGAIN.

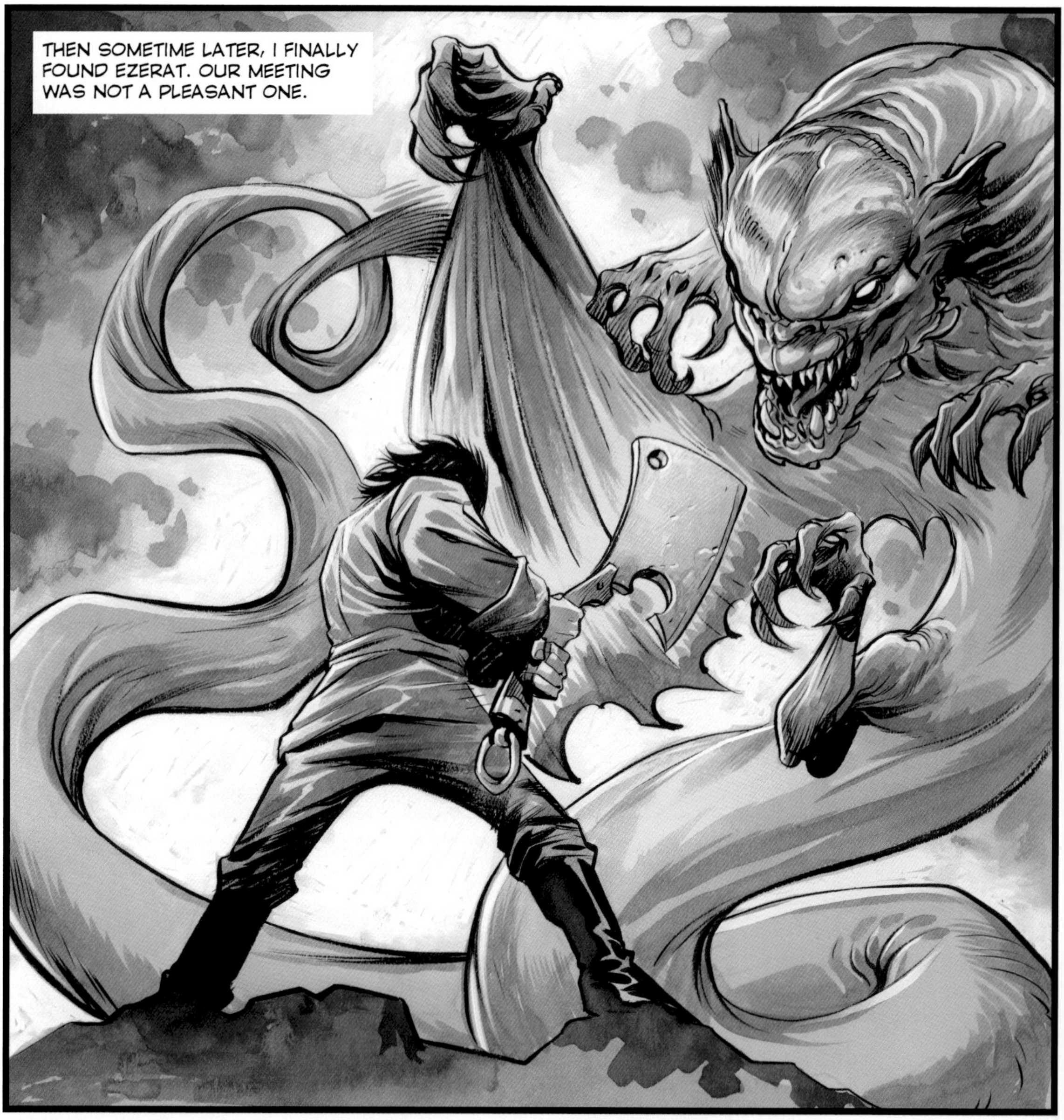
THEN SOMETIME LATER, I FINALLY FOUND EZERAT. OUR MEETING WAS NOT A PLEASANT ONE.

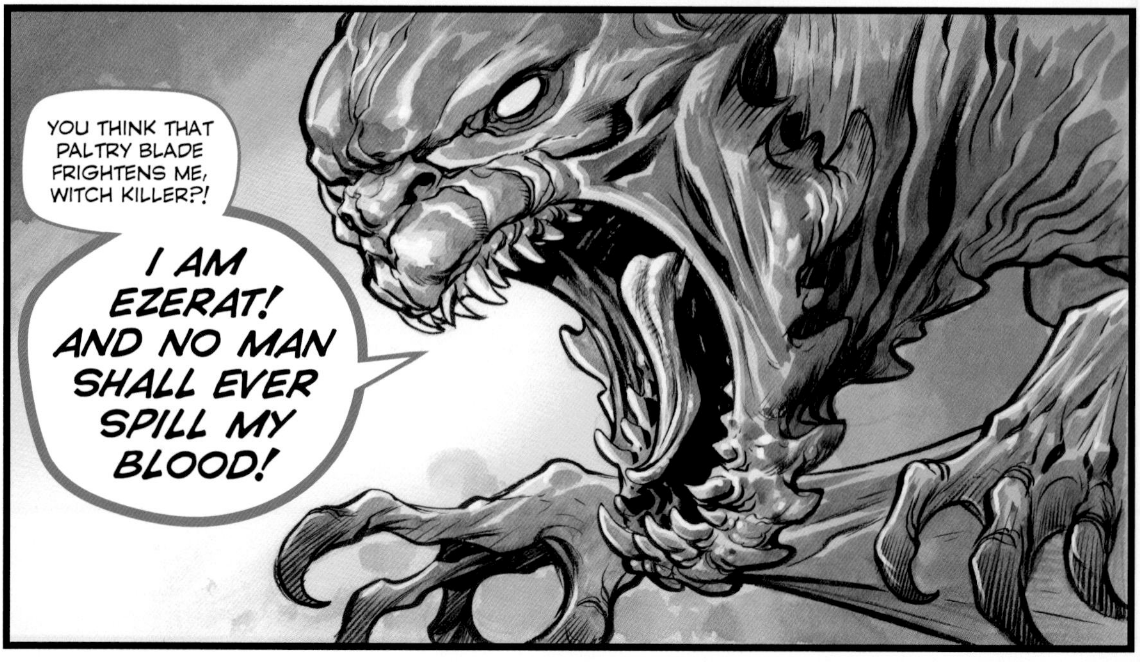
YOU THINK THAT PALTRY BLADE FRIGHTENS ME, WITCH KILLER?!
I AM EZERAT! AND NO MAN SHALL EVER SPILL MY BLOOD!

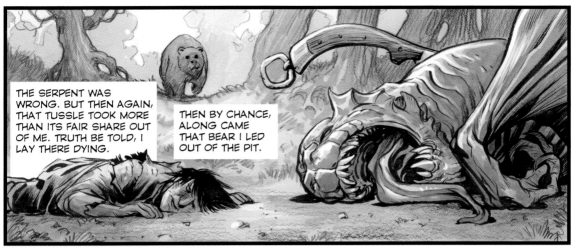

THE SERPENT WAS WRONG. BUT THEN AGAIN, THAT TUSSLE TOOK MORE THAN ITS FAIR SHARE OUT OF ME. TRUTH BE TOLD, I LAY THERE DYING.

THEN BY CHANCE, ALONG CAME THAT BEAR I LED OUT OF THE PIT.

SHE DRUG ME INTO THE HOLLOW OF A DEAD TREE AND NURSED ME BACK TO HEALTH.

NOW THAT YOU HAVE KILLED THE SERPENT, MAN, WHAT WILL YOU DO?

WELL, I RECKON I DON'T KNOW. SEE, I KIND OF JUST WANDER ABOUT MOSTLY.

SILLY MAN. THEN YOU BEST COME EAST WITH ME TO KEEP YOURSELF OUT OF TROUBLE.

THE WICKED.

I NEVER BEEN THIS FAR. WHAT KIND OF FOLKS YOU RECKON LIVE HERE?

WILL YOU LOOK AT THAT. RECKON THERE'S SOME WELL-TO-DO FOLKS THAT LIVE THERE.

THAT'S WHERE I'M HEADING.

MY MOTHER. THE MAN THAT KILLED HER LIVES THERE.

WHAT ON EARTH WOULD A GRIZ WANT WITH A PLACE LIKE THAT?

AND I'M GOING TO KILL HIM.

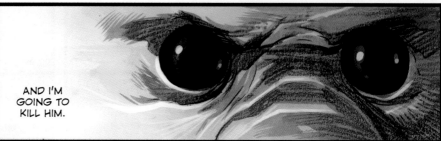

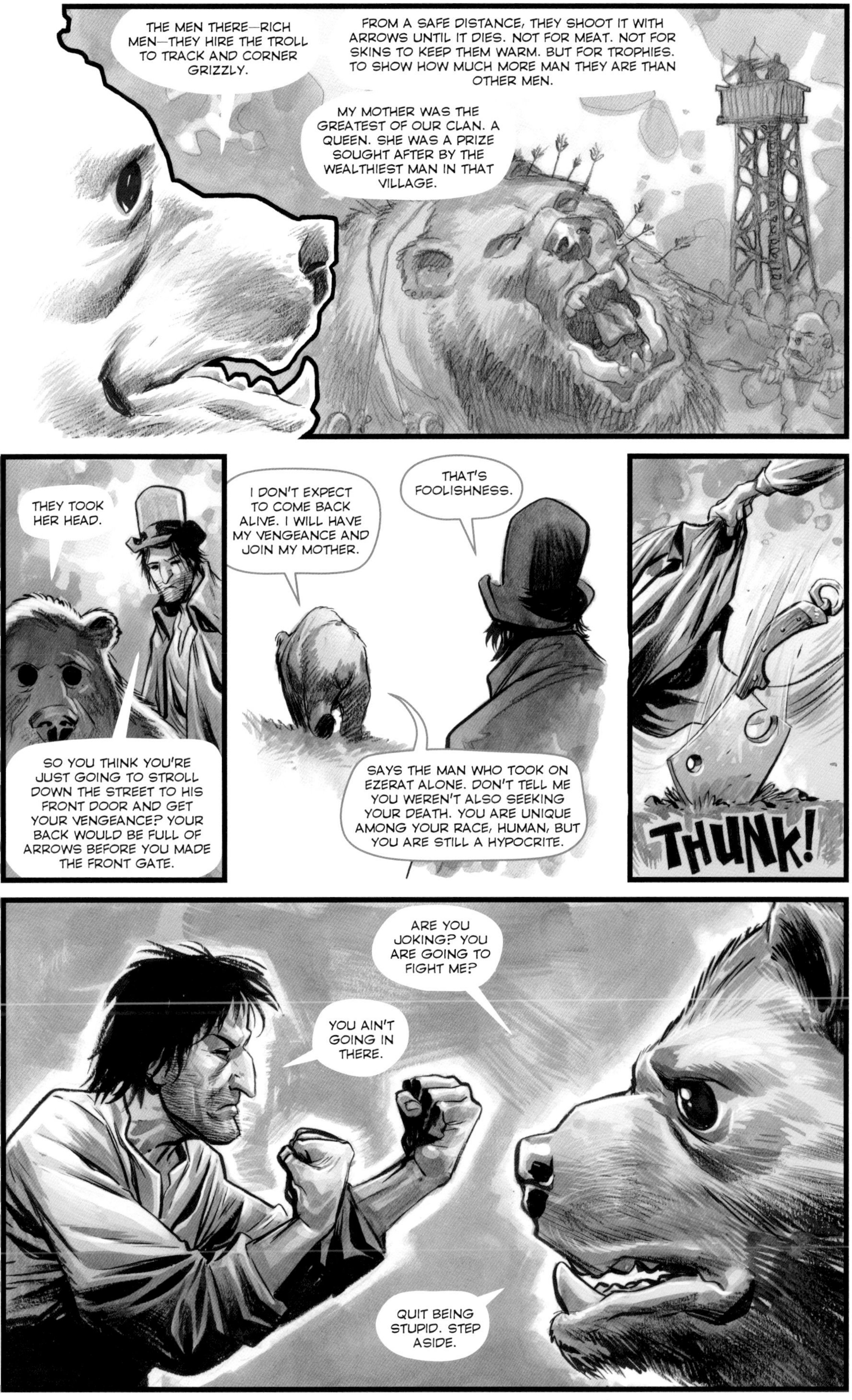
THE MEN THERE—RICH MEN—THEY HIRE THE TROLL TO TRACK AND CORNER GRIZZLY.
FROM A SAFE DISTANCE, THEY SHOOT IT WITH ARROWS UNTIL IT DIES. NOT FOR MEAT. NOT FOR SKINS TO KEEP THEM WARM. BUT FOR TROPHIES. TO SHOW HOW MUCH MORE MAN THEY ARE THAN OTHER MEN.
MY MOTHER WAS THE GREATEST OF OUR CLAN. A QUEEN. SHE WAS A PRIZE SOUGHT AFTER BY THE WEALTHIEST MAN IN THAT VILLAGE.
THEY TOOK HER HEAD.
SO YOU THINK YOU'RE JUST GOING TO STROLL DOWN THE STREET TO HIS FRONT DOOR AND GET YOUR VENGEANCE? YOUR BACK WOULD BE FULL OF ARROWS BEFORE YOU MADE THE FRONT GATE.
I DON'T EXPECT TO COME BACK ALIVE. I WILL HAVE MY VENGEANCE AND JOIN MY MOTHER.
THAT'S FOOLISHNESS.
SAYS THE MAN WHO TOOK ON EZERAT ALONE. DON'T TELL ME YOU WEREN'T ALSO SEEKING YOUR DEATH. YOU ARE UNIQUE AMONG YOUR RACE, HUMAN, BUT YOU ARE STILL A HYPOCRITE.
THUNK!
YOU AIN'T GOING IN THERE.
ARE YOU JOKING? YOU ARE GOING TO FIGHT ME?
QUIT BEING STUPID. STEP ASIDE.

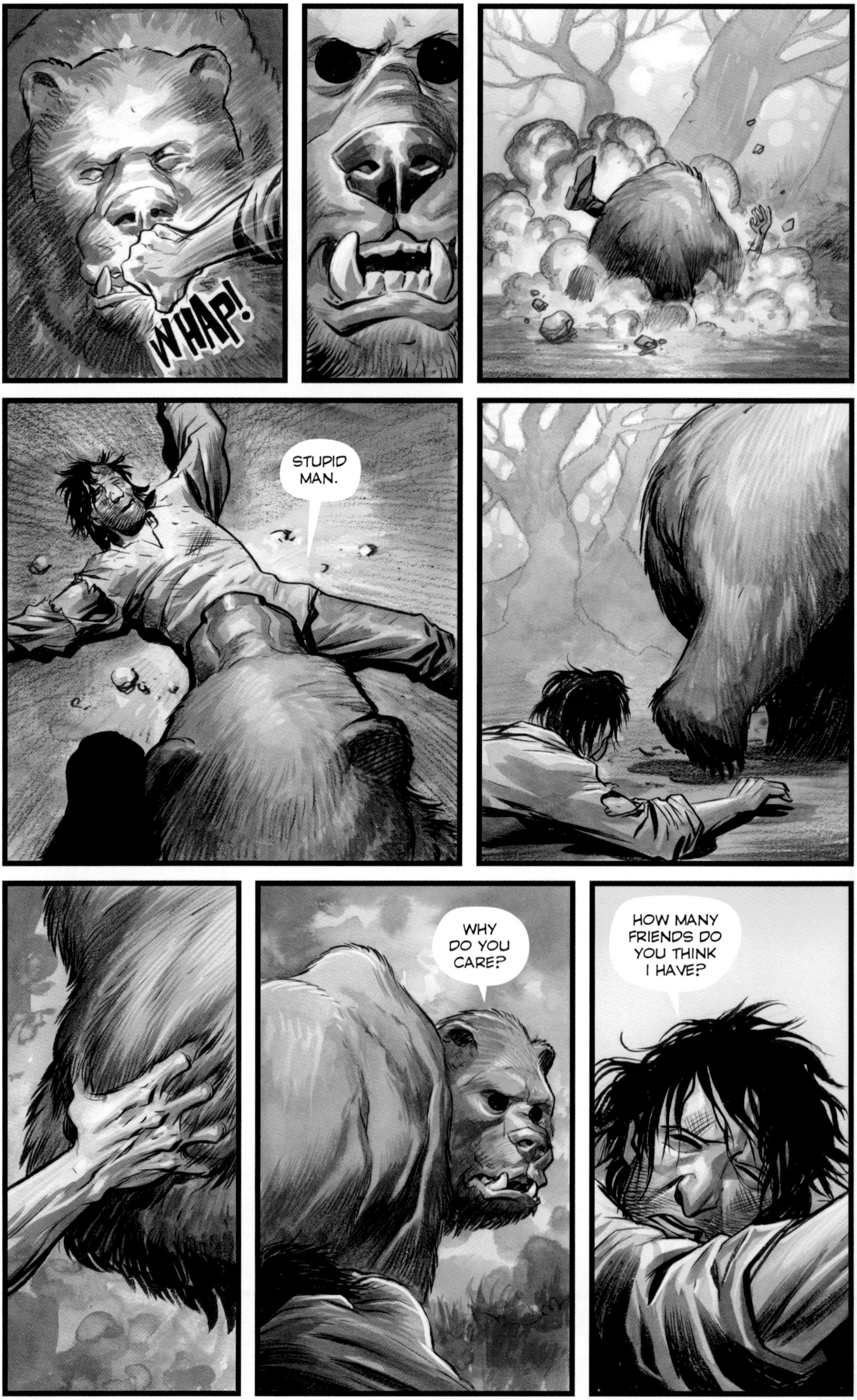
WHAP!
STUPID MAN.
WHY DO YOU CARE?
HOW MANY FRIENDS DO YOU THINK I HAVE?

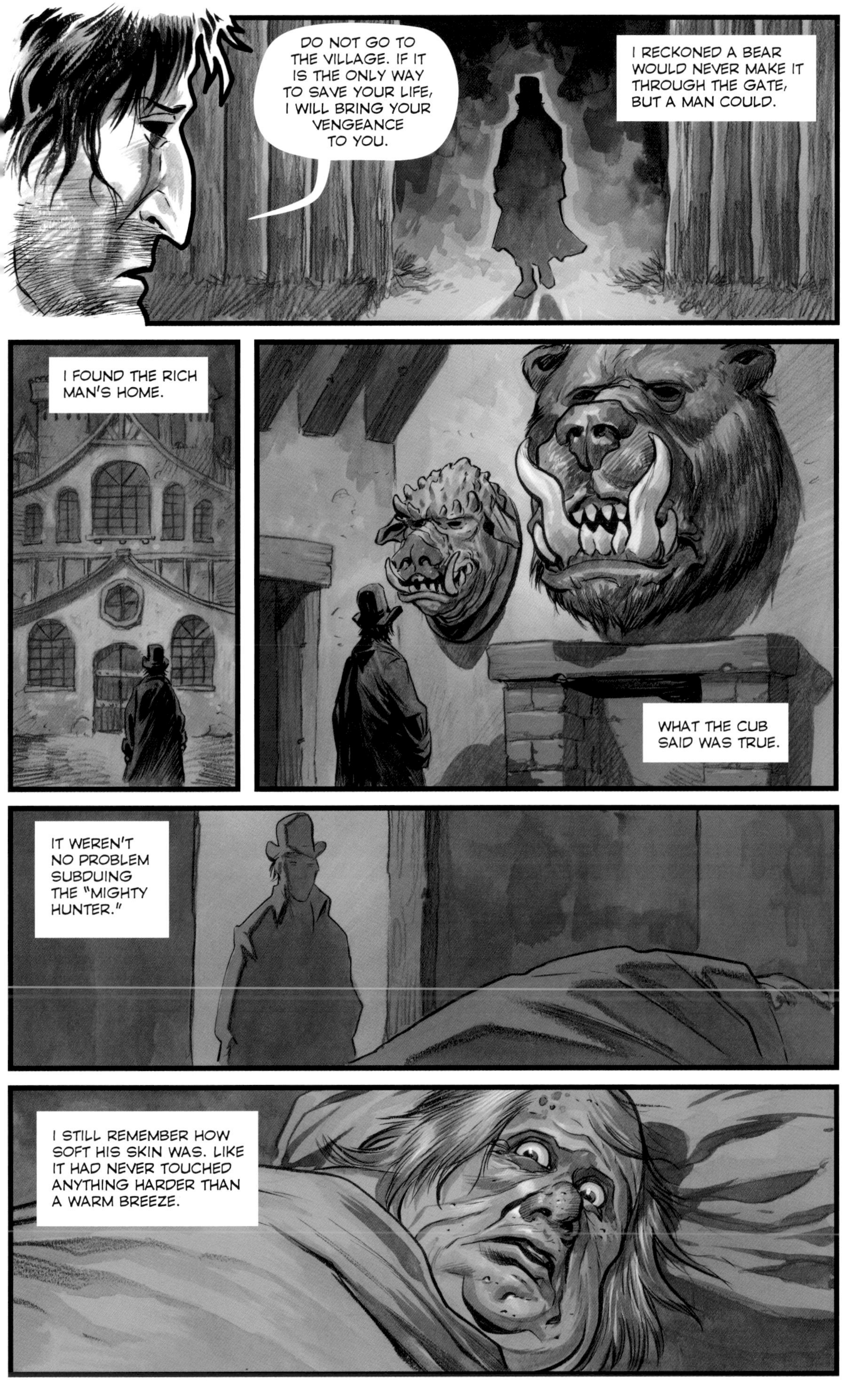
DO NOT GO TO THE VILLAGE. IF IT IS THE ONLY WAY TO SAVE YOUR LIFE, I WILL BRING YOUR VENGEANCE TO YOU.
I RECKONED A BEAR WOULD NEVER MAKE IT THROUGH THE GATE, BUT A MAN COULD.
I FOUND THE RICH MAN'S HOME.
WHAT THE CUB SAID WAS TRUE.
IT WEREN'T NO PROBLEM SUBDUING THE "MIGHTY HUNTER."
I STILL REMEMBER HOW SOFT HIS SKIN WAS. LIKE IT HAD NEVER TOUCHED ANYTHING HARDER THAN A WARM BREEZE.

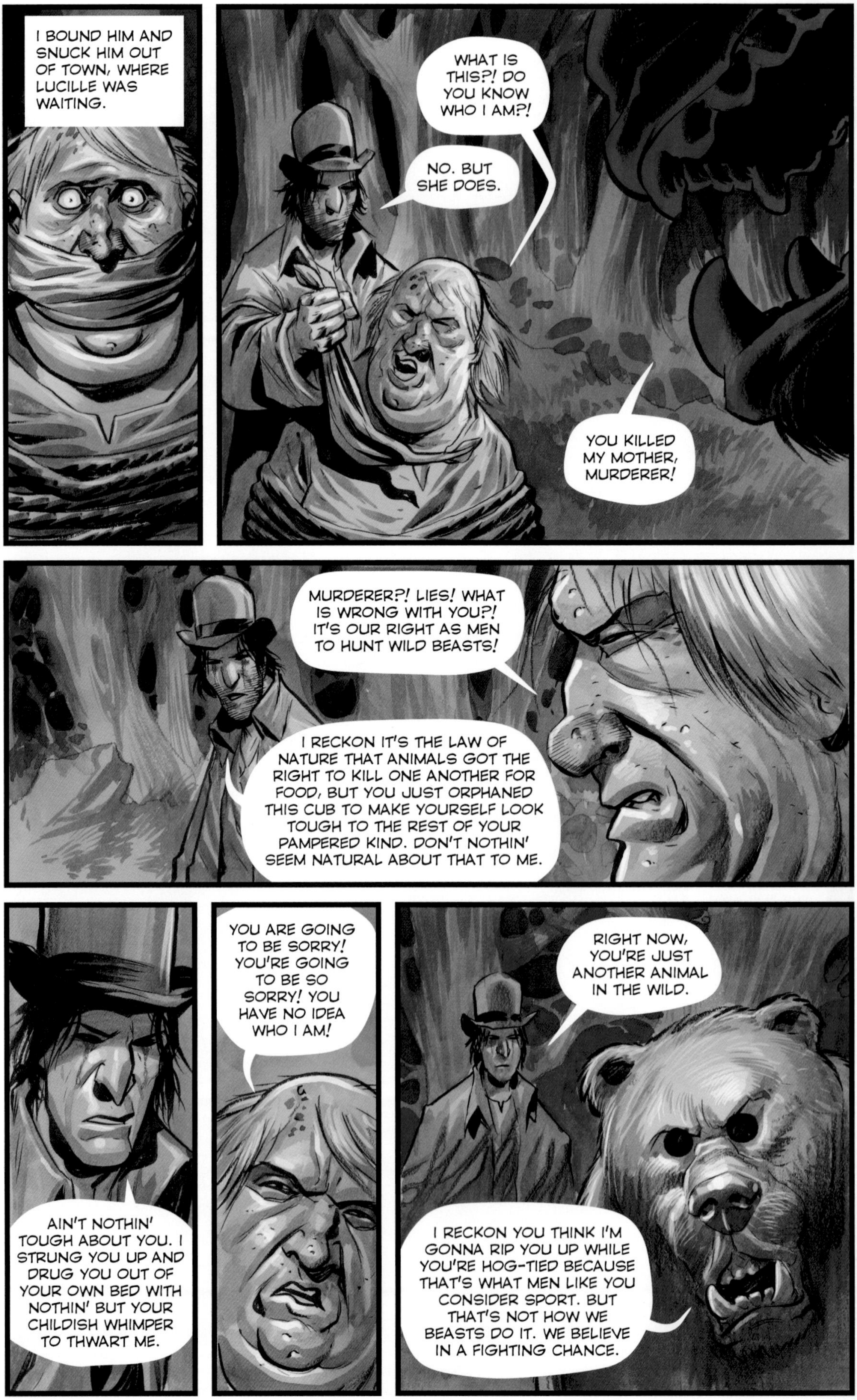
I BOUND HIM AND SNUCK HIM OUT OF TOWN, WHERE LUCILLE WAS WAITING.
WHAT IS THIS?! DO YOU KNOW WHO I AM?!
NO. BUT SHE DOES.
YOU KILLED MY MOTHER, MURDERER!
MURDERER?! LIES! WHAT IS WRONG WITH YOU?! IT'S OUR RIGHT AS MEN TO HUNT WILD BEASTS!
I RECKON IT'S THE LAW OF NATURE THAT ANIMALS GOT THE RIGHT TO KILL ONE ANOTHER FOR FOOD, BUT YOU JUST ORPHANED THIS CUB TO MAKE YOURSELF LOOK TOUGH TO THE REST OF YOUR PAMPERED KIND. DON'T NOTHIN' SEEM NATURAL ABOUT THAT TO ME.
AIN'T NOTHIN' TOUGH ABOUT YOU. I STRUNG YOU UP AND DRUG YOU OUT OF YOUR OWN BED WITH NOTHIN' BUT YOUR CHILDISH WHIMPER TO THWART ME.
YOU ARE GOING TO BE SORRY! YOU'RE GOING TO BE SO SORRY! YOU HAVE NO IDEA WHO I AM!
RIGHT NOW, YOU'RE JUST ANOTHER ANIMAL IN THE WILD.
I RECKON YOU THINK I'M GONNA RIP YOU UP WHILE YOU'RE HOG-TIED BECAUSE THAT'S WHAT MEN LIKE YOU CONSIDER SPORT. BUT THAT'S NOT HOW WE BEASTS DO IT. WE BELIEVE IN A FIGHTING CHANCE.

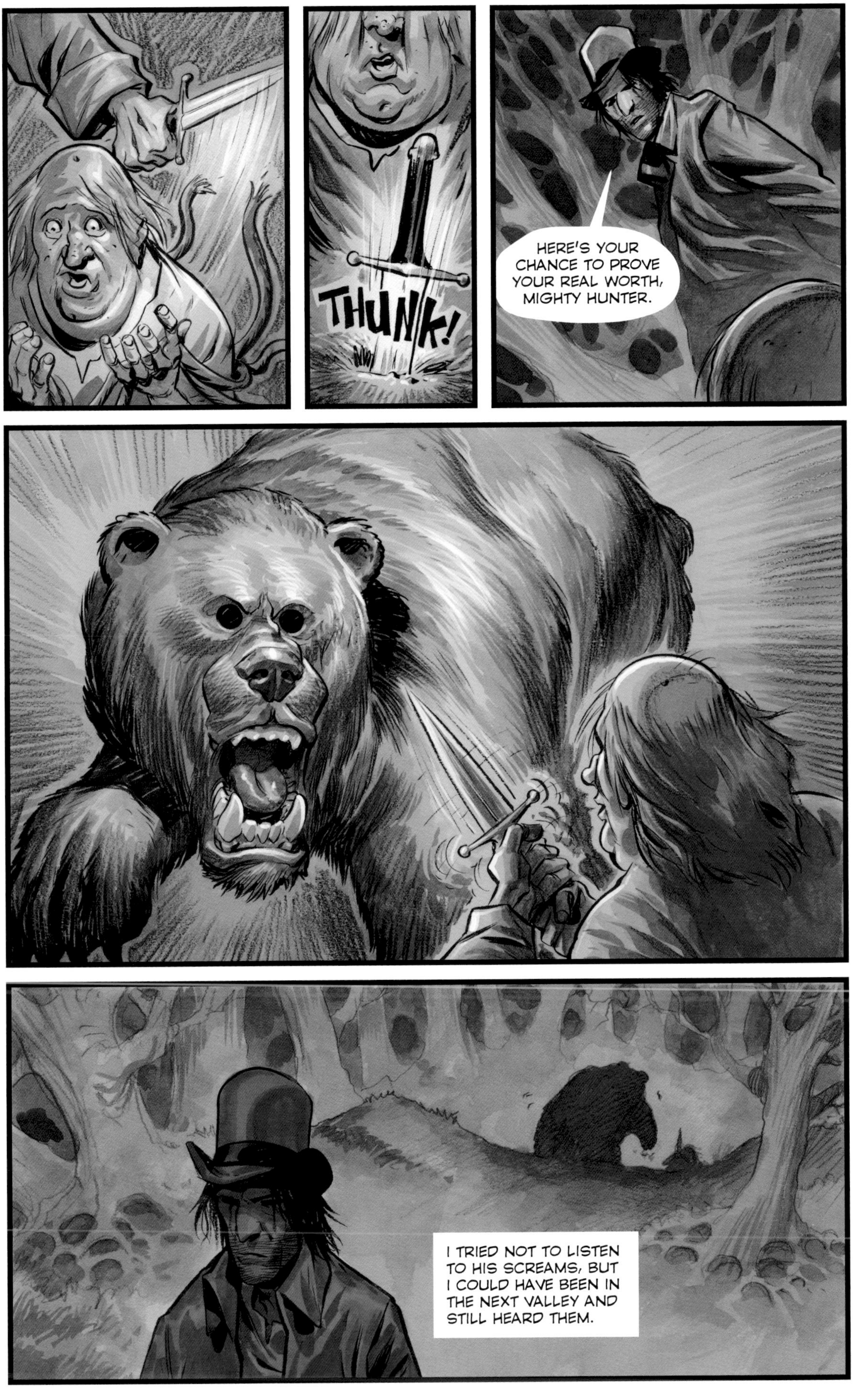
THUNK!
HERE'S YOUR CHANCE TO PROVE YOUR REAL WORTH, MIGHTY HUNTER.
I TRIED NOT TO LISTEN TO HIS SCREAMS, BUT I COULD HAVE BEEN IN THE NEXT VALLEY AND STILL HEARD THEM.

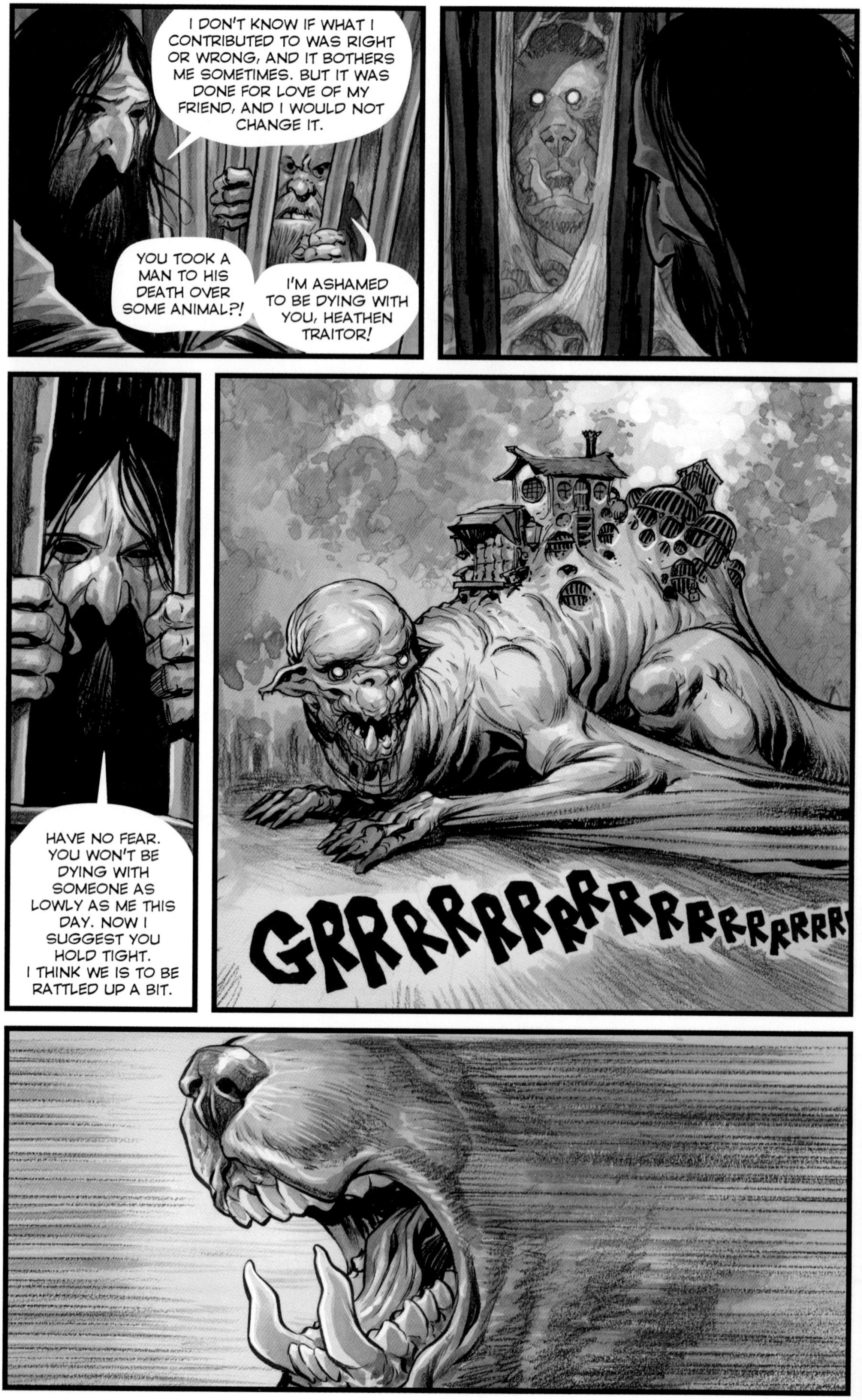
I DON'T KNOW IF WHAT I CONTRIBUTED TO WAS RIGHT OR WRONG, AND IT BOTHERS ME SOMETIMES. BUT IT WAS DONE FOR LOVE OF MY FRIEND, AND I WOULD NOT CHANGE IT.
YOU TOOK A MAN TO HIS DEATH OVER SOME ANIMAL?!
I'M ASHAMED TO BE DYING WITH YOU, HEATHEN TRAITOR!
HAVE NO FEAR. YOU WON'T BE DYING WITH SOMEONE AS LOWLY AS ME THIS DAY. NOW I SUGGEST YOU HOLD TIGHT. I THINK WE IS TO BE RATTLED UP A BIT.
GRRRRRRRRRRRRRRR

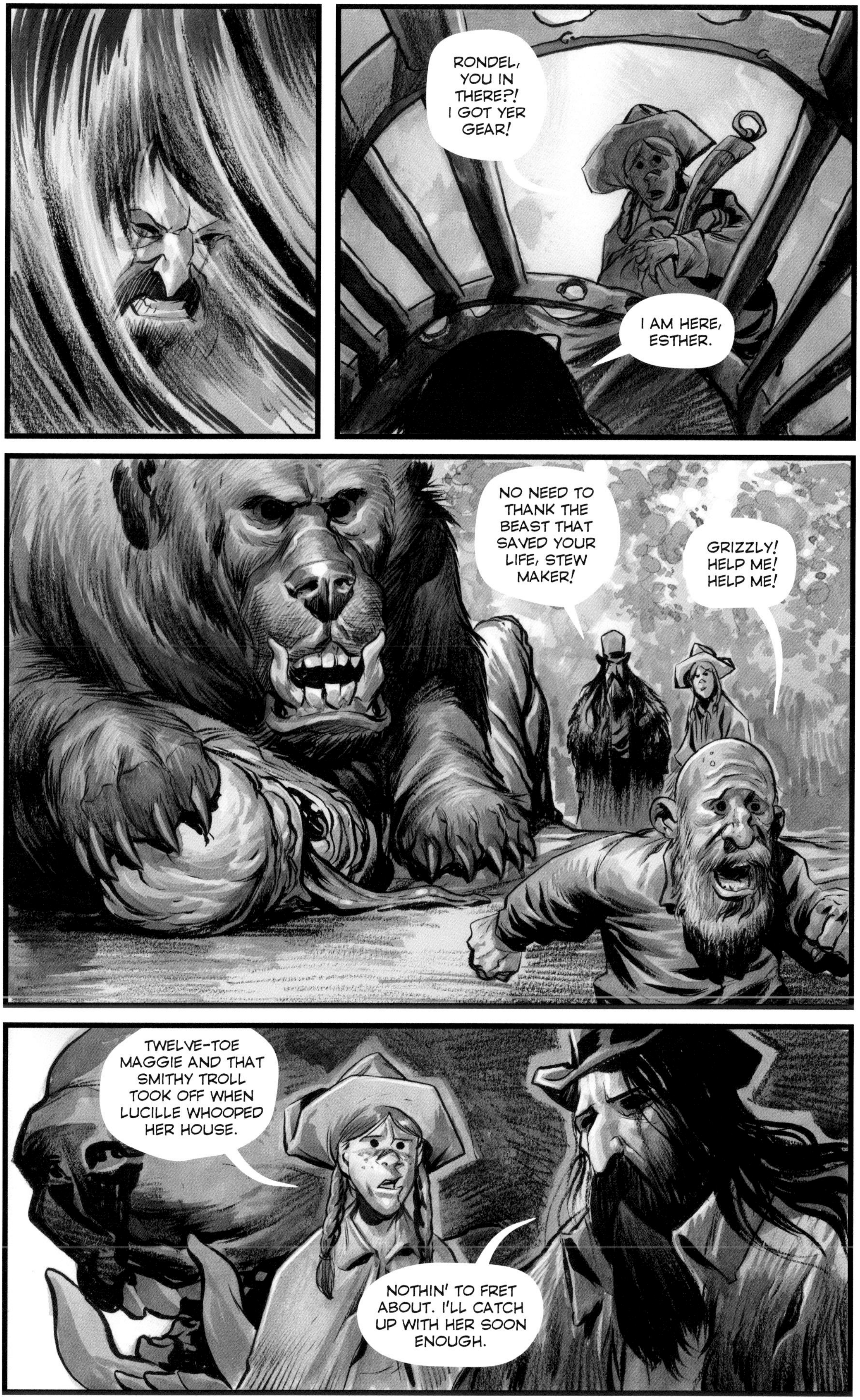
RONDEL, YOU IN THERE?! I GOT YER GEAR!
I AM HERE, ESTHER.
NO NEED TO THANK THE BEAST THAT SAVED YOUR LIFE, STEW MAKER!
GRIZZLY! HELP ME! HELP ME!
TWELVE-TOE MAGGIE AND THAT SMITHY TROLL TOOK OFF WHEN LUCILLE WHOOPED HER HOUSE.
NOTHIN' TO FRET ABOUT. I'LL CATCH UP WITH HER SOON ENOUGH.

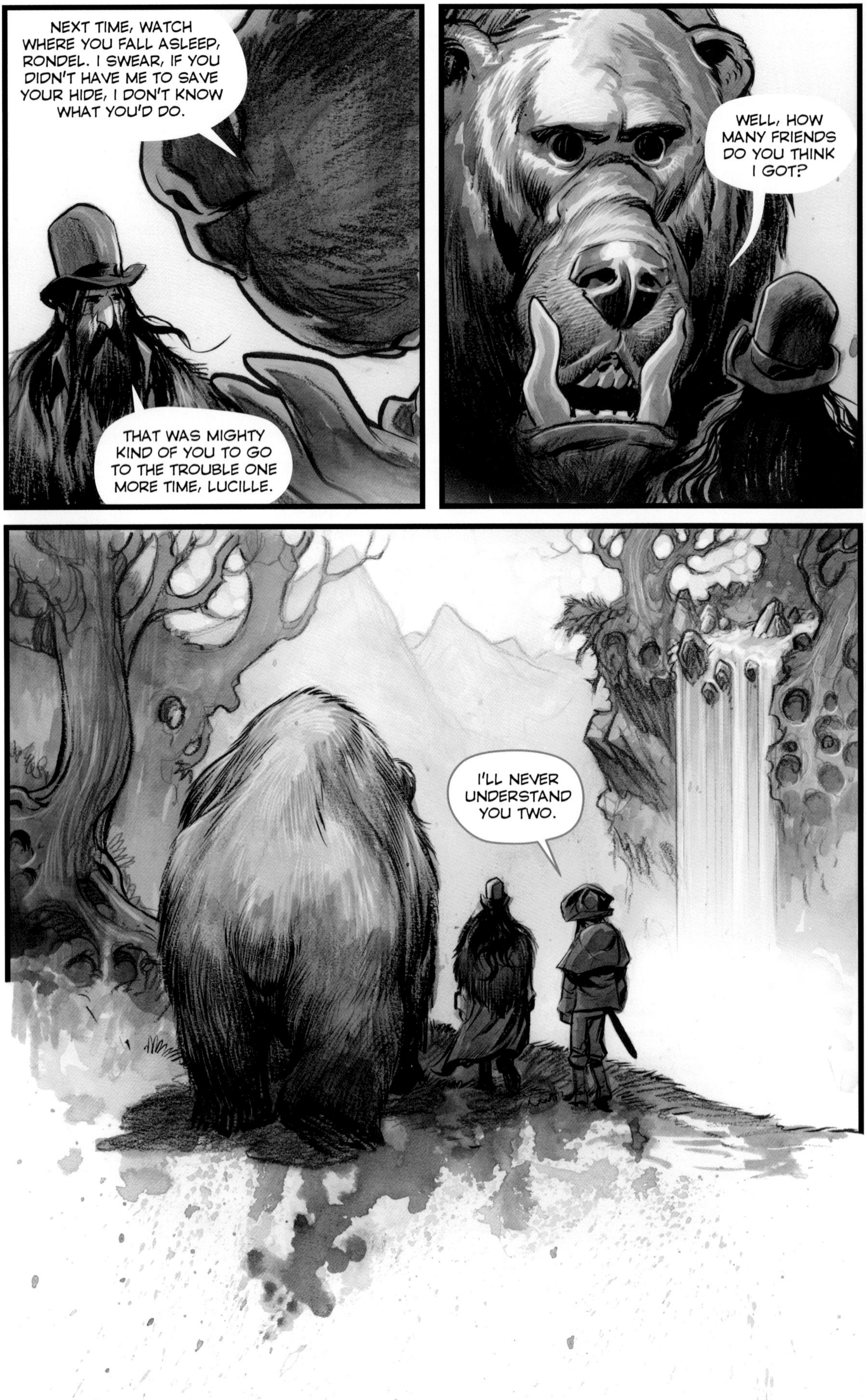
NEXT TIME, WATCH WHERE YOU FALL ASLEEP, RONDEL. I SWEAR, IF YOU DIDN'T HAVE ME TO SAVE YOUR HIDE, I DON'T KNOW WHAT YOU'D DO.
THAT WAS MIGHTY KIND OF YOU TO GO TO THE TROUBLE ONE MORE TIME, LUCILLE.
WELL, HOW MANY FRIENDS DO YOU THINK I GOT?
I'LL NEVER UNDERSTAND YOU TWO.

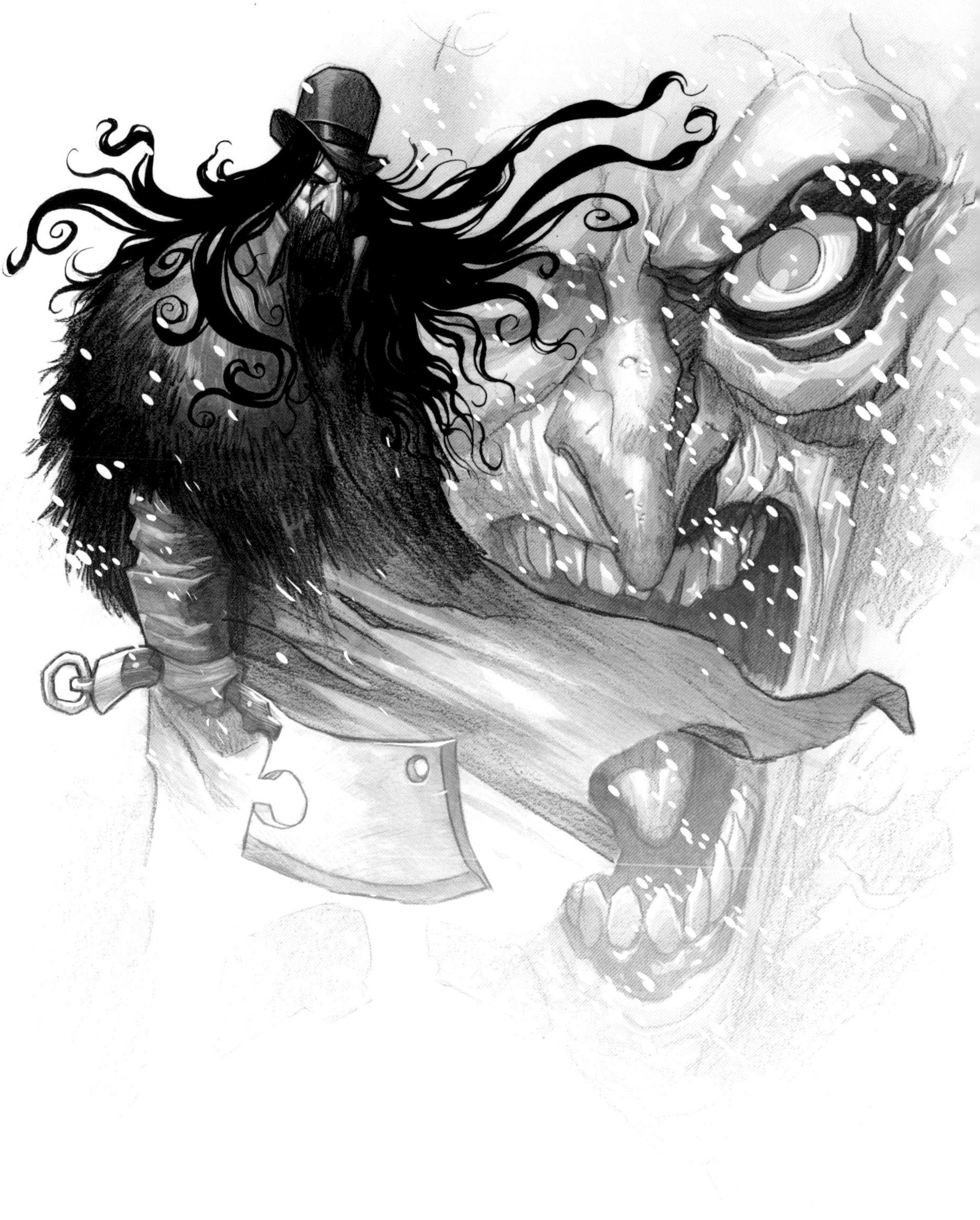
Eric Powell -16

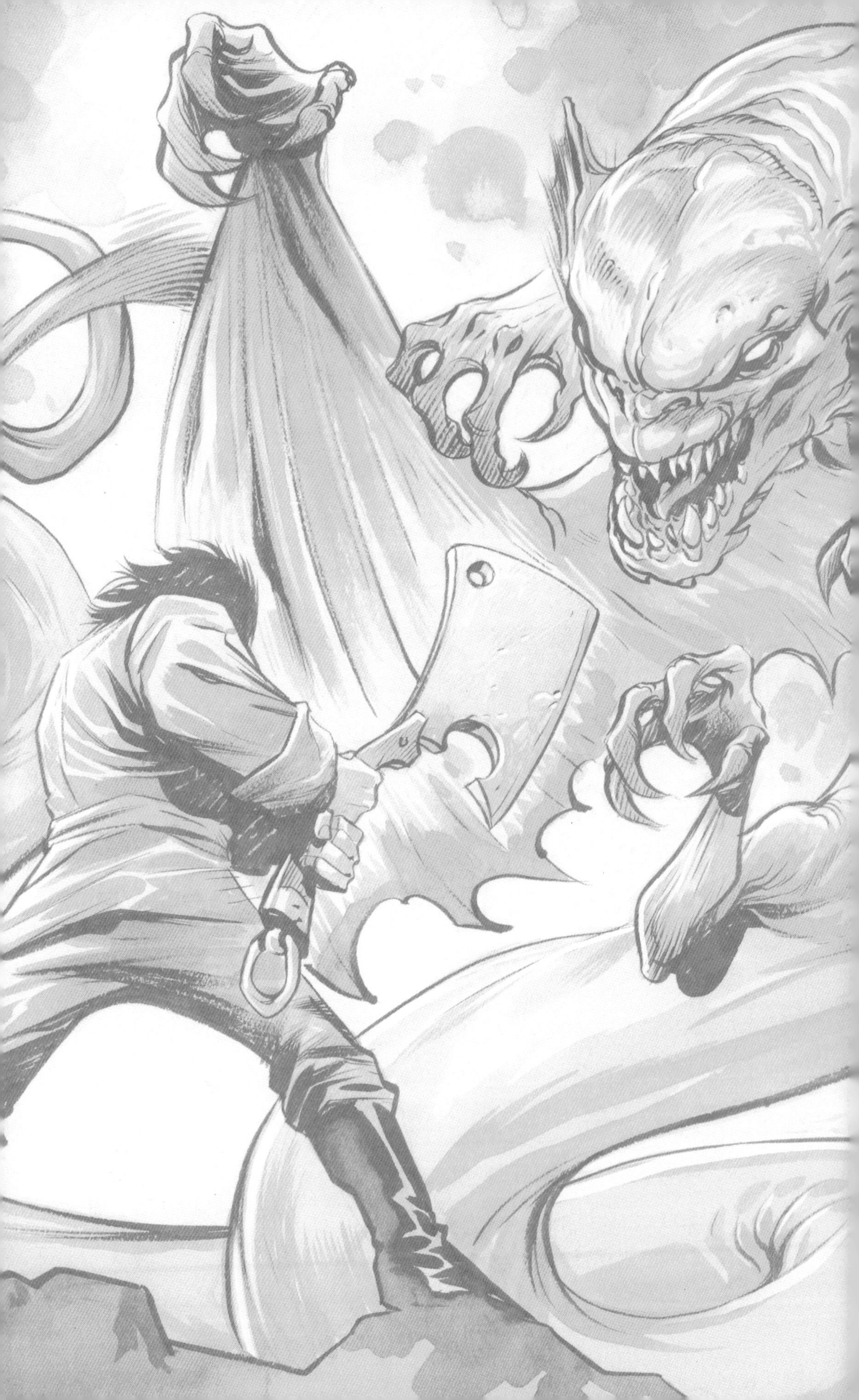

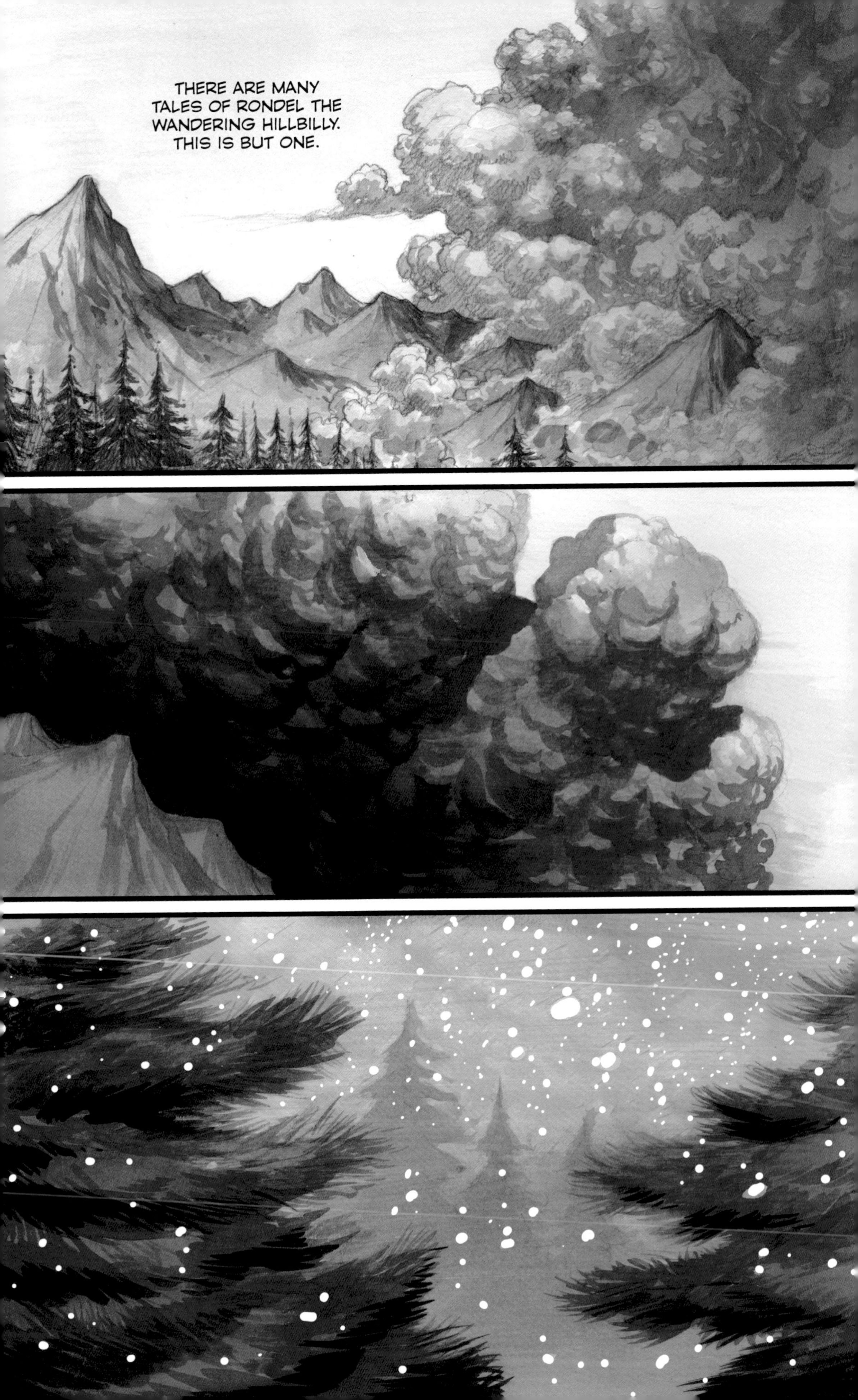
THERE ARE MANY TALES OF RONDEL THE WANDERING HILLBILLY. THIS IS BUT ONE.

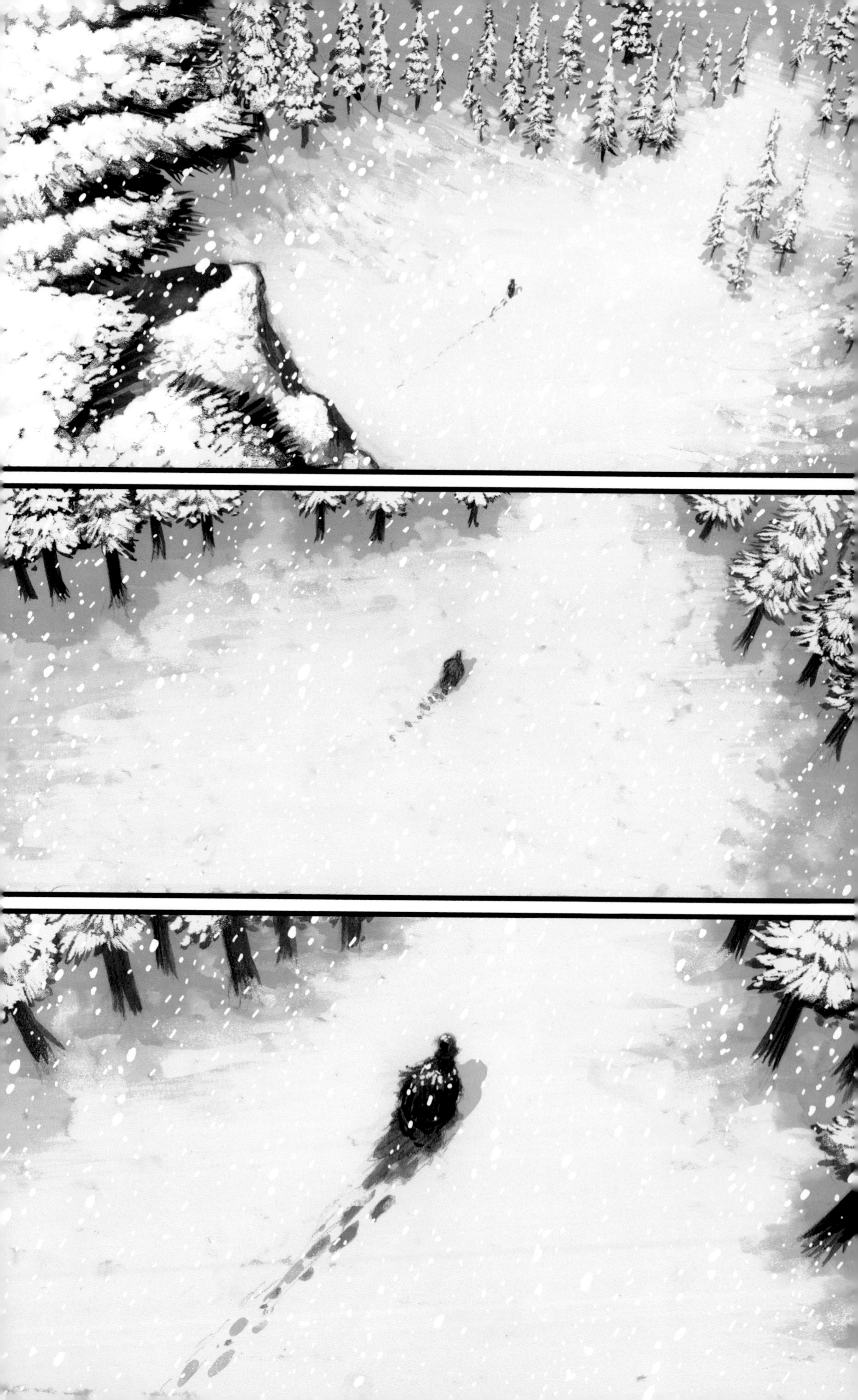

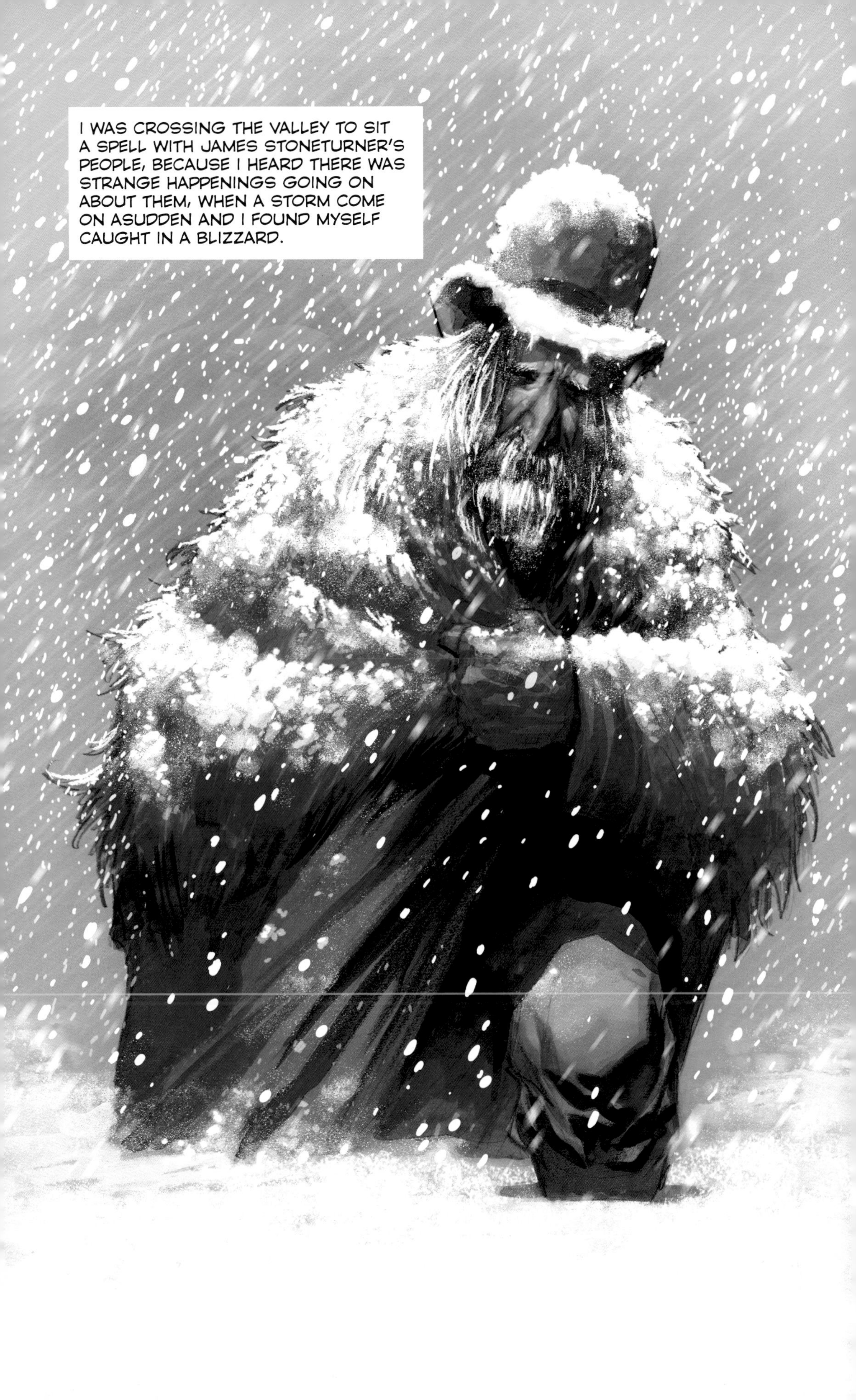
I WAS CROSSING THE VALLEY TO SIT A SPELL WITH JAMES STONETURNER'S PEOPLE, BECAUSE I HEARD THERE WAS STRANGE HAPPENINGS GOING ON ABOUT THEM, WHEN A STORM COME ON ASUDDEN AND I FOUND MYSELF CAUGHT IN A BLIZZARD.

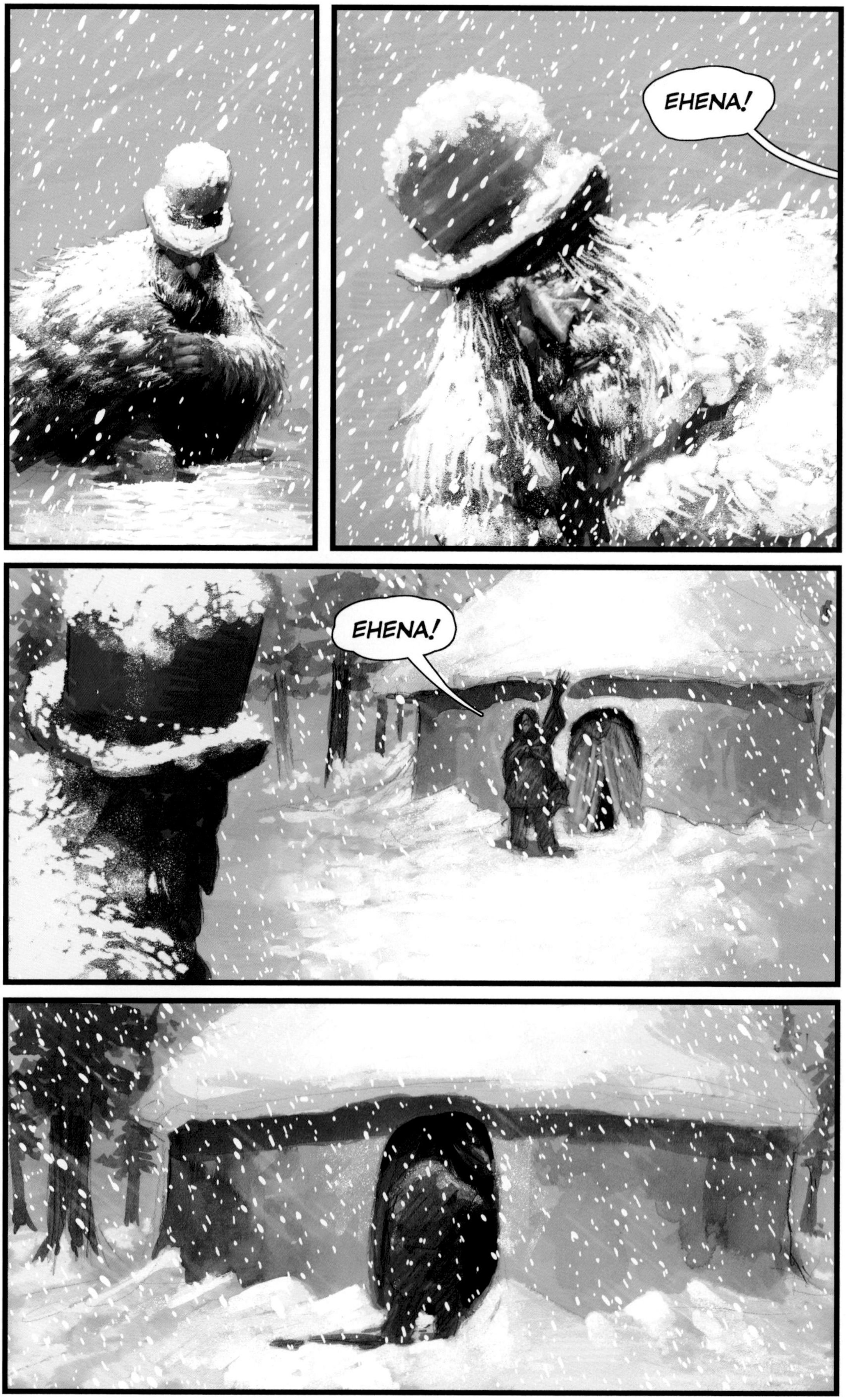
EHENA!
EHENA!

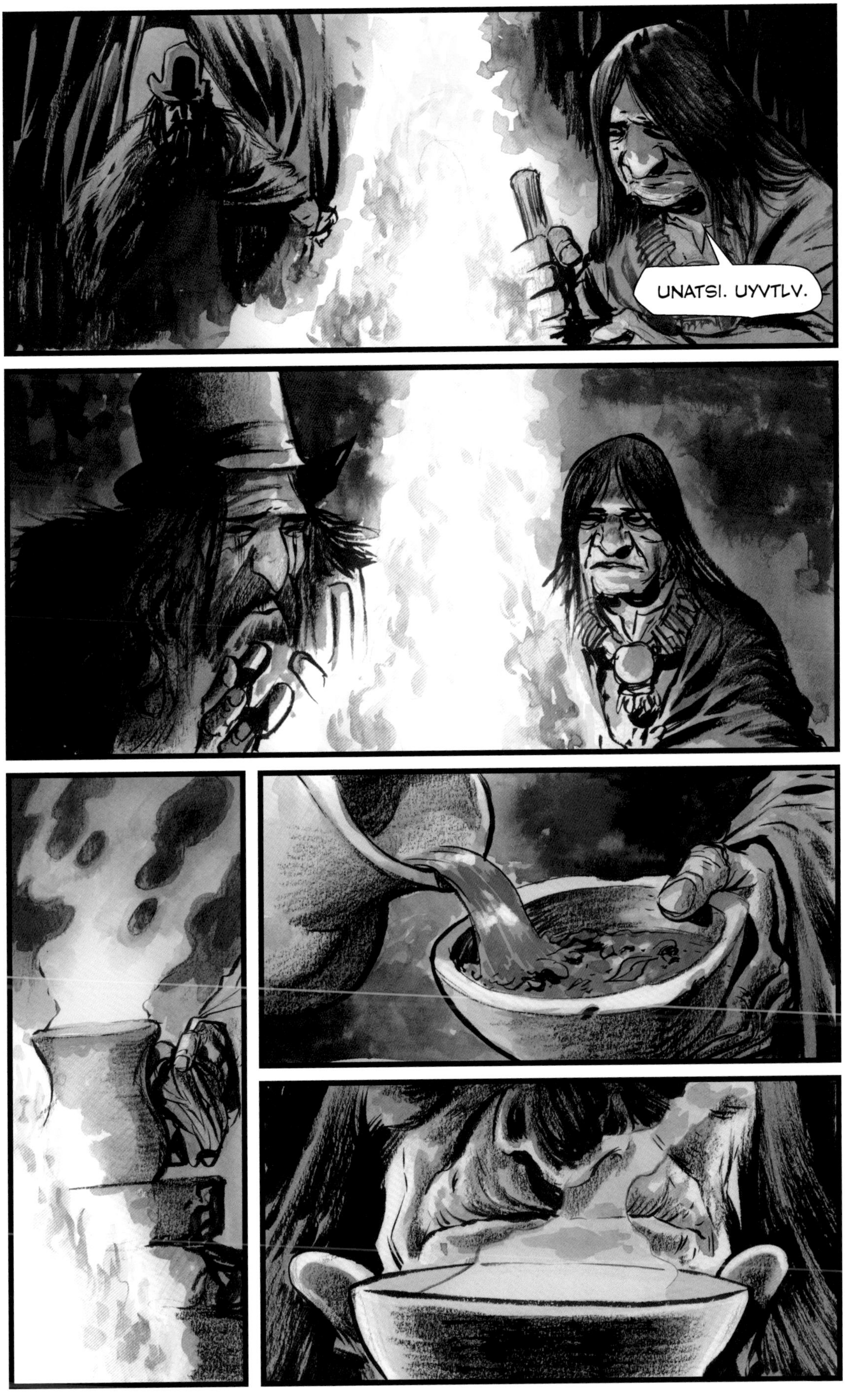
UNATSI. UYVTLV.

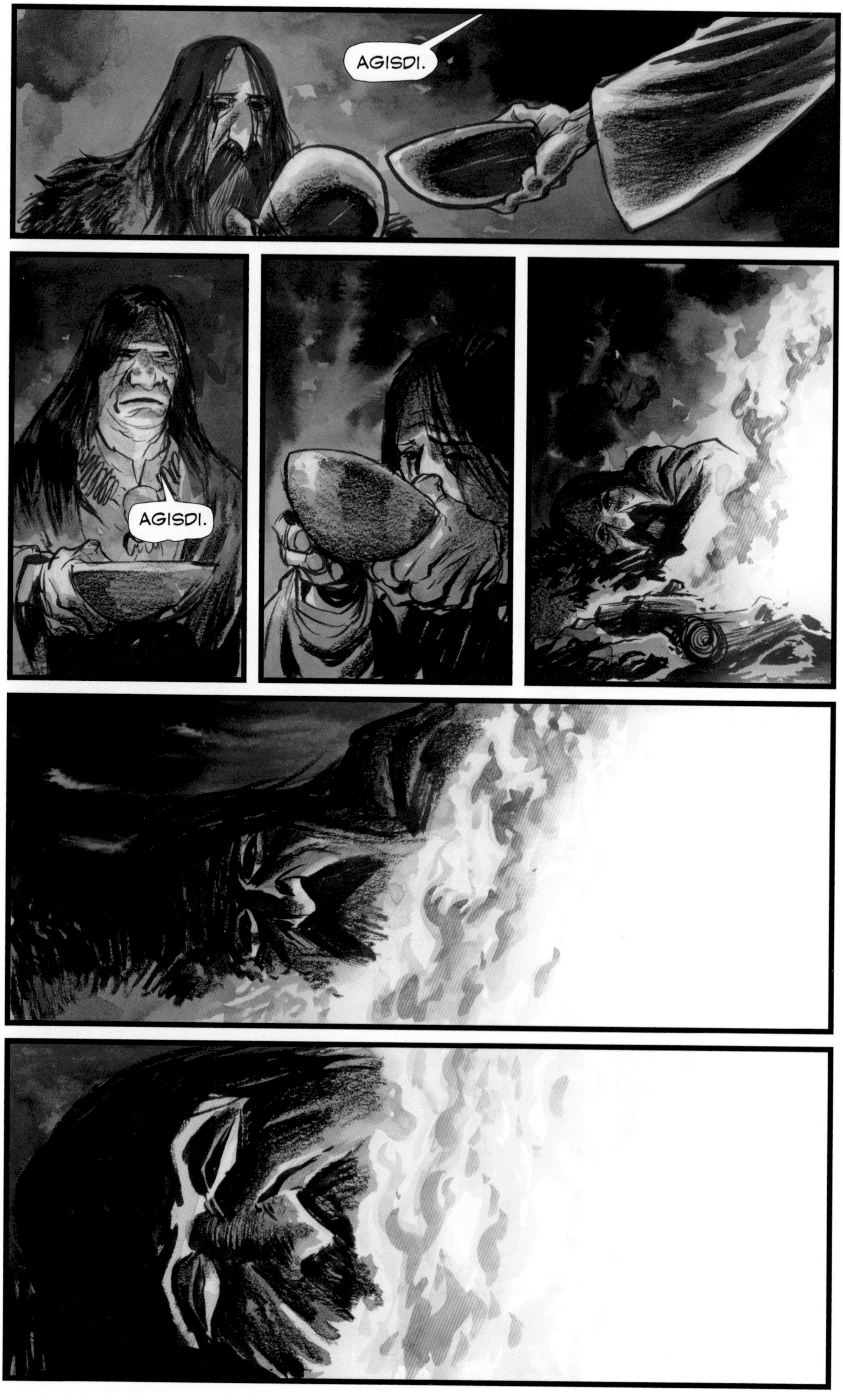
AGISDI.
AGISDI.

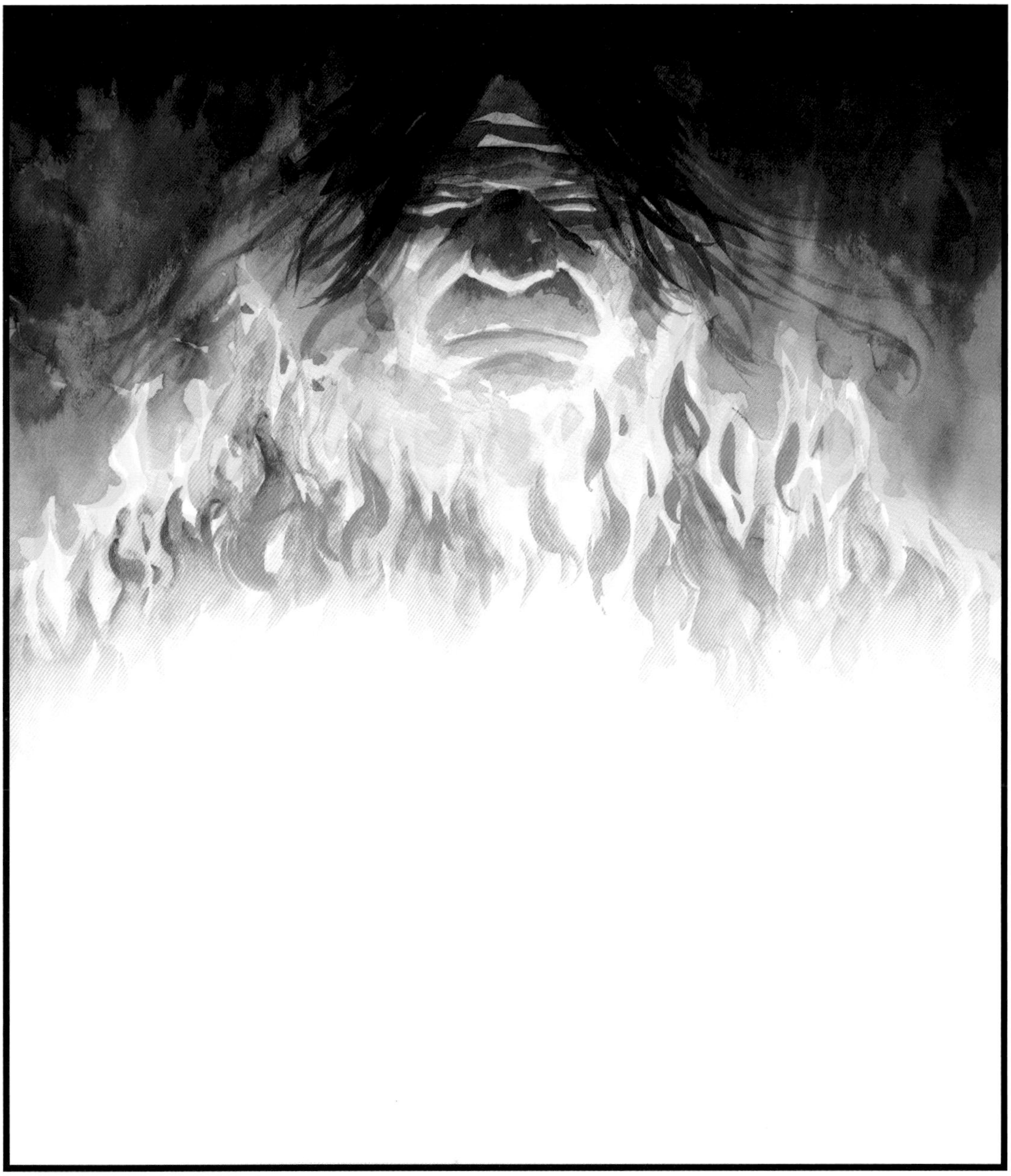
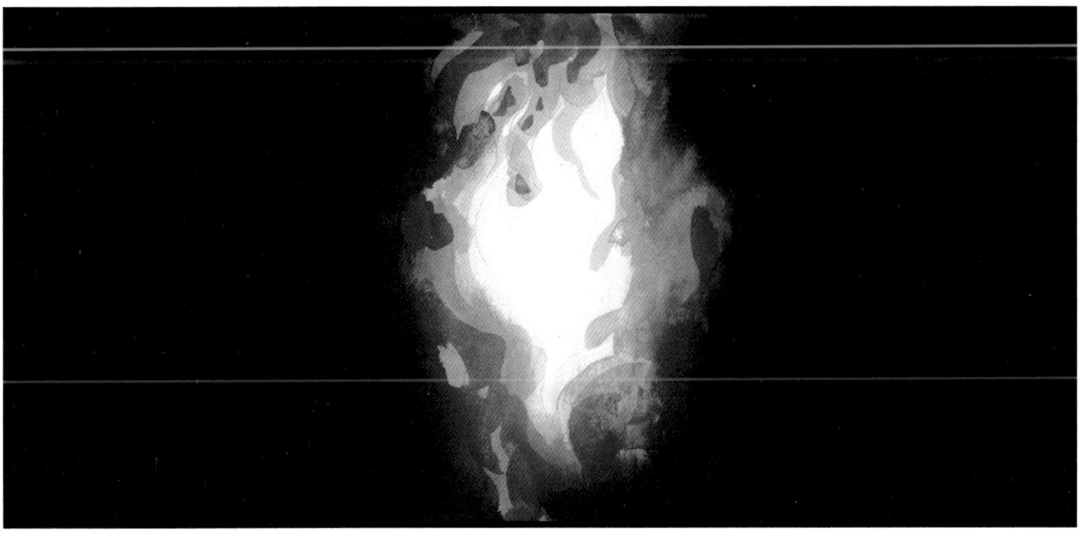

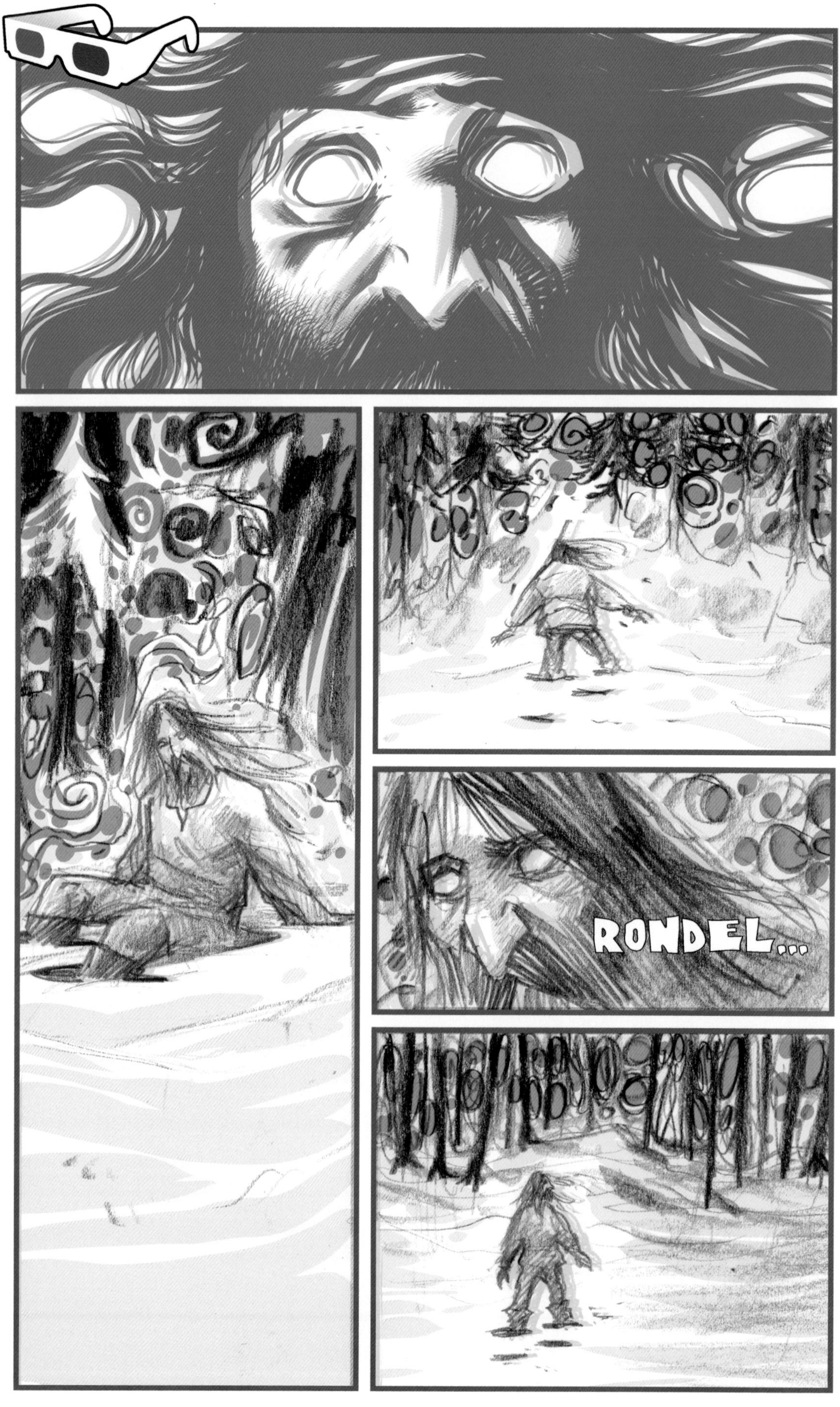
RONDEL...

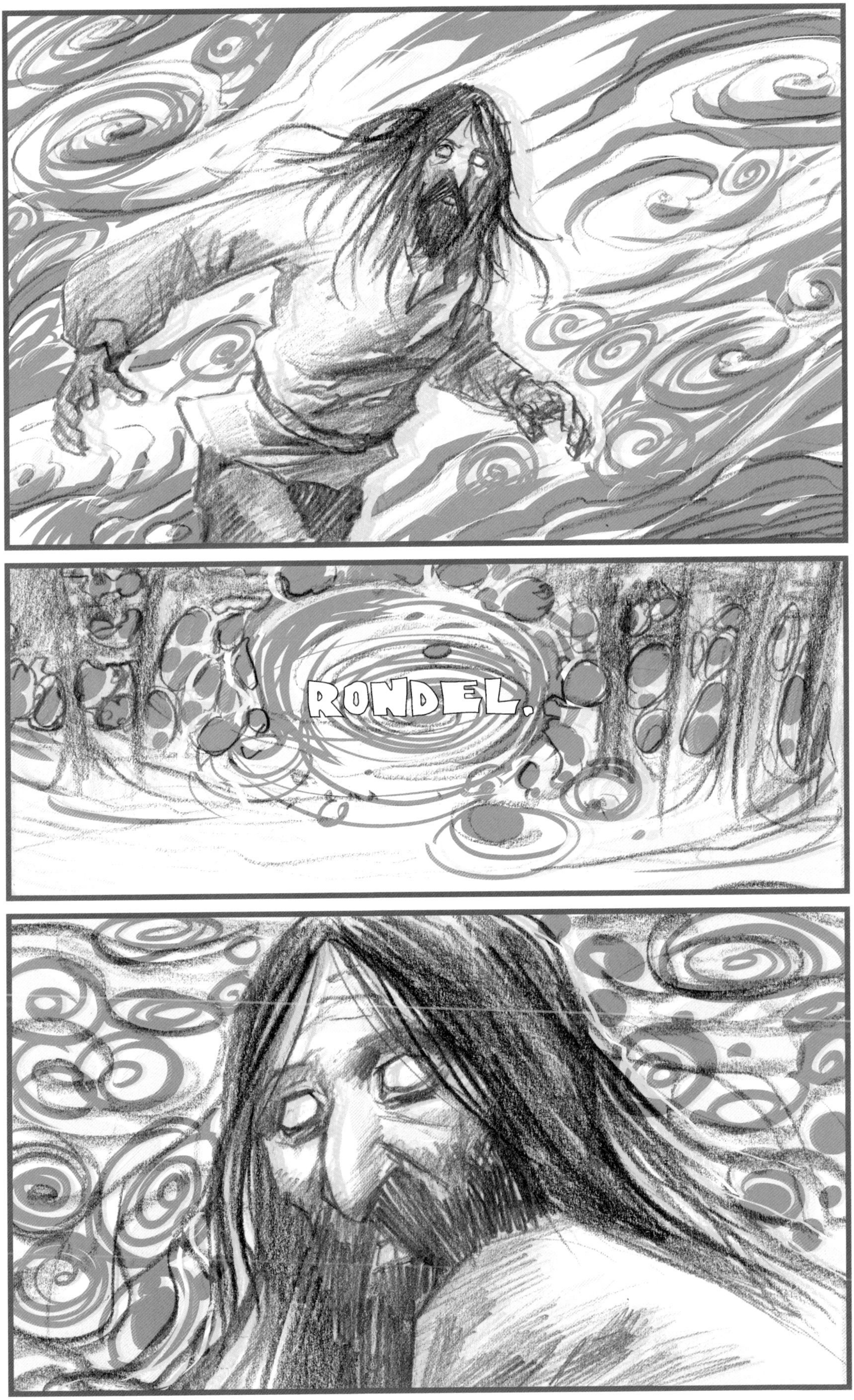
RONDEL.

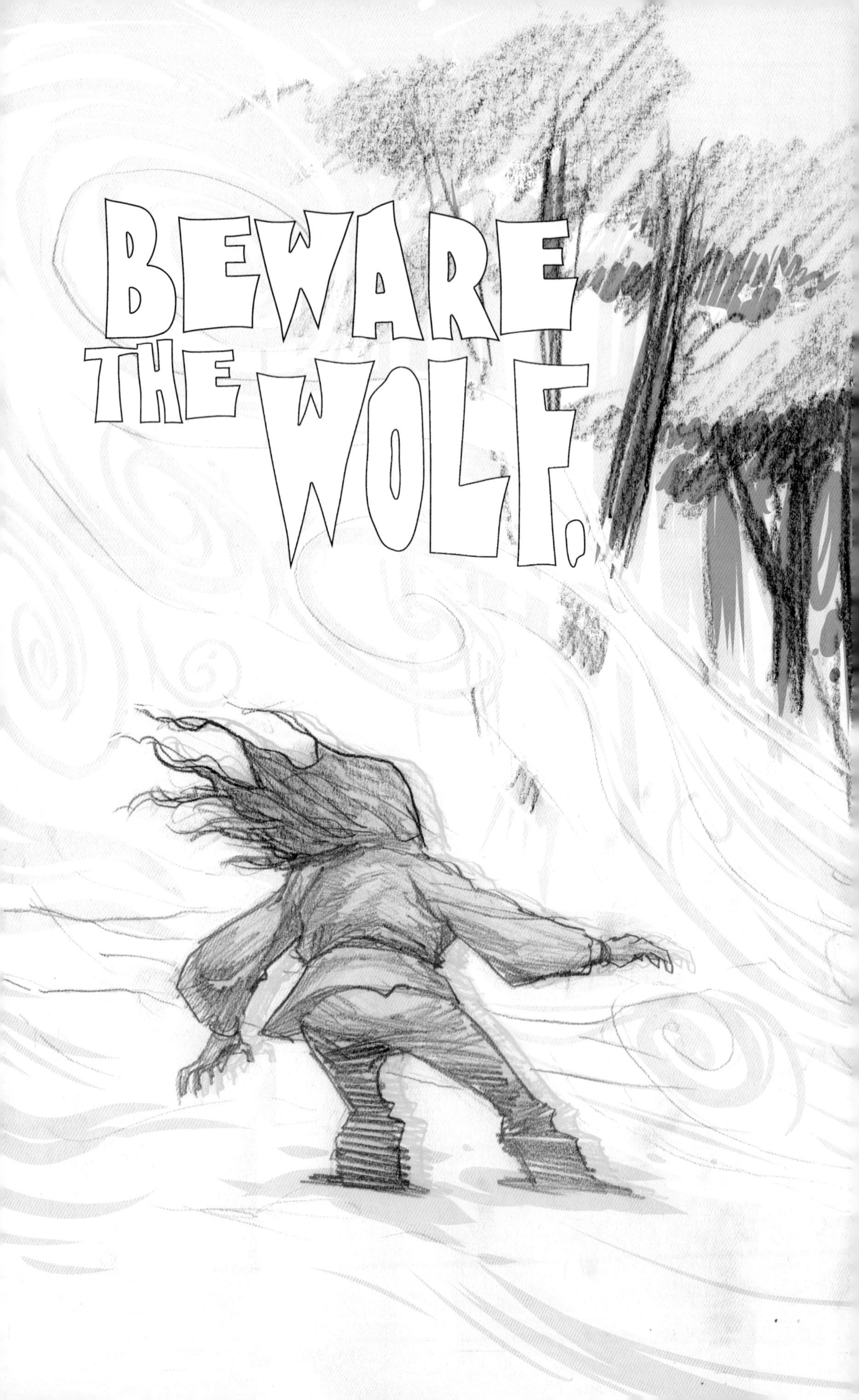
BEWARE
THE WOLF.

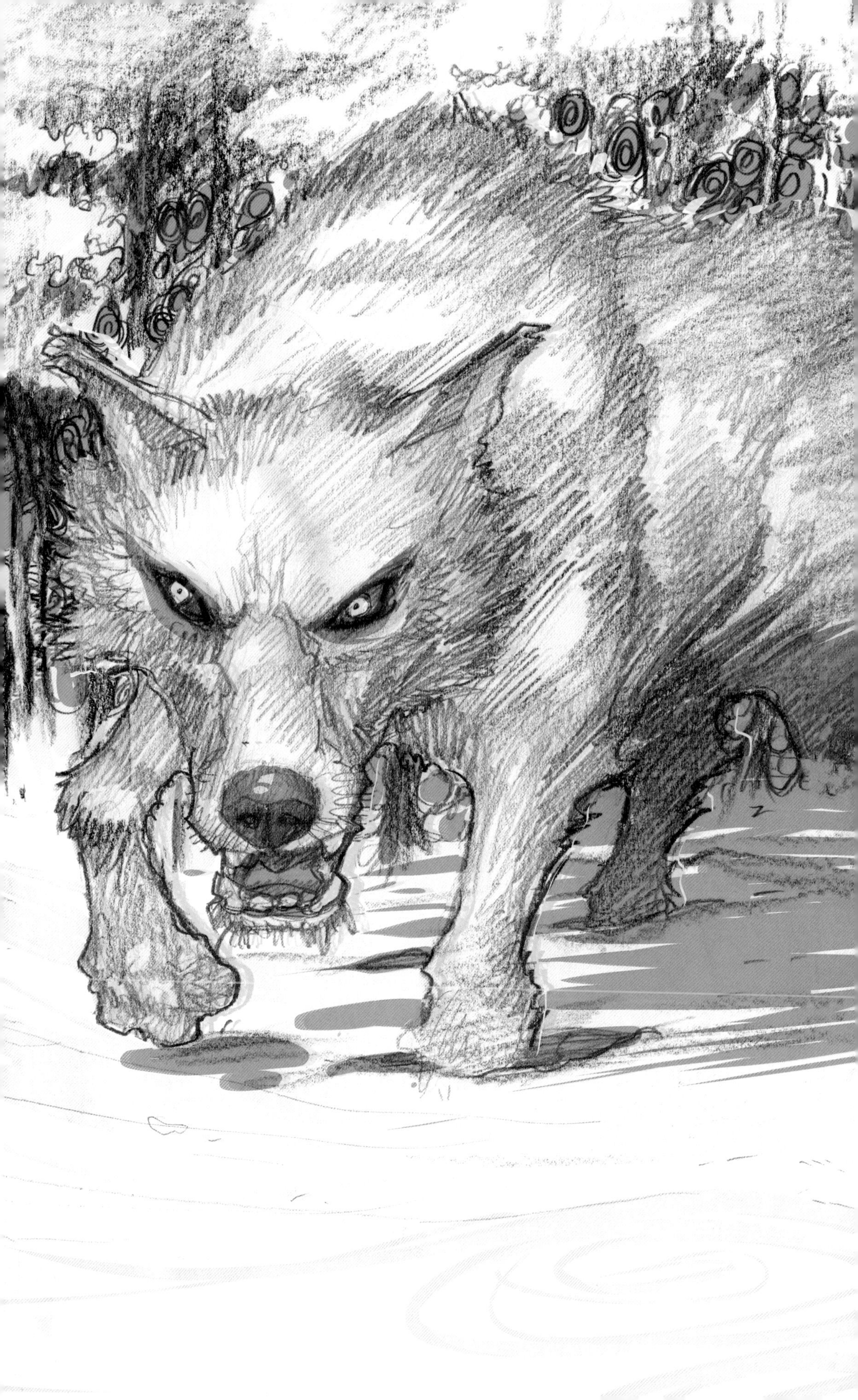

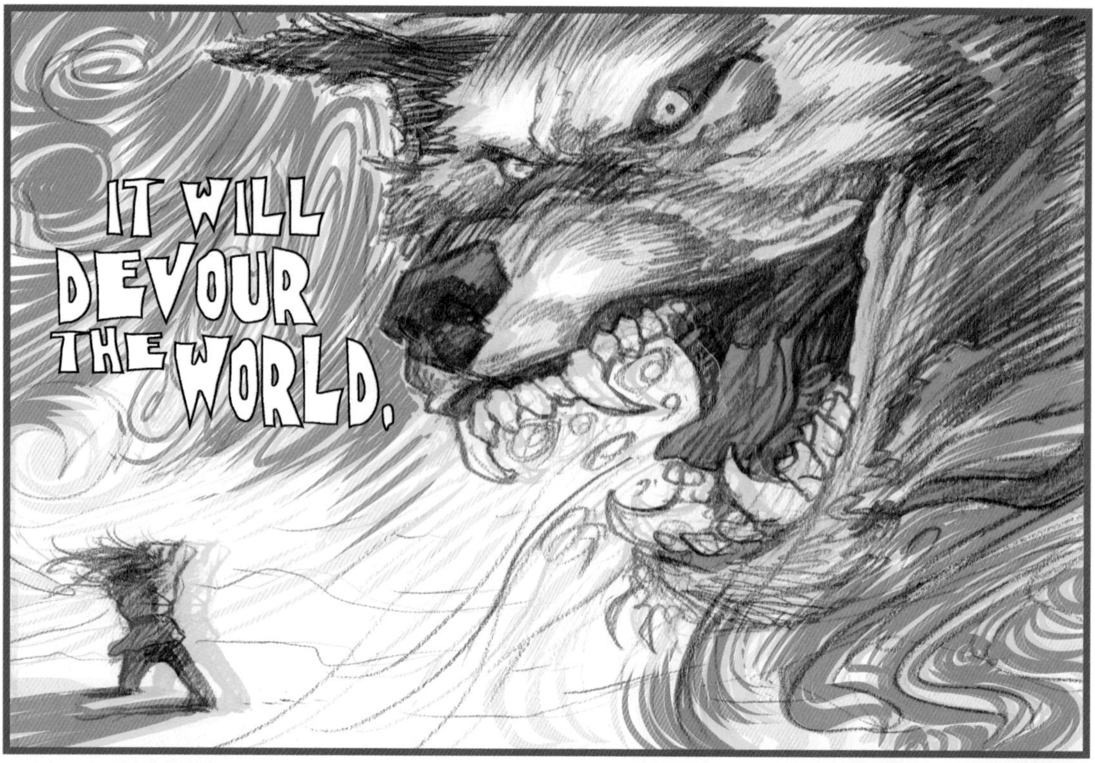
IT WILL DEVOUR THE WORLD.
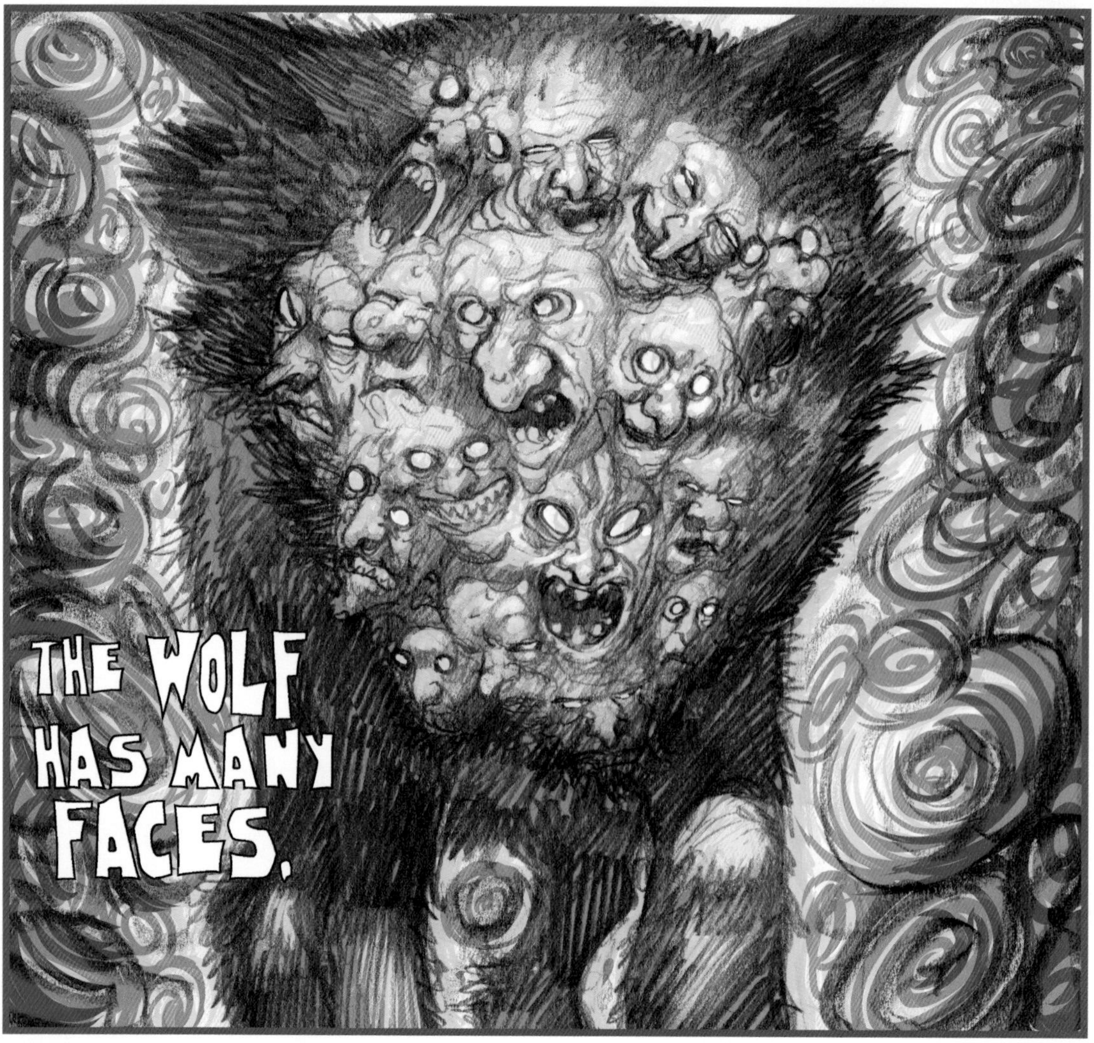
THE WOLF HAS MANY FACES.

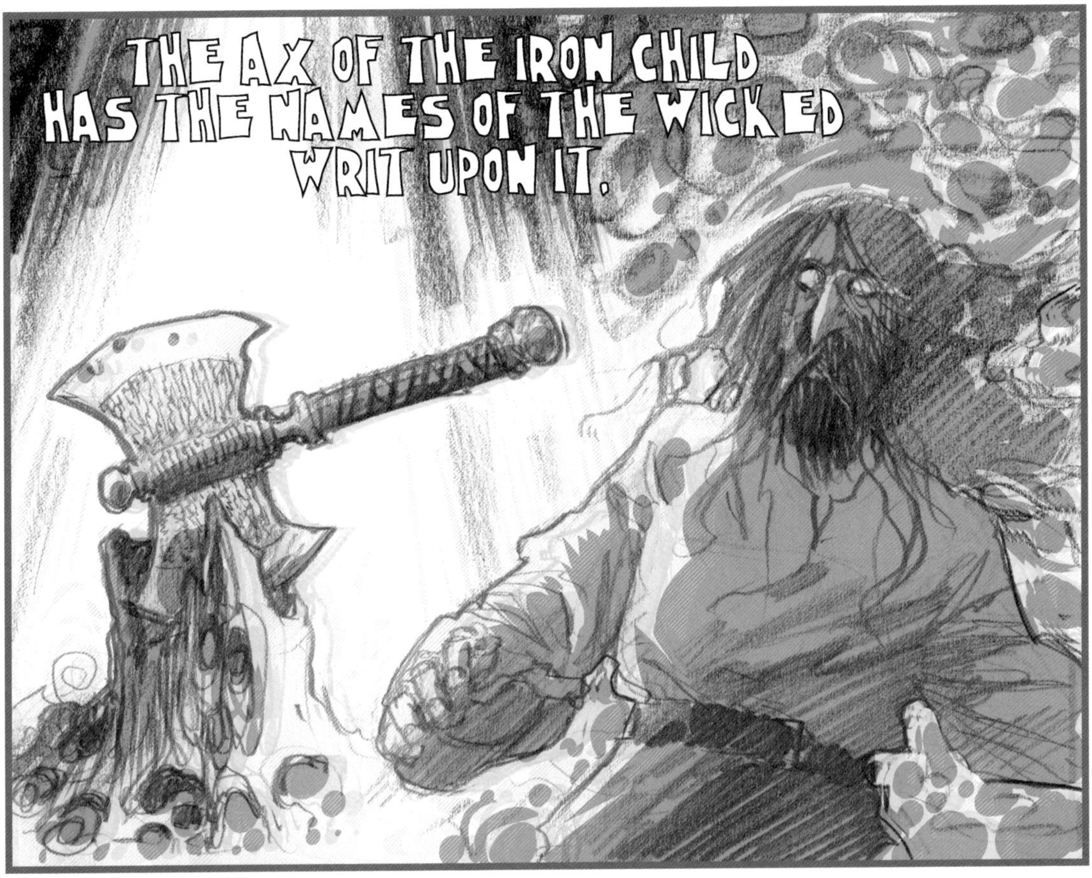
THE AX OF THE IRON CHILD HAS THE NAMES OF THE WICKED WRIT UPON IT.

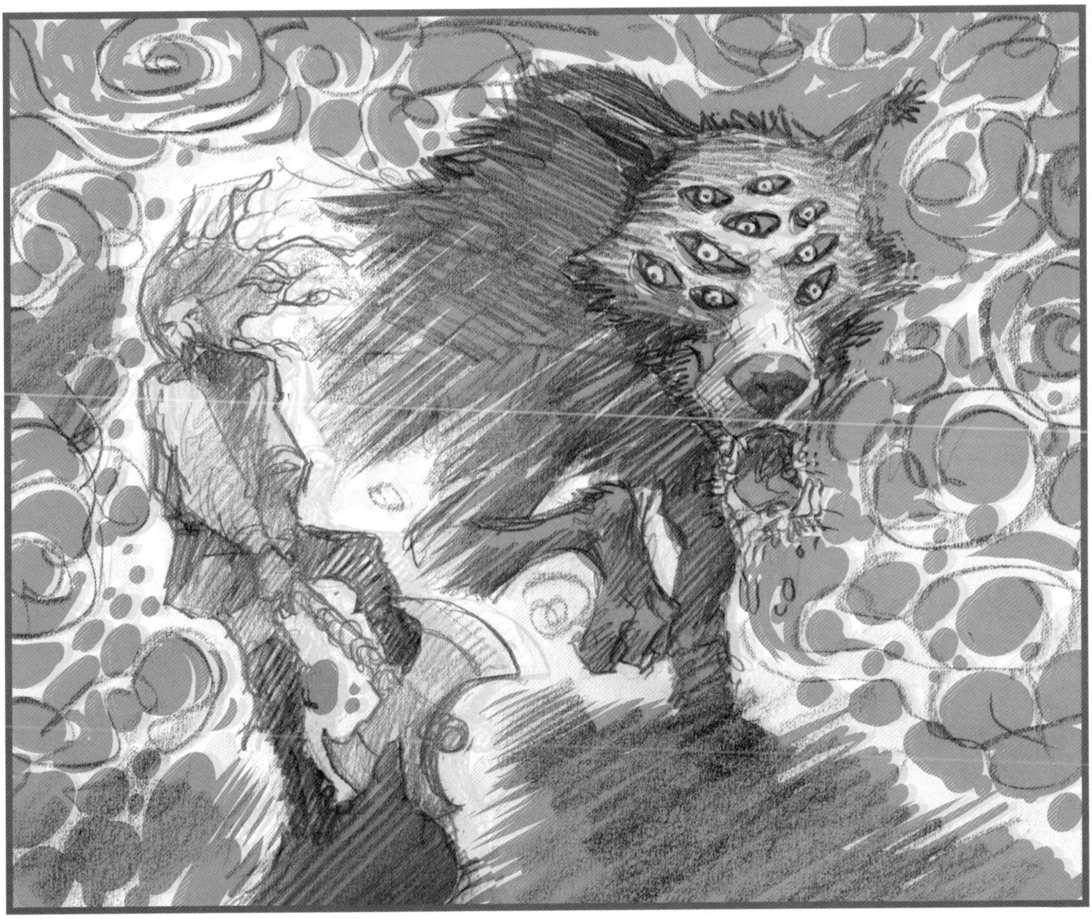

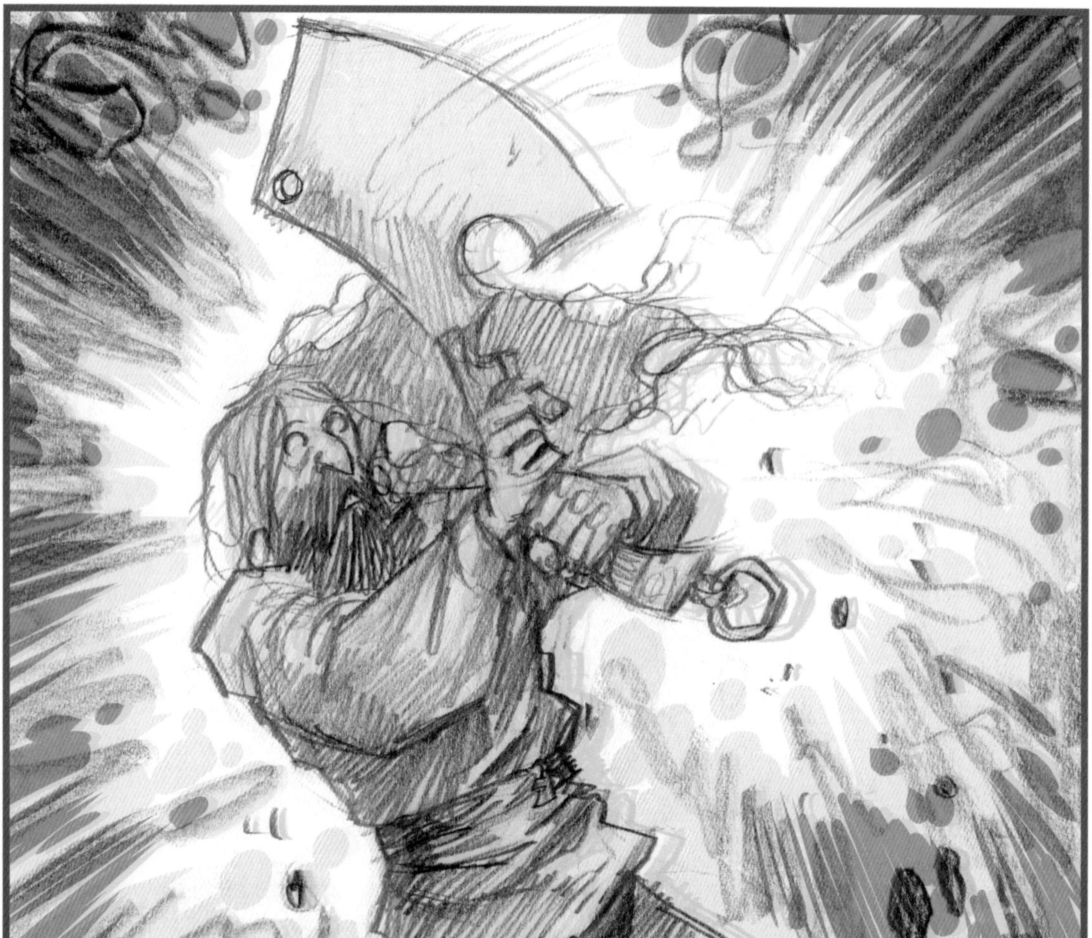

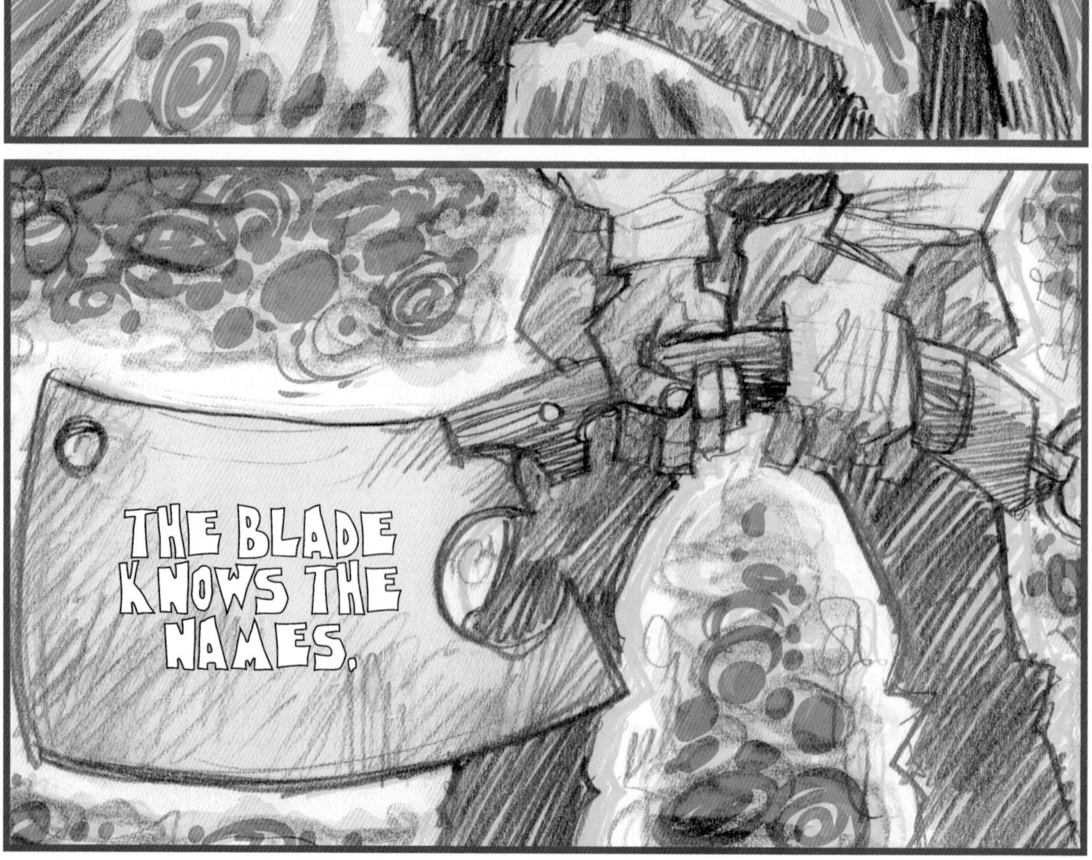
THE BLADE KNOWS THE NAMES.

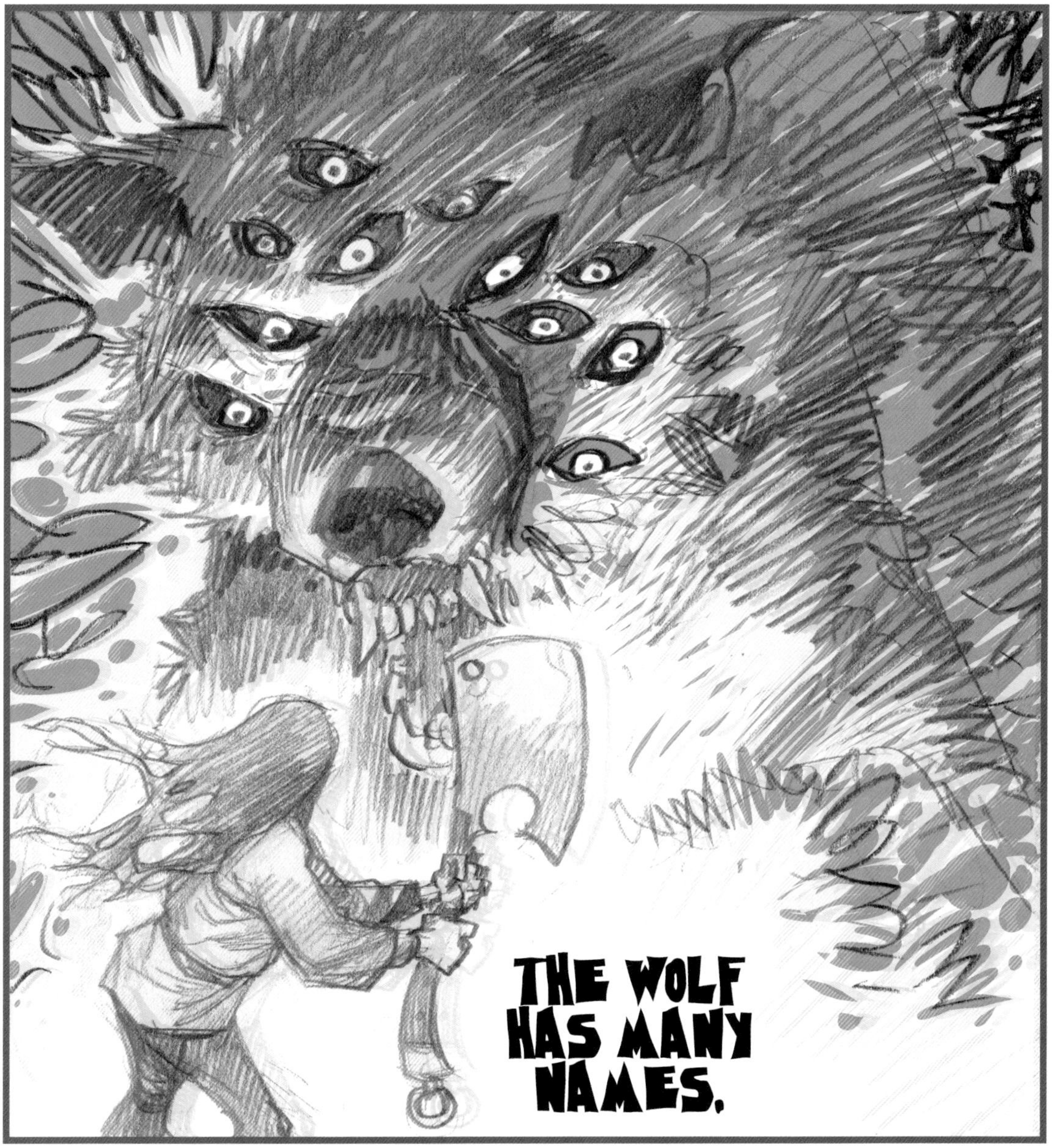
THE WOLF HAS MANY NAMES.

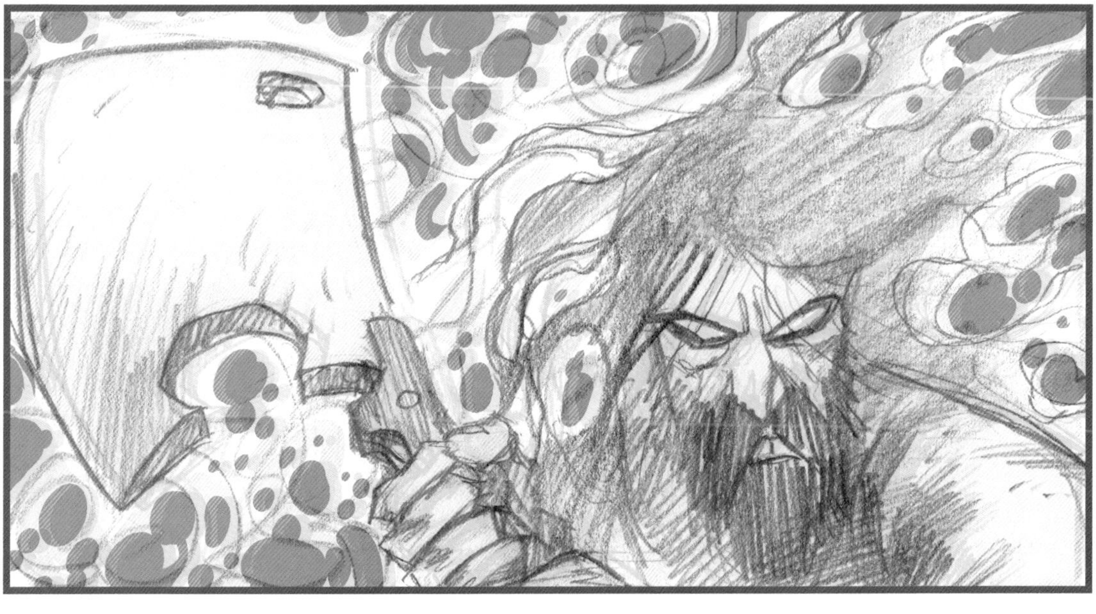

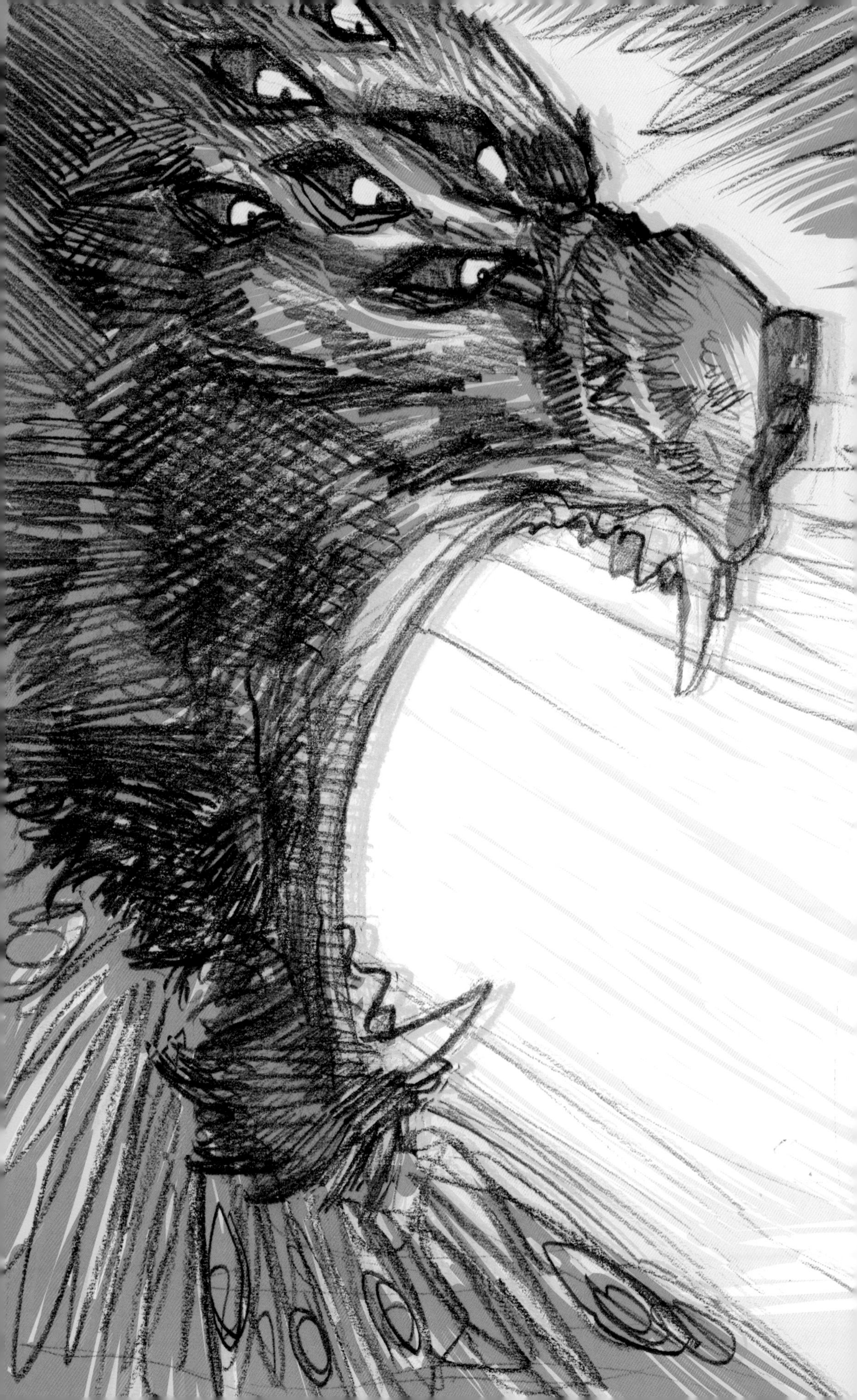

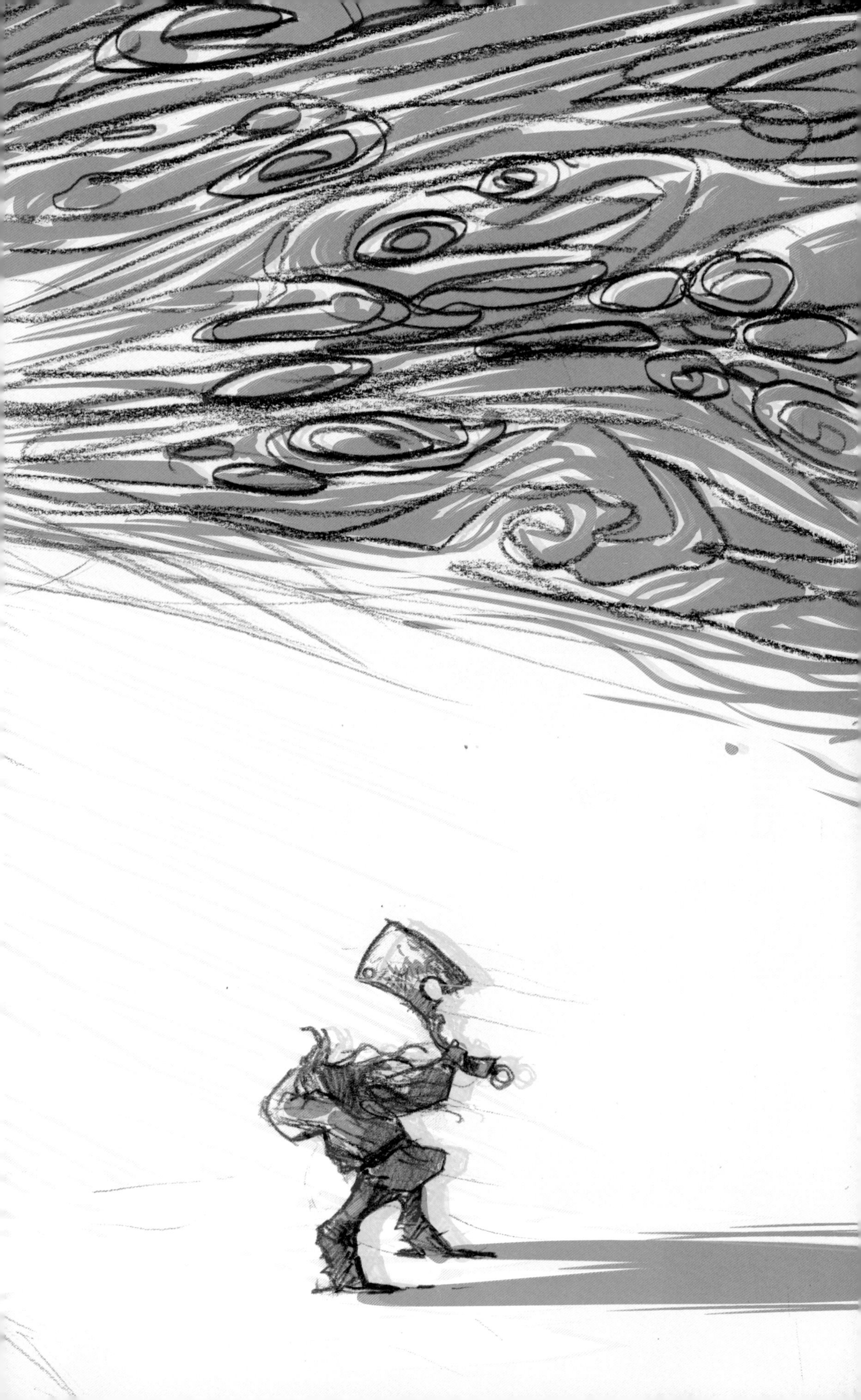

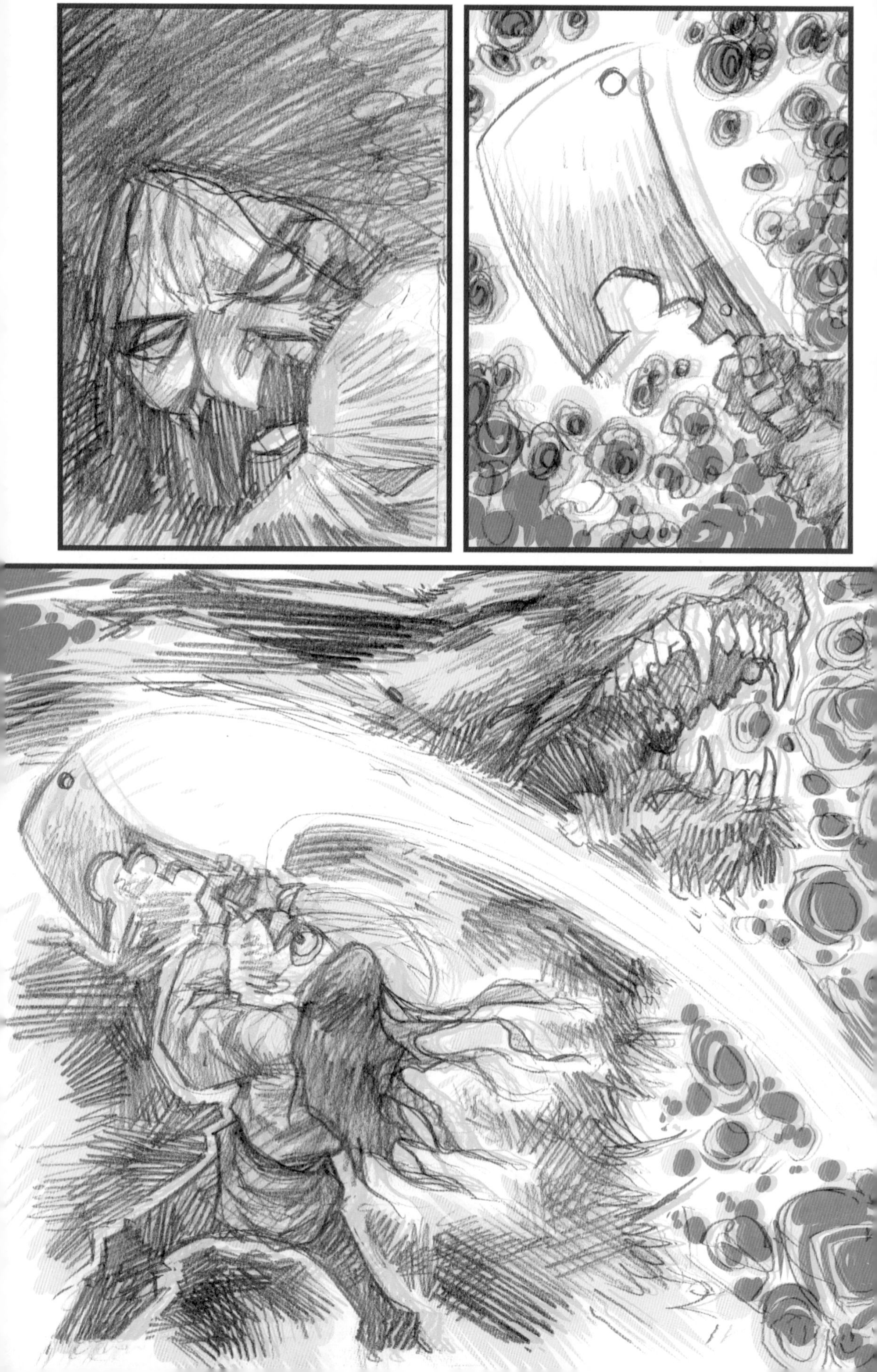

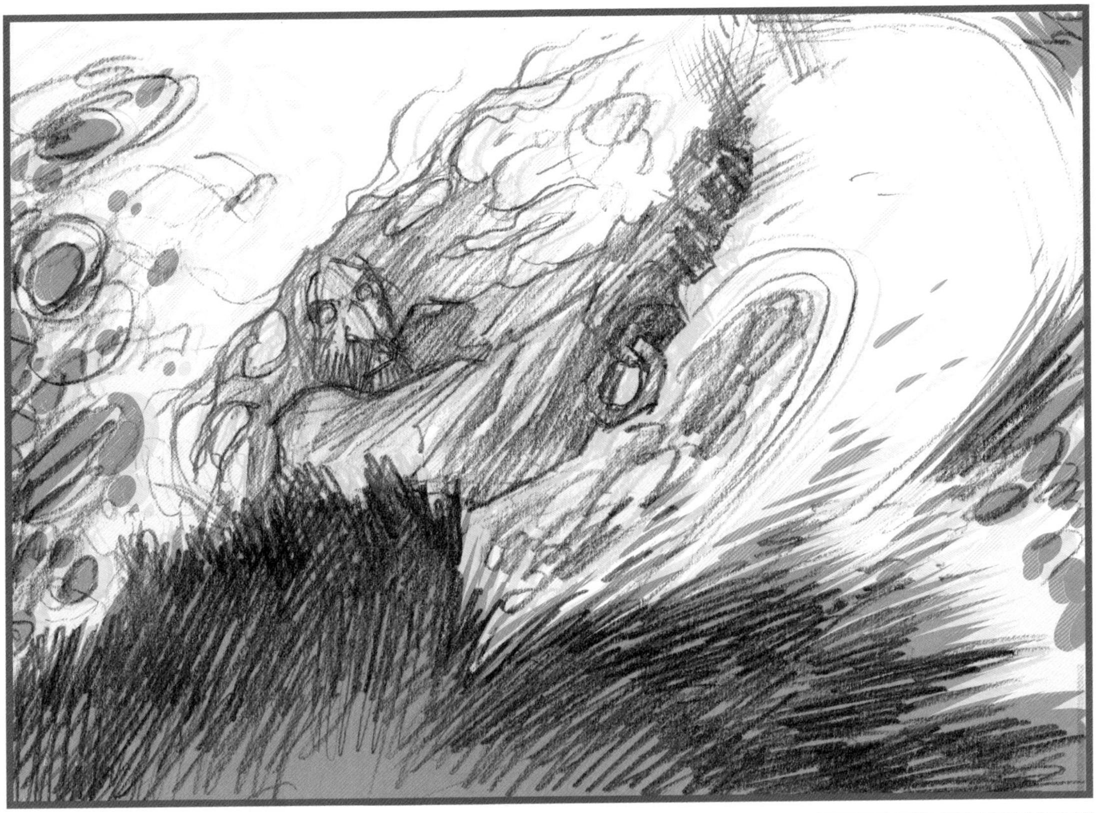
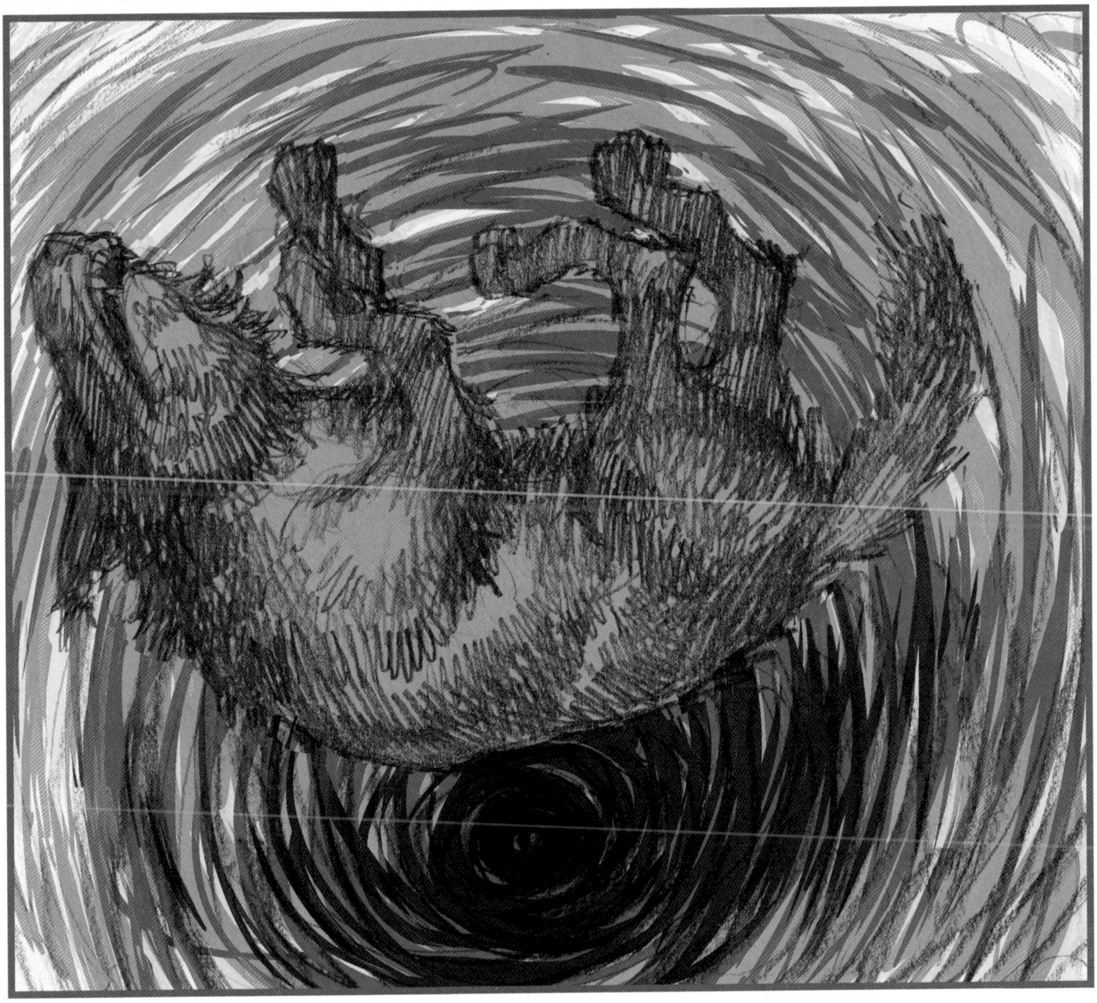

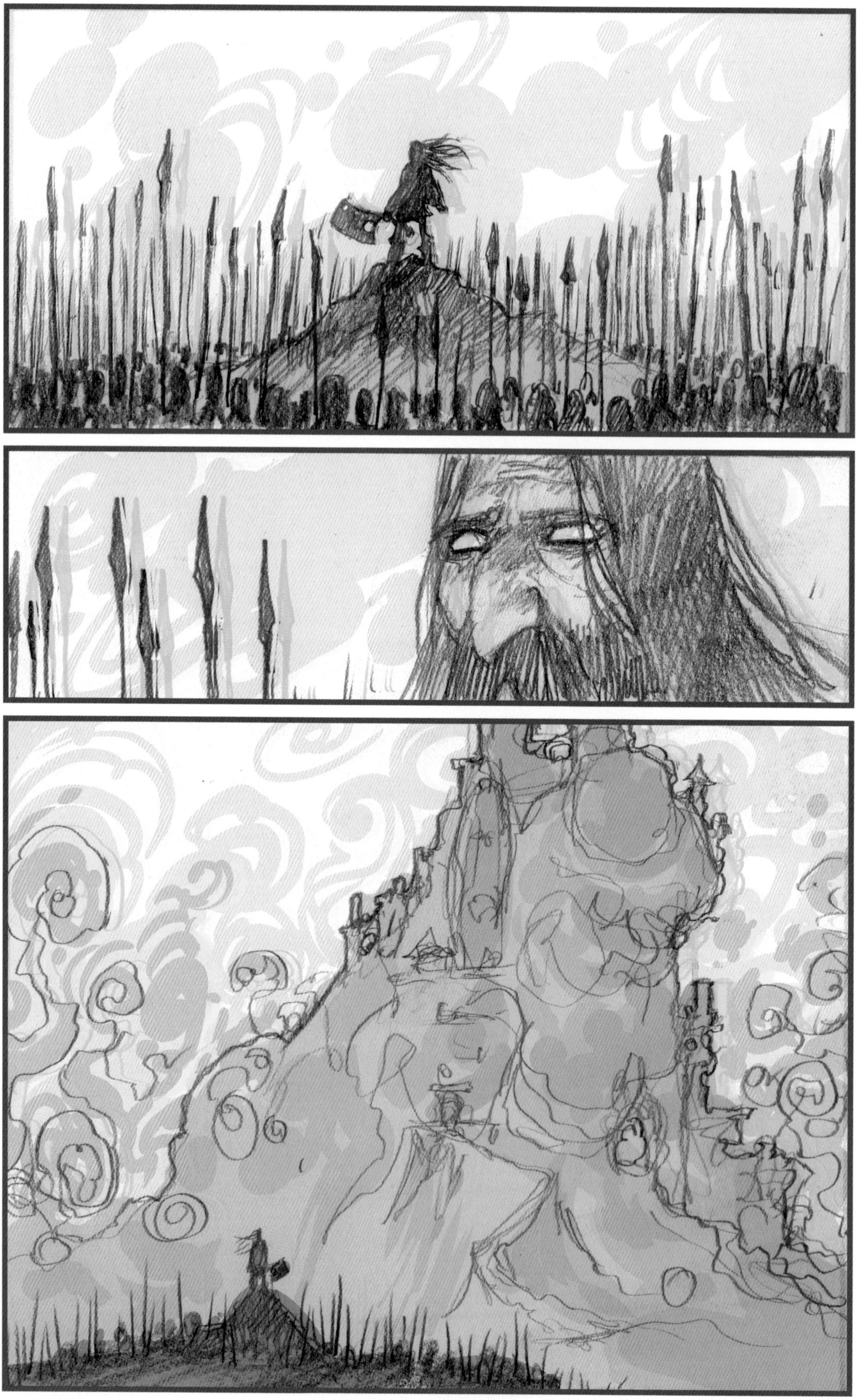

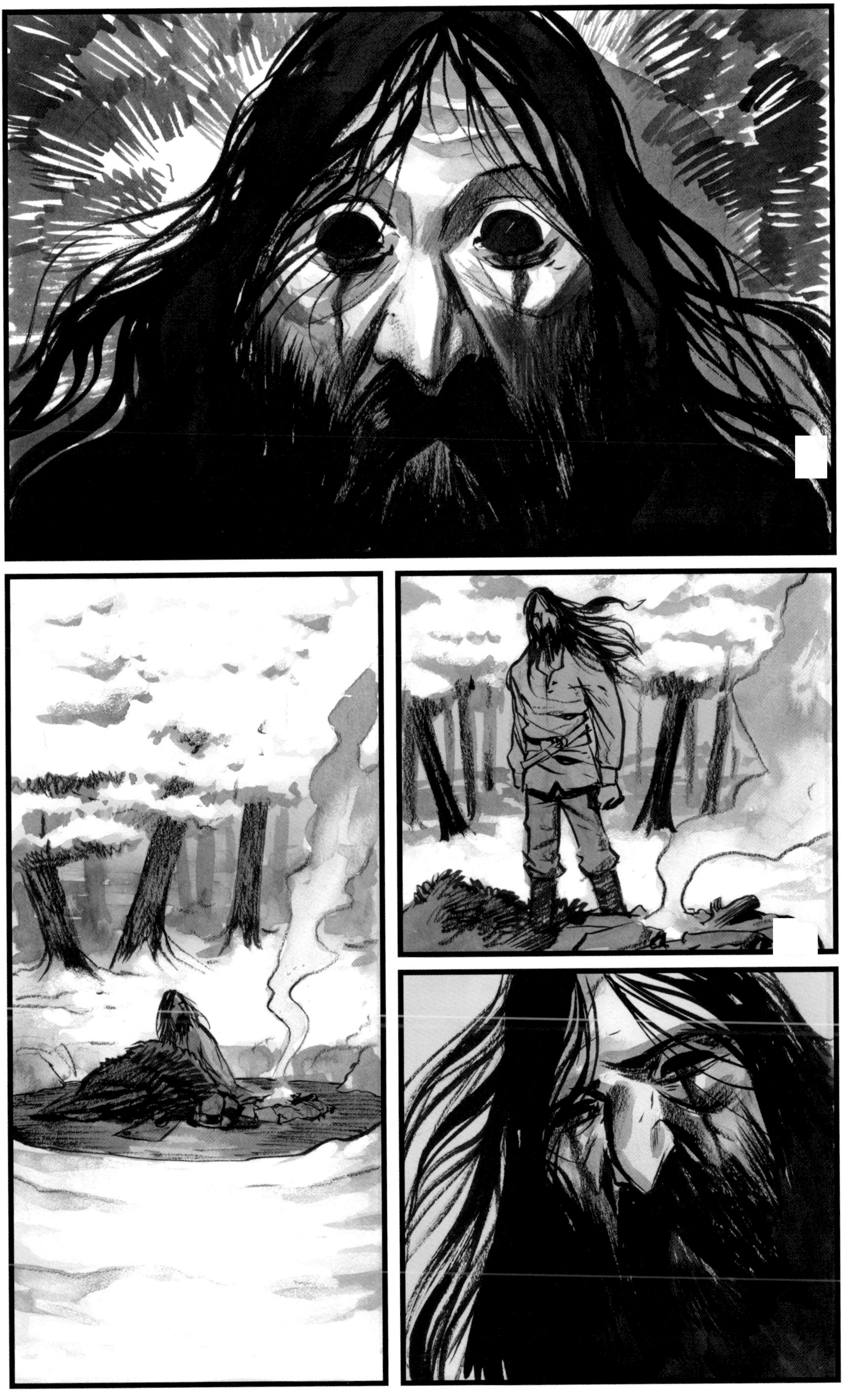

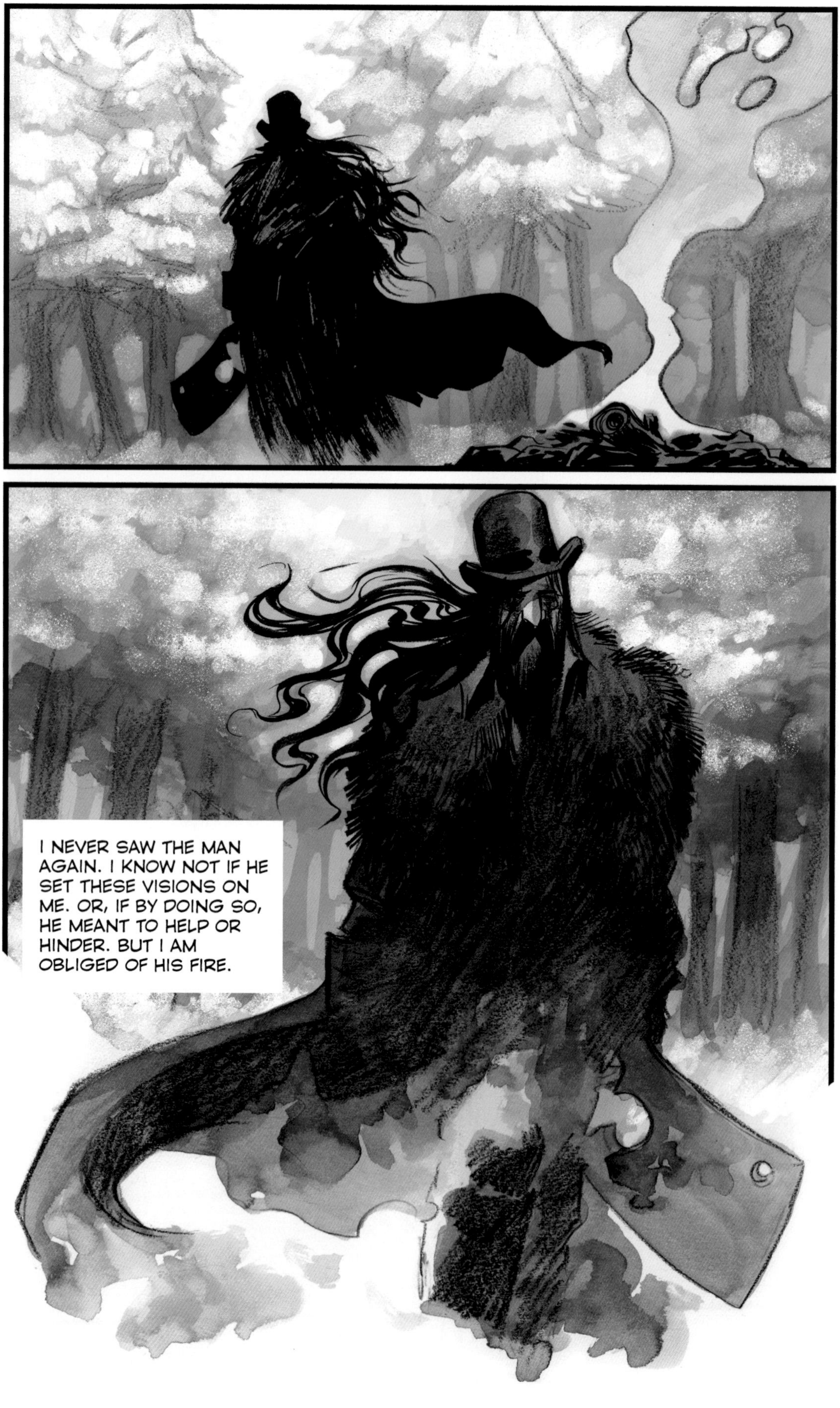
I NEVER SAW THE MAN AGAIN. I KNOW NOT IF HE SET THESE VISIONS ON ME. OR, IF BY DOING SO, HE MEANT TO HELP OR HINDER. BUT I AM OBLIGED OF HIS FIRE.

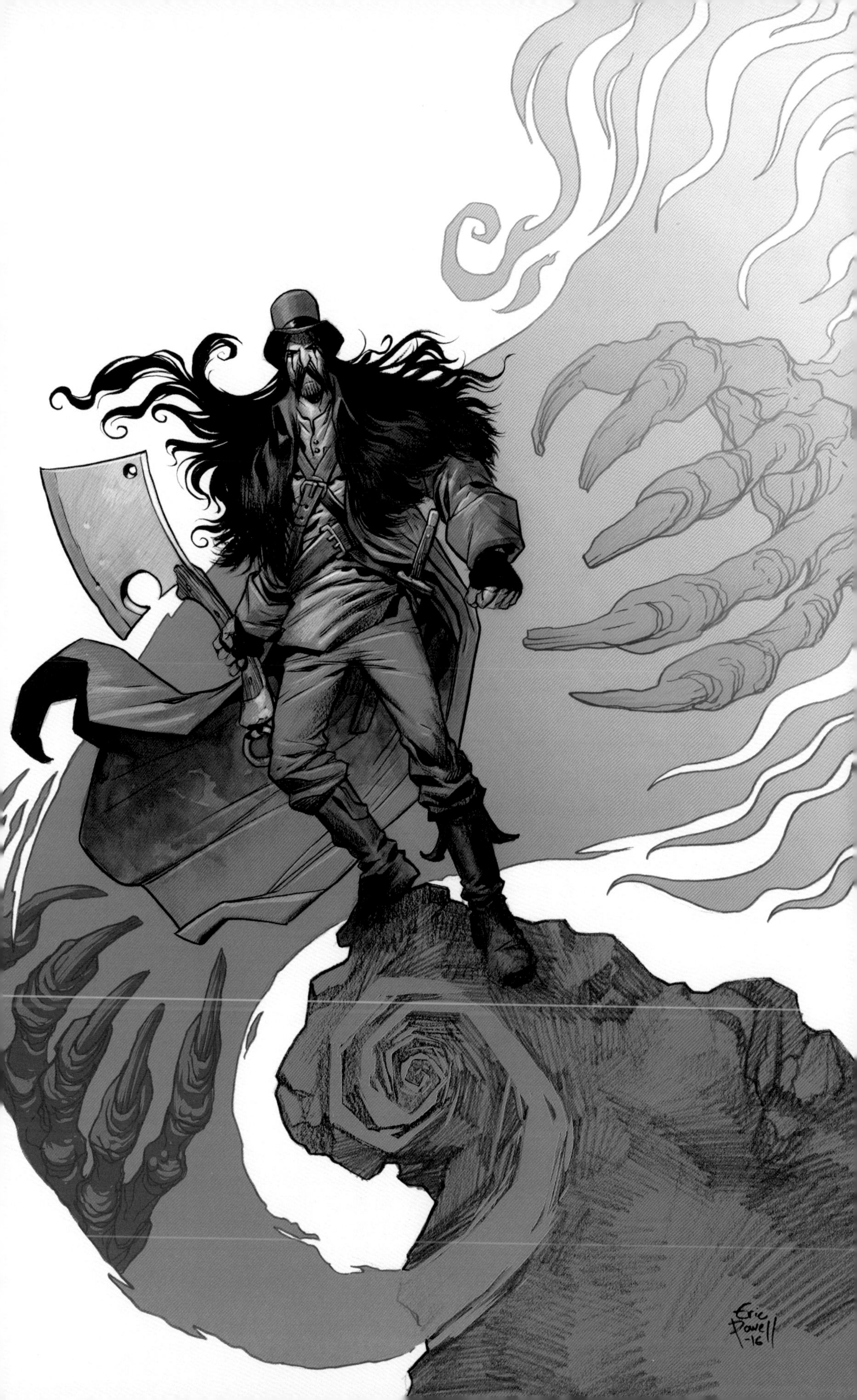
Eric
Powell
-16

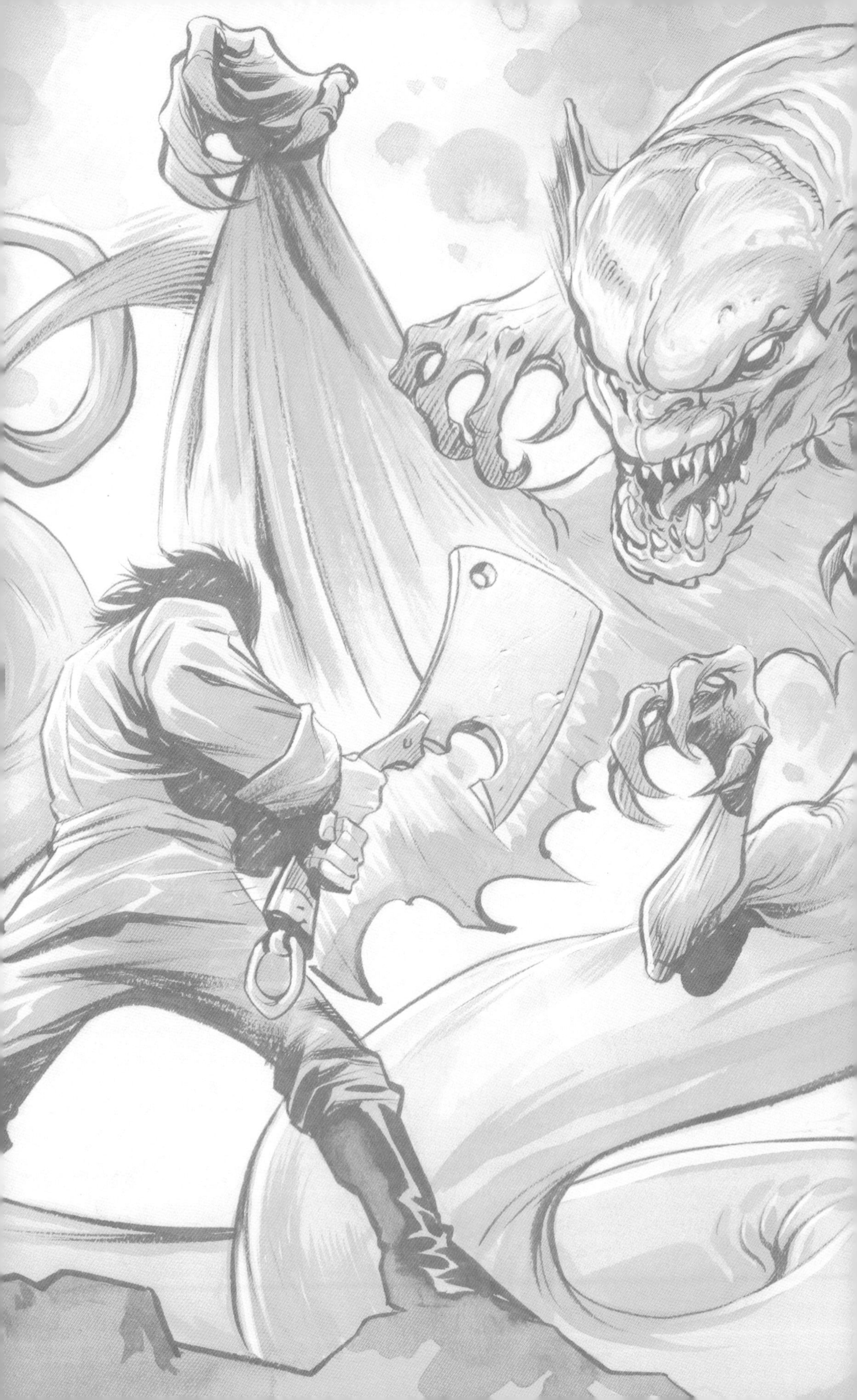

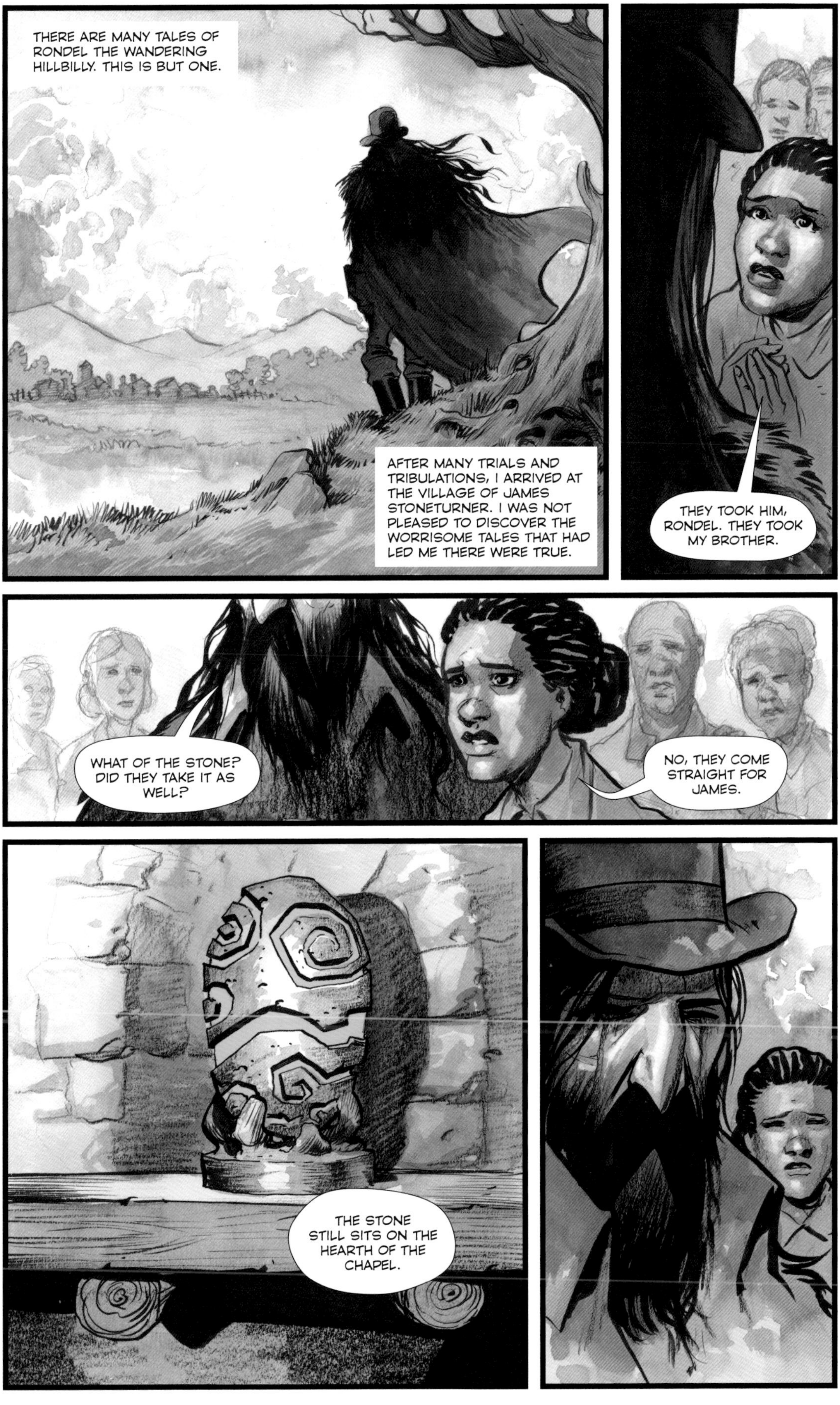
THERE ARE MANY TALES OF RONDEL THE WANDERING HILLBILLY. THIS IS BUT ONE.
AFTER MANY TRIALS AND TRIBULATIONS, I ARRIVED AT THE VILLAGE OF JAMES STONETURNER. I WAS NOT PLEASED TO DISCOVER THE WORRISOME TALES THAT HAD LED ME THERE WERE TRUE.
THEY TOOK HIM, RONDEL. THEY TOOK MY BROTHER.
WHAT OF THE STONE? DID THEY TAKE IT AS WELL?
NO, THEY COME STRAIGHT FOR JAMES.
THE STONE STILL SITS ON THE HEARTH OF THE CHAPEL.

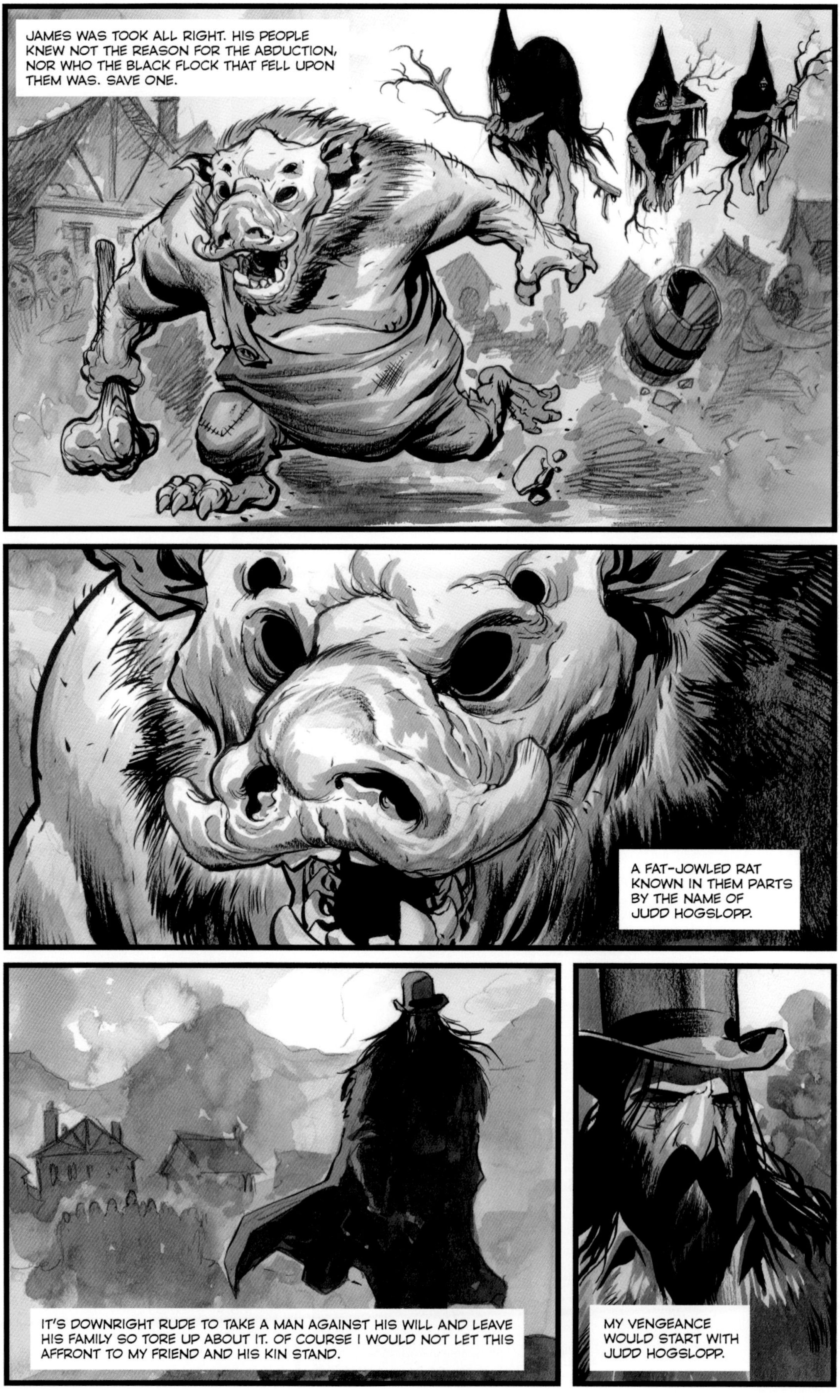
JAMES WAS TOOK ALL RIGHT. HIS PEOPLE KNEW NOT THE REASON FOR THE ABDUCTION, NOR WHO THE BLACK FLOCK THAT FELL UPON THEM WAS. SAVE ONE.
A FAT-JOWLED RAT KNOWN IN THEM PARTS BY THE NAME OF JUDD HOGSLOPP.
IT'S DOWNRIGHT RUDE TO TAKE A MAN AGAINST HIS WILL AND LEAVE HIS FAMILY SO TORE UP ABOUT IT. OF COURSE I WOULD NOT LET THIS AFFRONT TO MY FRIEND AND HIS KIN STAND.
MY VENGEANCE WOULD START WITH JUDD HOGSLOPP.

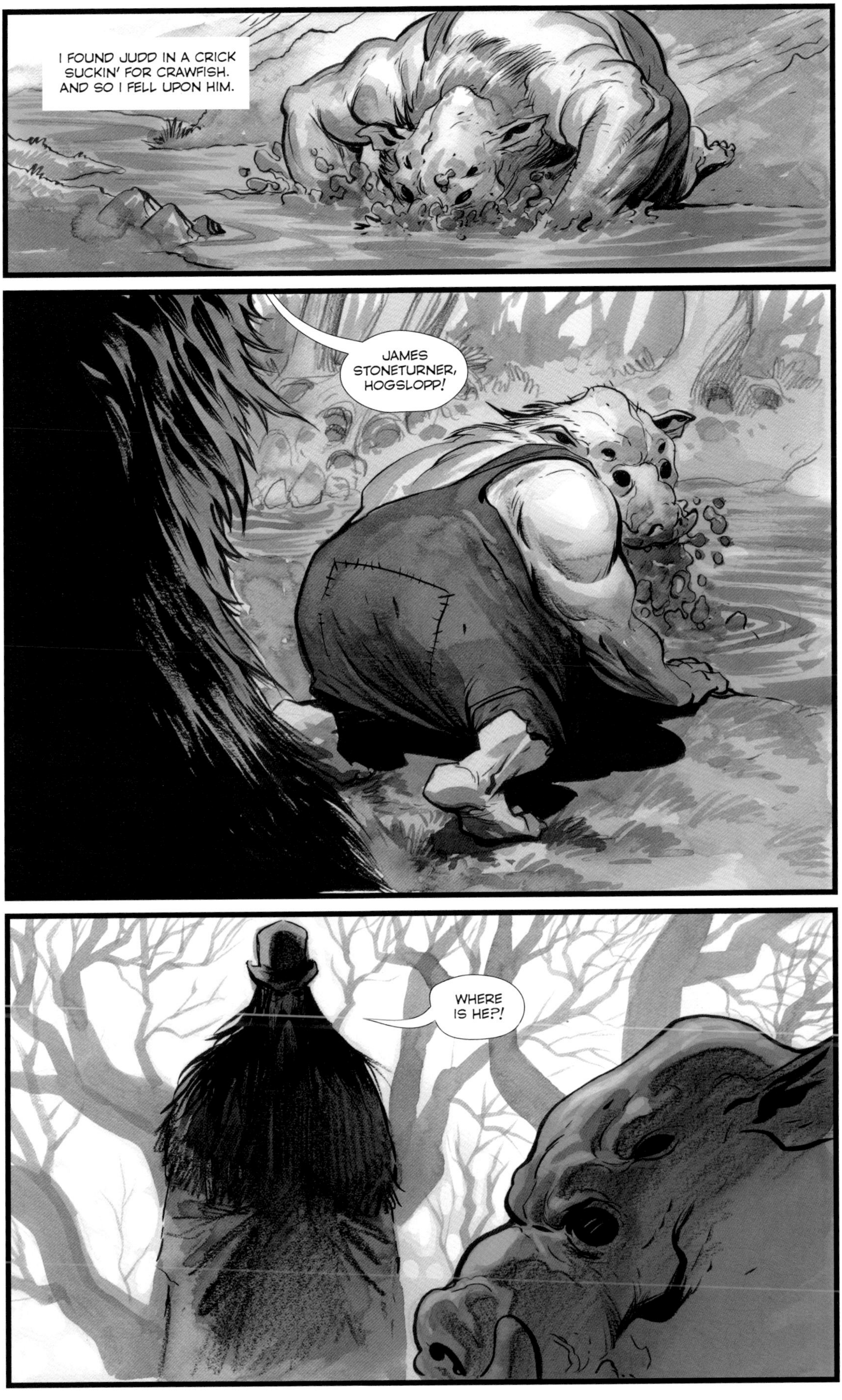
I FOUND JUDD IN A CRICK SUCKIN' FOR CRAWFISH. AND SO I FELL UPON HIM.
JAMES STONETURNER, HOGSLOPP!
WHERE IS HE?!

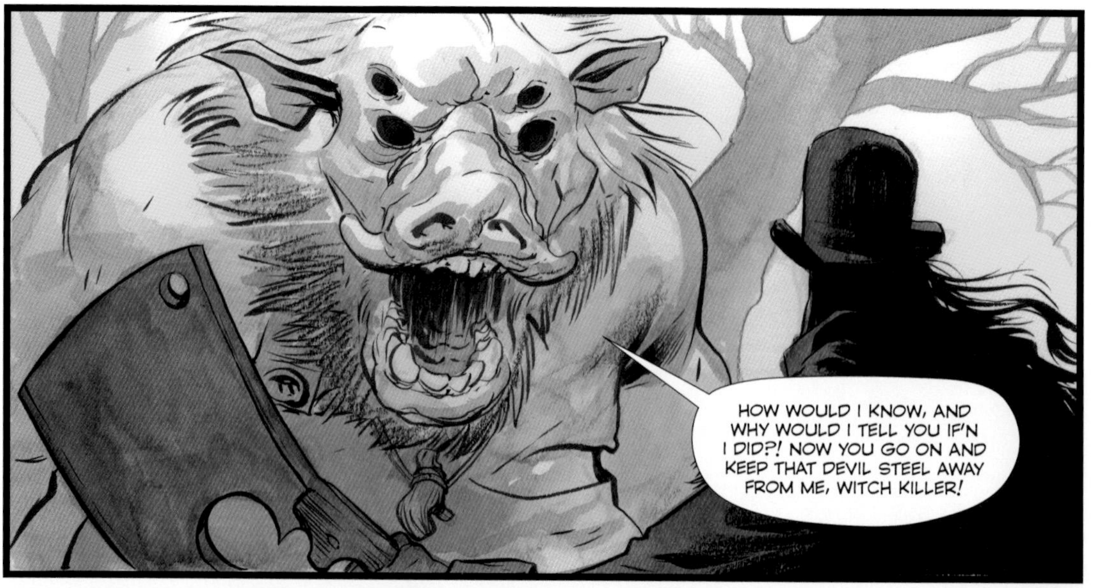
HOW WOULD I KNOW, AND WHY WOULD I TELL YOU IF'N I DID?! NOW YOU GO ON AND KEEP THAT DEVIL STEEL AWAY FROM ME, WITCH KILLER!

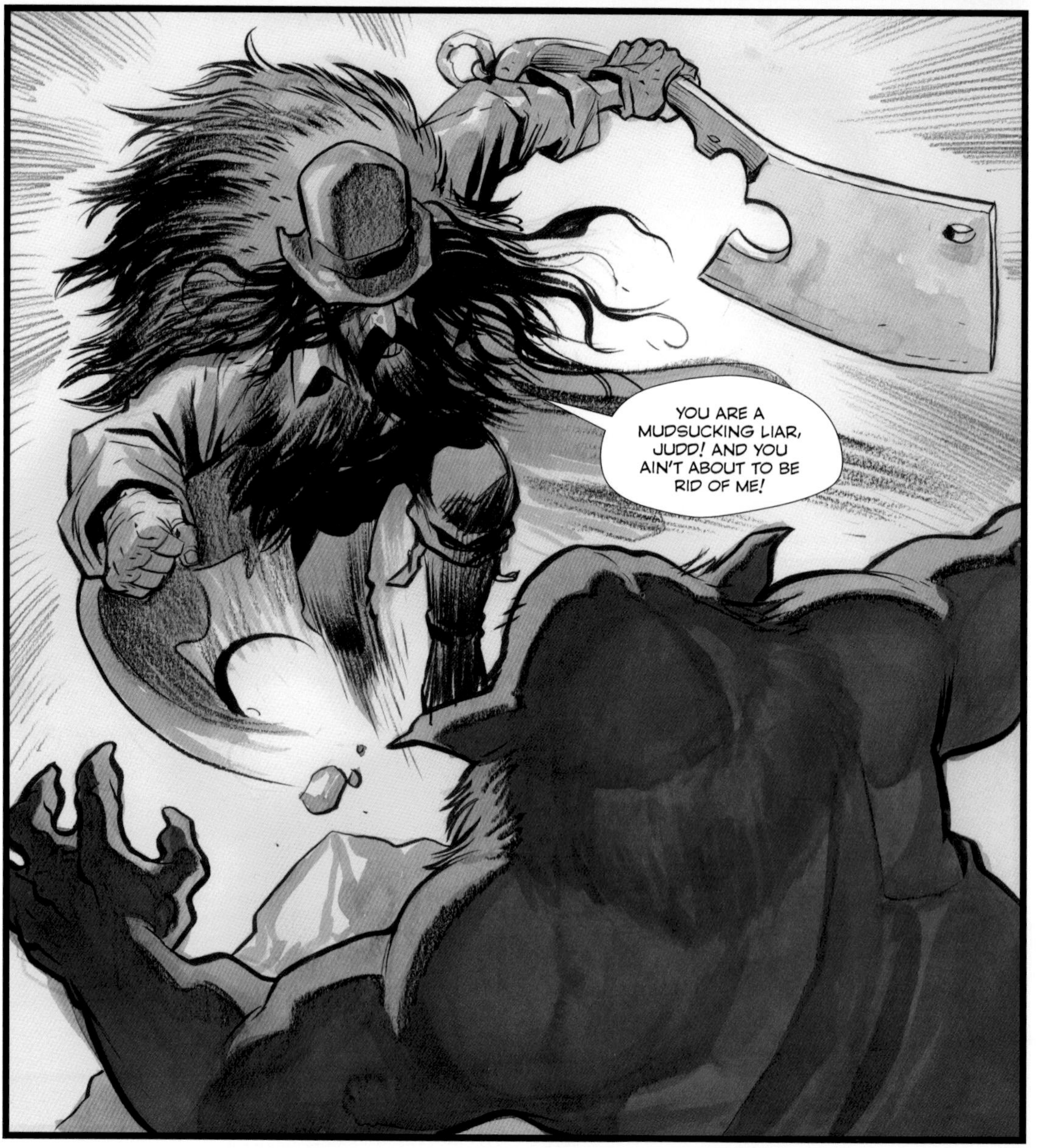
YOU ARE A MUDSUCKING LIAR, JUDD! AND YOU AIN'T ABOUT TO BE RID OF ME!

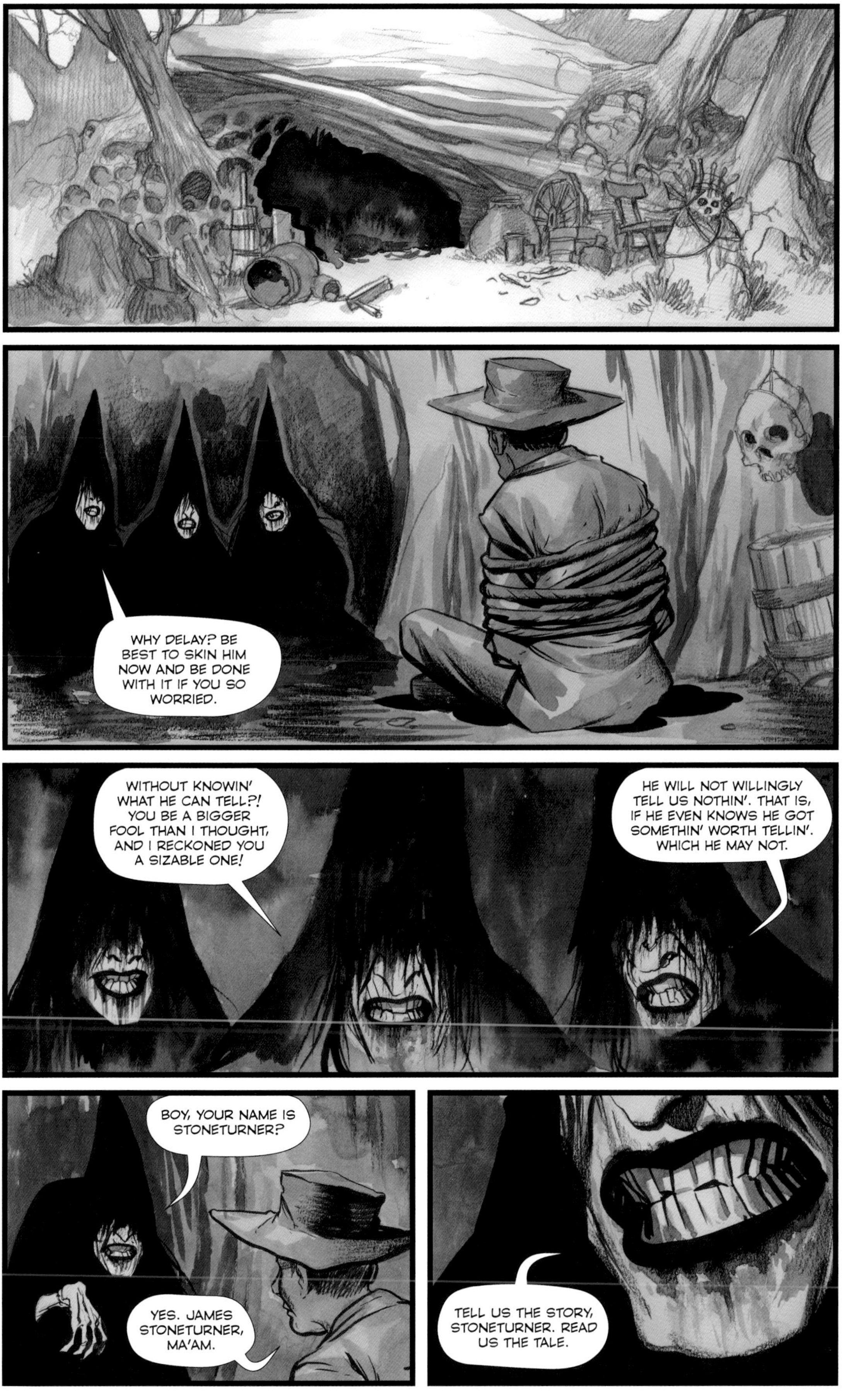
WHY DELAY? BE BEST TO SKIN HIM NOW AND BE DONE WITH IT IF YOU SO WORRIED.
WITHOUT KNOWIN' WHAT HE CAN TELL?! YOU BE A BIGGER FOOL THAN I THOUGHT, AND I RECKONED YOU A SIZABLE ONE!
HE WILL NOT WILLINGLY TELL US NOTHIN'. THAT IS, IF HE EVEN KNOWS HE GOT SOMETHIN' WORTH TELLIN'. WHICH HE MAY NOT.
BOY, YOUR NAME IS STONETURNER?
YES. JAMES STONETURNER, MA'AM.
TELL US THE STORY, STONETURNER. READ US THE TALE.

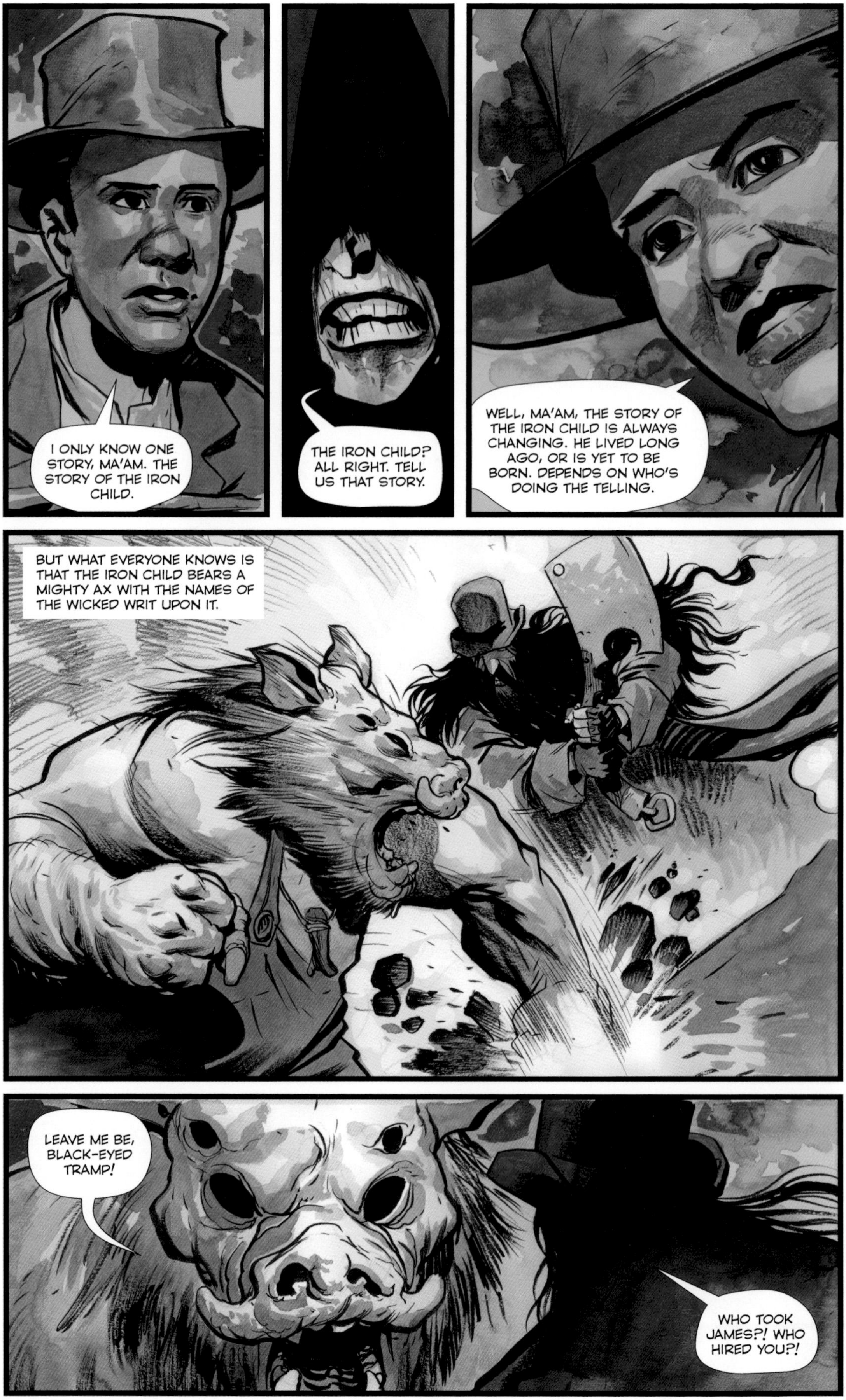
I ONLY KNOW ONE STORY, MA'AM. THE STORY OF THE IRON CHILD.
THE IRON CHILD? ALL RIGHT. TELL US THAT STORY.
WELL, MA'AM, THE STORY OF THE IRON CHILD IS ALWAYS CHANGING. HE LIVED LONG AGO, OR IS YET TO BE BORN. DEPENDS ON WHO'S DOING THE TELLING.
BUT WHAT EVERYONE KNOWS IS THAT THE IRON CHILD BEARS A MIGHTY AX WITH THE NAMES OF THE WICKED WRIT UPON IT.
LEAVE ME BE, BLACK-EYED TRAMP!
WHO TOOK JAMES?! WHO HIRED YOU?!

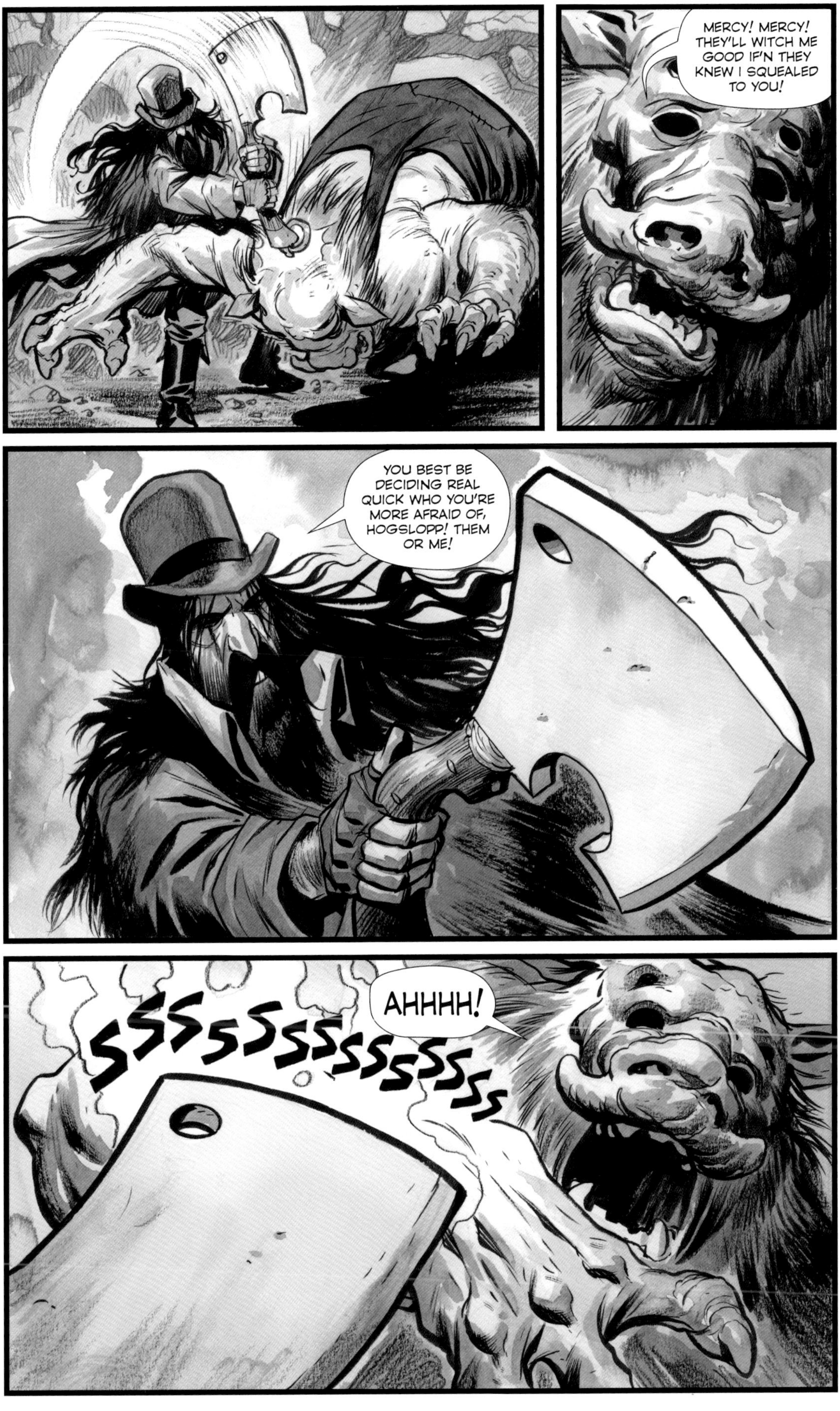
MERCY! MERCY! THEY'LL WITCH ME GOOD IF'N THEY KNEW I SQUEALED TO YOU!
YOU BEST BE DECIDING REAL QUICK WHO YOU'RE MORE AFRAID OF, HOGSLOPP! THEM OR ME!
SSSSSSSSSSSSSS
AHHHH!

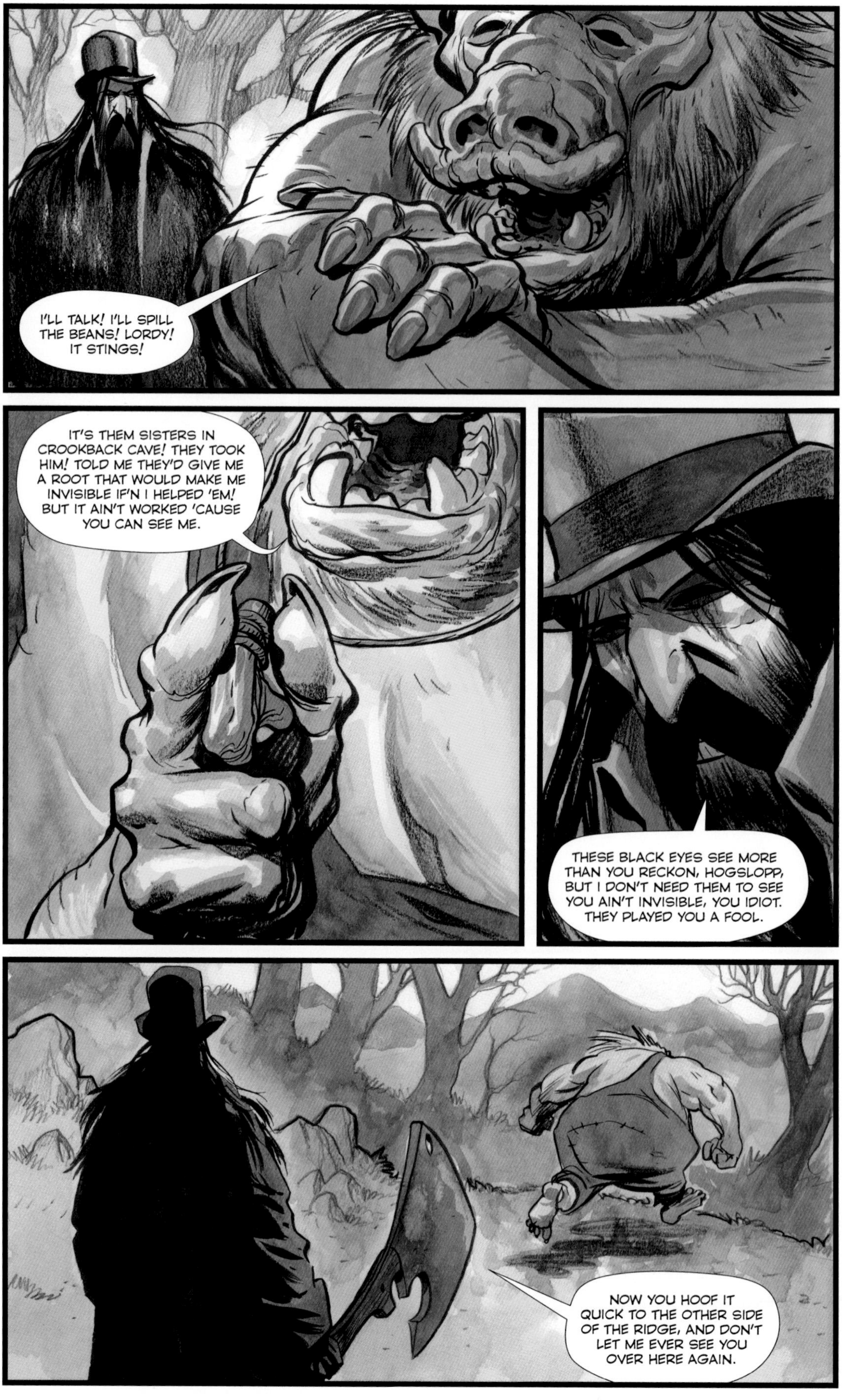
I'LL TALK! I'LL SPILL THE BEANS! LORDY! IT STINGS!
IT'S THEM SISTERS IN CROOKBACK CAVE! THEY TOOK HIM! TOLD ME THEY'D GIVE ME A ROOT THAT WOULD MAKE ME INVISIBLE IF'N I HELPED 'EM! BUT IT AIN'T WORKED 'CAUSE YOU CAN SEE ME.
THESE BLACK EYES SEE MORE THAN YOU RECKON, HOGSLOPP, BUT I DON'T NEED THEM TO SEE YOU AIN'T INVISIBLE, YOU IDIOT. THEY PLAYED YOU A FOOL.
NOW YOU HOOF IT QUICK TO THE OTHER SIDE OF THE RIDGE, AND DON'T LET ME EVER SEE YOU OVER HERE AGAIN.

AND THEN THE IRON CHILD WHOOPED THE TREE OF SORROWS AND RUN THE DOG-EATER OFF INTO THE SWAMP WHERE IT WAS NEVER HEARD OF AGAIN.

FAIRY TALES. WHAT DOES THIS MATTER? WE WASTE TIME. WE SHOULD KILL THE STONETURNER NOW.

BUT WAIT. THERE IS MORE TO THE STORY.

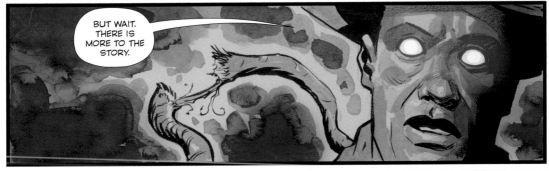

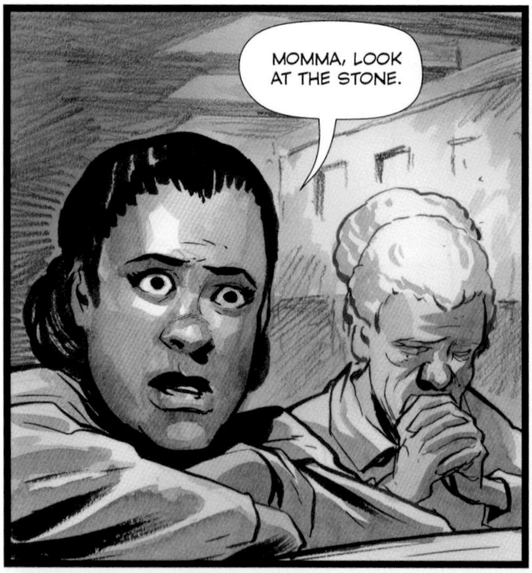
MOMMA, LOOK
AT THE STONE.

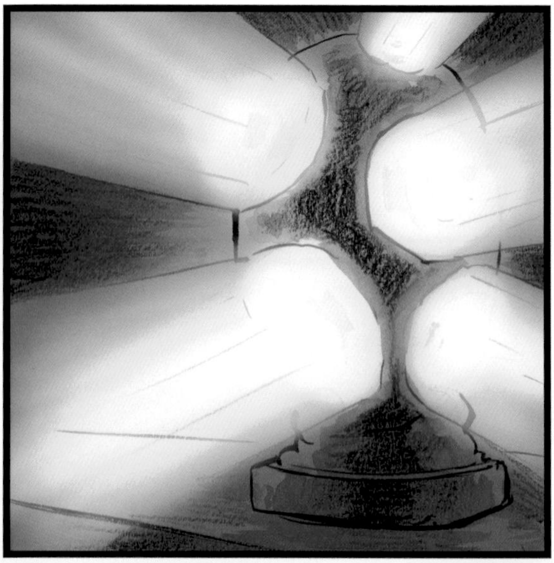

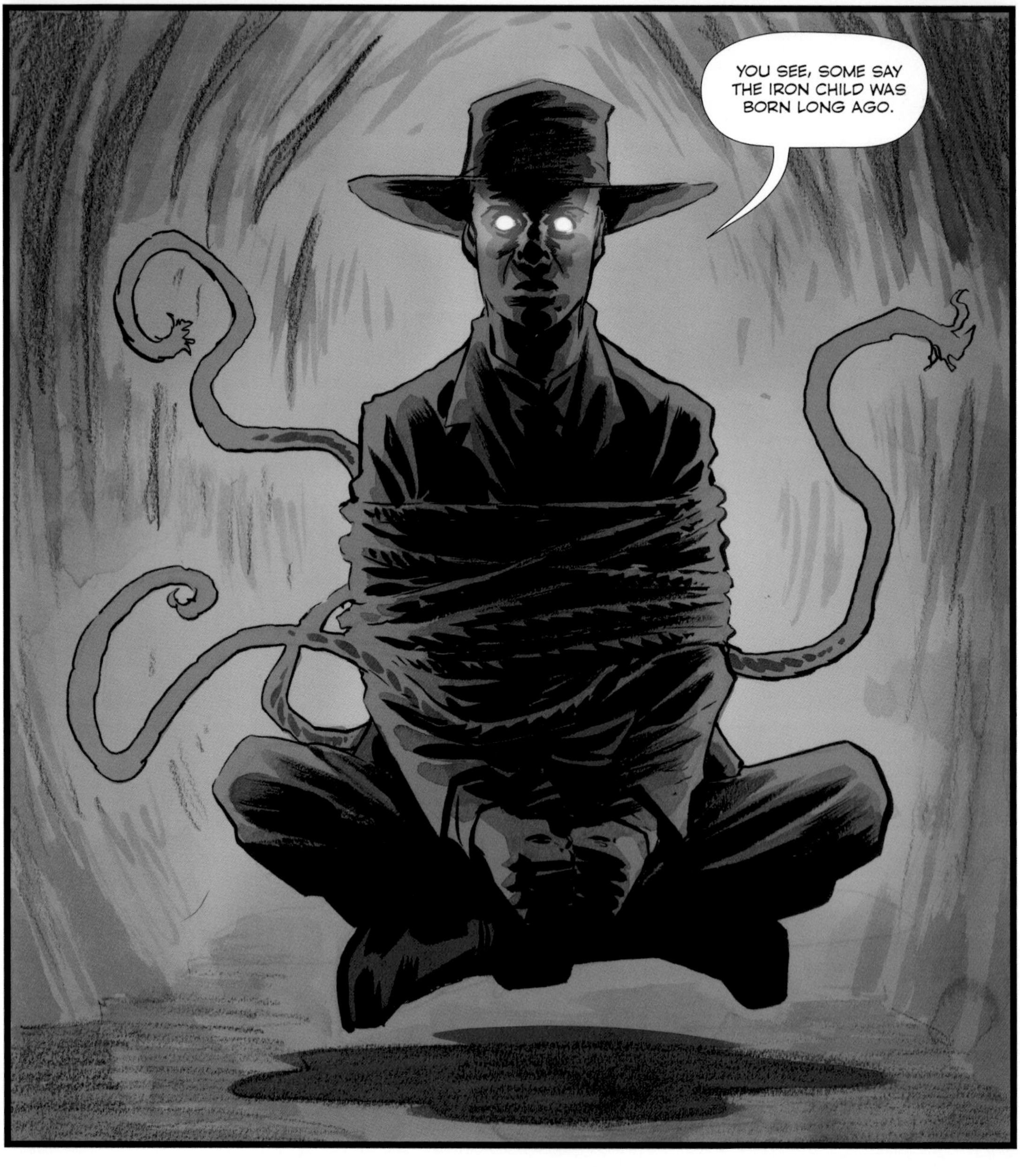
YOU SEE, SOME SAY
THE IRON CHILD WAS
BORN LONG AGO.

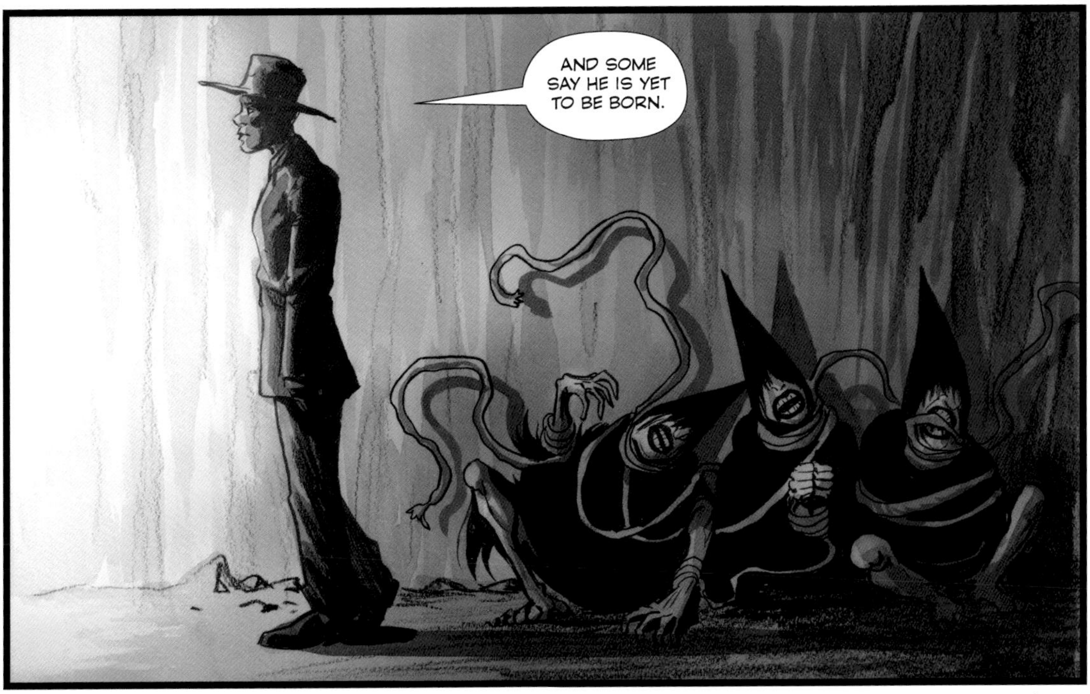
AND SOME SAY HE IS YET TO BE BORN.

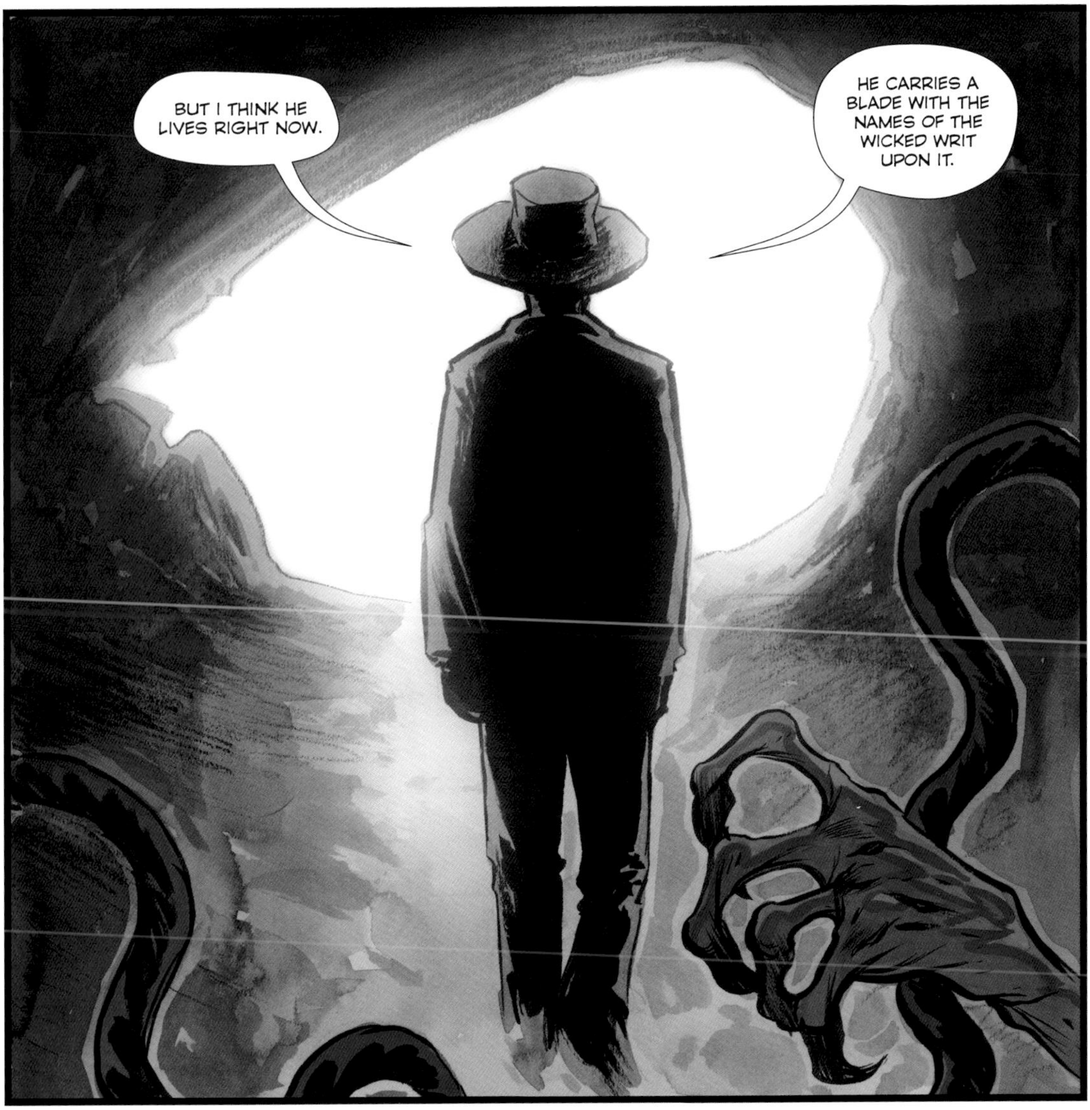
BUT I THINK HE LIVES RIGHT NOW.
HE CARRIES A BLADE WITH THE NAMES OF THE WICKED WRIT UPON IT.

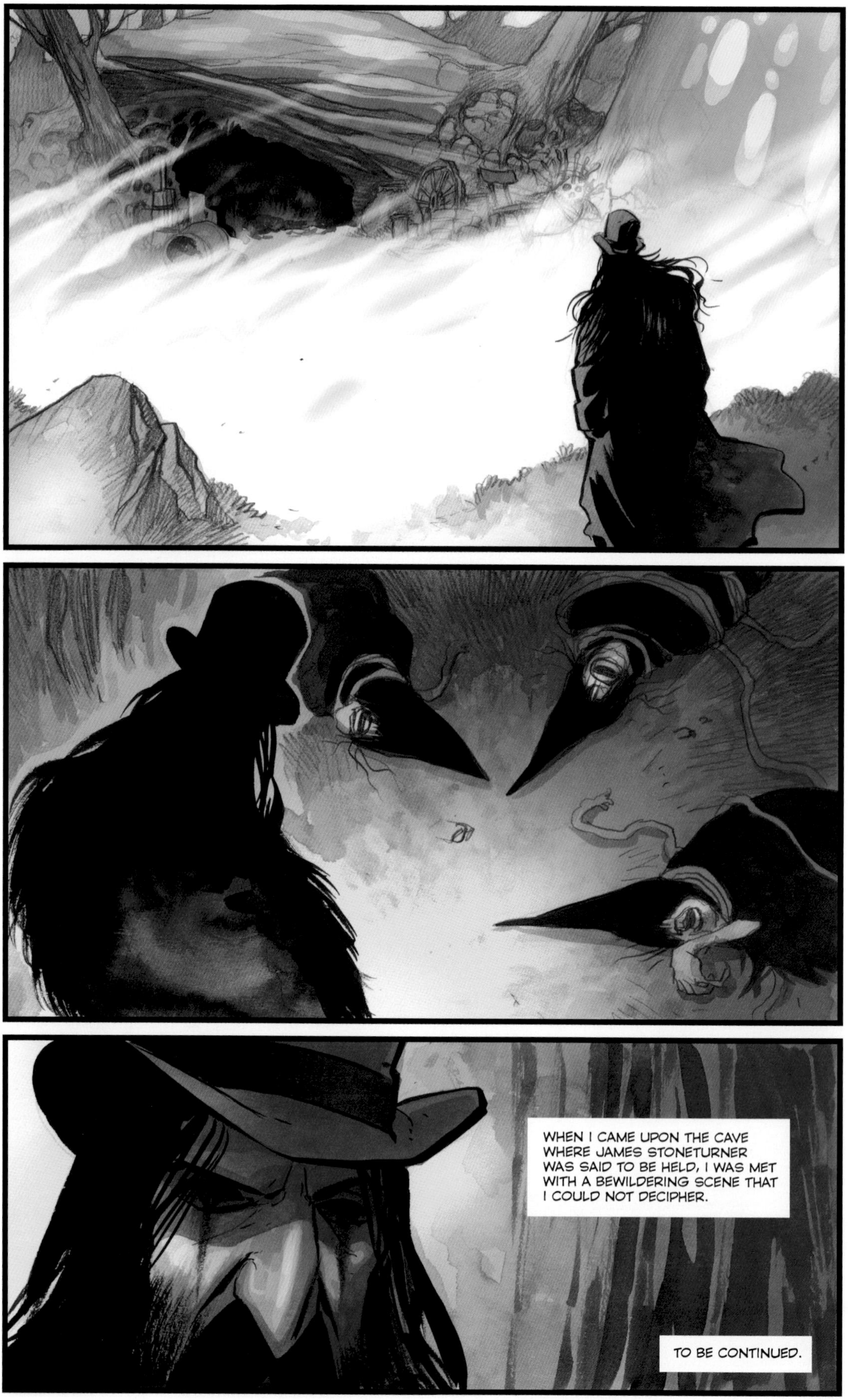
WHEN I CAME UPON THE CAVE WHERE JAMES STONETURNER WAS SAID TO BE HELD, I WAS MET WITH A BEWILDERING SCENE THAT I COULD NOT DECIPHER.
TO BE CONTINUED.

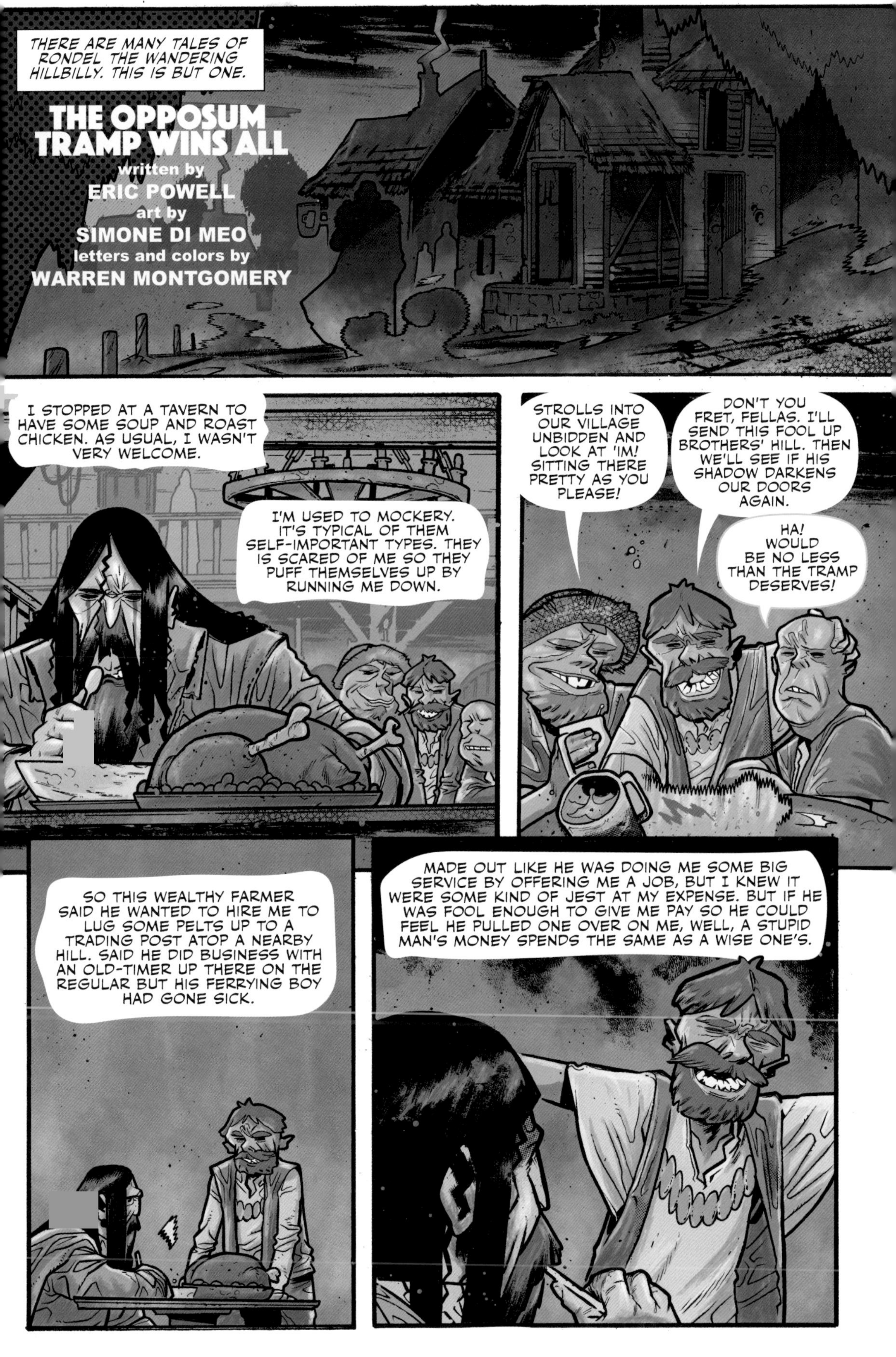
THERE ARE MANY TALES OF RONDEL THE WANDERING HILLBILLY. THIS IS BUT ONE.
THE OPPOSUM TRAMP WINS ALL
written by ERIC POWELL
art by SIMONE DI MEO
letters and colors by WARREN MONTGOMERY
I STOPPED AT A TAVERN TO HAVE SOME SOUP AND ROAST CHICKEN. AS USUAL, I WASN'T VERY WELCOME.
I'M USED TO MOCKERY. IT'S TYPICAL OF THEM SELF-IMPORTANT TYPES. THEY IS SCARED OF ME SO THEY PUFF THEMSELVES UP BY RUNNING ME DOWN.
STROLLS INTO OUR VILLAGE UNBIDDEN AND LOOK AT 'IM! SITTING THERE PRETTY AS YOU PLEASE!
DON'T YOU FRET, FELLAS. I'LL SEND THIS FOOL UP BROTHERS' HILL. THEN WE'LL SEE IF HIS SHADOW DARKENS OUR DOORS AGAIN.
HA! WOULD BE NO LESS THAN THE TRAMP DESERVES!
SO THIS WEALTHY FARMER SAID HE WANTED TO HIRE ME TO LUG SOME PELTS UP TO A TRADING POST ATOP A NEARBY HILL. SAID HE DID BUSINESS WITH AN OLD-TIMER UP THERE ON THE REGULAR BUT HIS FERRYING BOY HAD GONE SICK.
MADE OUT LIKE HE WAS DOING ME SOME BIG SERVICE BY OFFERING ME A JOB, BUT I KNEW IT WERE SOME KIND OF JEST AT MY EXPENSE. BUT IF HE WAS FOOL ENOUGH TO GIVE ME PAY SO HE COULD FEEL HE PULLED ONE OVER ON ME, WELL, A STUPID MAN'S MONEY SPENDS THE SAME AS A WISE ONE'S.

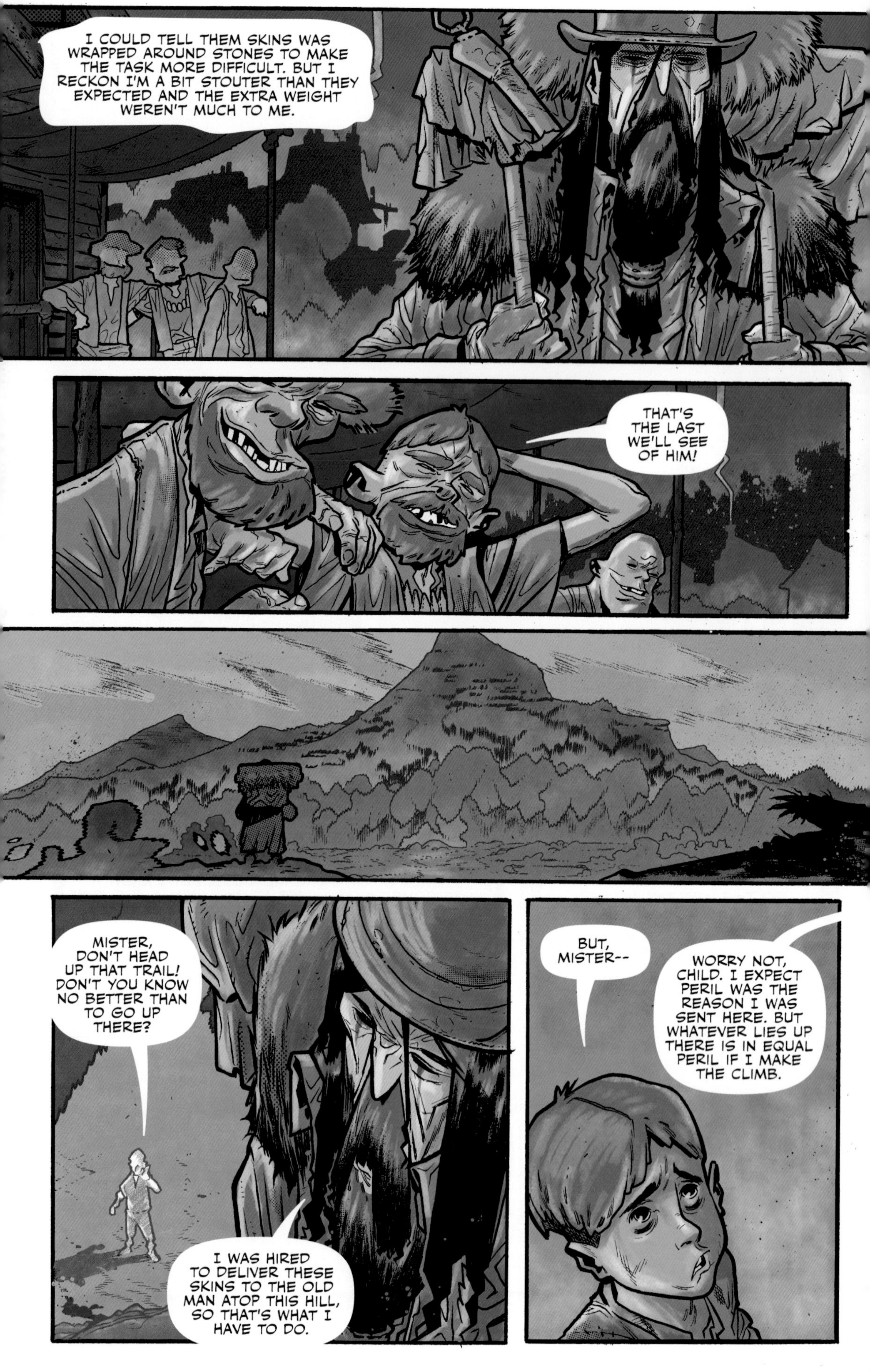
I COULD TELL THEM SKINS WAS WRAPPED AROUND STONES TO MAKE THE TASK MORE DIFFICULT. BUT I RECKON I'M A BIT STOUTER THAN THEY EXPECTED AND THE EXTRA WEIGHT WEREN'T MUCH TO ME.
THAT'S THE LAST WE'LL SEE OF HIM!
MISTER, DON'T HEAD UP THAT TRAIL! DON'T YOU KNOW NO BETTER THAN TO GO UP THERE?
I WAS HIRED TO DELIVER THESE SKINS TO THE OLD MAN ATOP THIS HILL, SO THAT'S WHAT I HAVE TO DO.
BUT, MISTER--
WORRY NOT, CHILD. I EXPECT PERIL WAS THE REASON I WAS SENT HERE. BUT WHATEVER LIES UP THERE IS IN EQUAL PERIL IF I MAKE THE CLIMB.

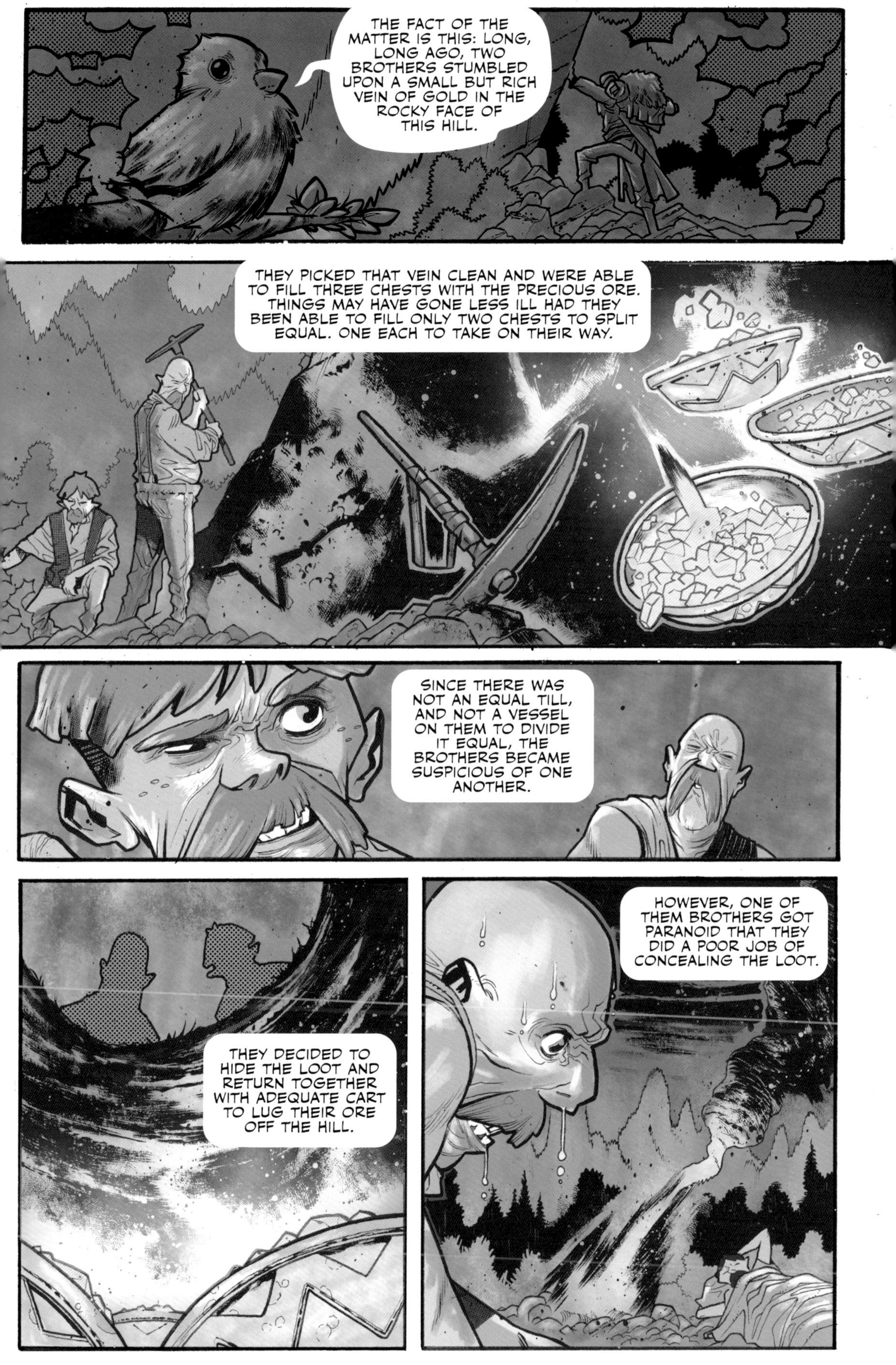
THE FACT OF THE MATTER IS THIS: LONG, LONG AGO, TWO BROTHERS STUMBLED UPON A SMALL BUT RICH VEIN OF GOLD IN THE ROCKY FACE OF THIS HILL.
THEY PICKED THAT VEIN CLEAN AND WERE ABLE TO FILL THREE CHESTS WITH THE PRECIOUS ORE. THINGS MAY HAVE GONE LESS ILL HAD THEY BEEN ABLE TO FILL ONLY TWO CHESTS TO SPLIT EQUAL. ONE EACH TO TAKE ON THEIR WAY.
SINCE THERE WAS NOT AN EQUAL TILL, AND NOT A VESSEL ON THEM TO DIVIDE IT EQUAL, THE BROTHERS BECAME SUSPICIOUS OF ONE ANOTHER.
THEY DECIDED TO HIDE THE LOOT AND RETURN TOGETHER WITH ADEQUATE CART TO LUG THEIR ORE OFF THE HILL.
HOWEVER, ONE OF THEM BROTHERS GOT PARANOID THAT THEY DID A POOR JOB OF CONCEALING THE LOOT.

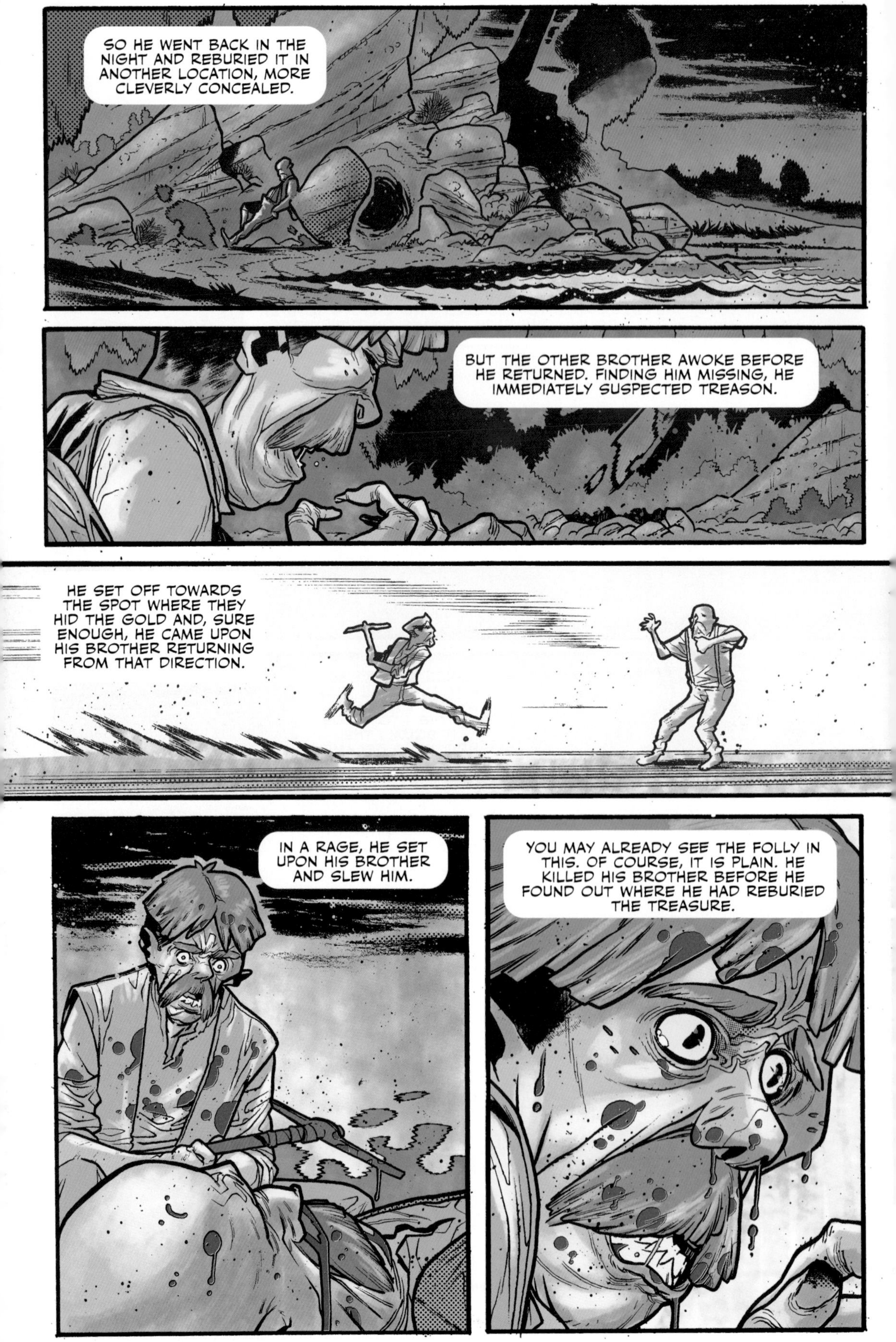
SO HE WENT BACK IN THE NIGHT AND REBURIED IT IN ANOTHER LOCATION, MORE CLEVERLY CONCEALED.
BUT THE OTHER BROTHER AWOKE BEFORE HE RETURNED. FINDING HIM MISSING, HE IMMEDIATELY SUSPECTED TREASON.
HE SET OFF TOWARDS THE SPOT WHERE THEY HID THE GOLD AND, SURE ENOUGH, HE CAME UPON HIS BROTHER RETURNING FROM THAT DIRECTION.
IN A RAGE, HE SET UPON HIS BROTHER AND SLEW HIM.
YOU MAY ALREADY SEE THE FOLLY IN THIS. OF COURSE, IT IS PLAIN. HE KILLED HIS BROTHER BEFORE HE FOUND OUT WHERE HE HAD REBURIED THE TREASURE.

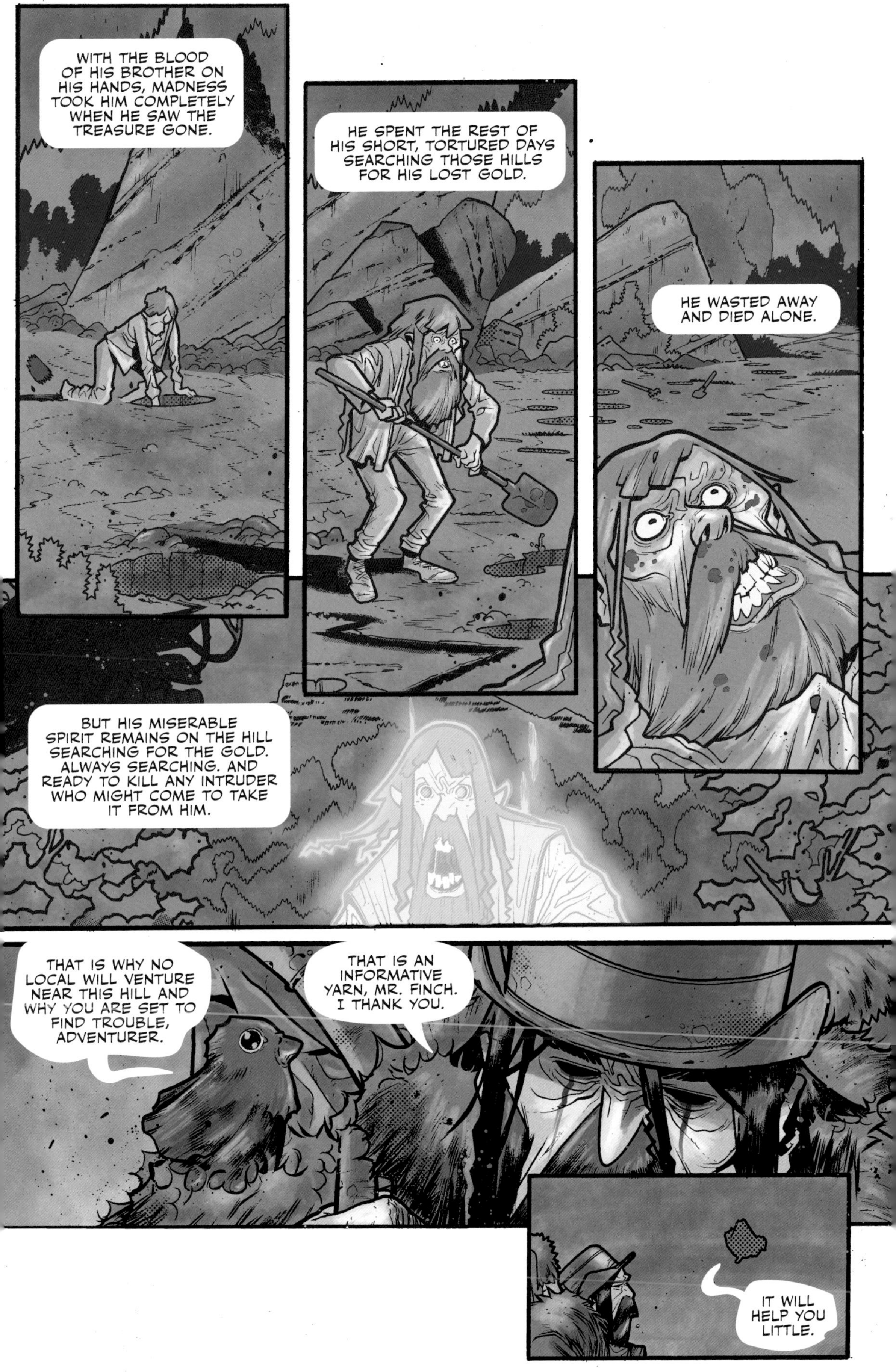
WITH THE BLOOD OF HIS BROTHER ON HIS HANDS, MADNESS TOOK HIM COMPLETELY WHEN HE SAW THE TREASURE GONE.
HE SPENT THE REST OF HIS SHORT, TORTURED DAYS SEARCHING THOSE HILLS FOR HIS LOST GOLD.
HE WASTED AWAY AND DIED ALONE.
BUT HIS MISERABLE SPIRIT REMAINS ON THE HILL SEARCHING FOR THE GOLD. ALWAYS SEARCHING. AND READY TO KILL ANY INTRUDER WHO MIGHT COME TO TAKE IT FROM HIM.
THAT IS WHY NO LOCAL WILL VENTURE NEAR THIS HILL AND WHY YOU ARE SET TO FIND TROUBLE, ADVENTURER.
THAT IS AN INFORMATIVE YARN, MR. FINCH. I THANK YOU.
IT WILL HELP YOU LITTLE.

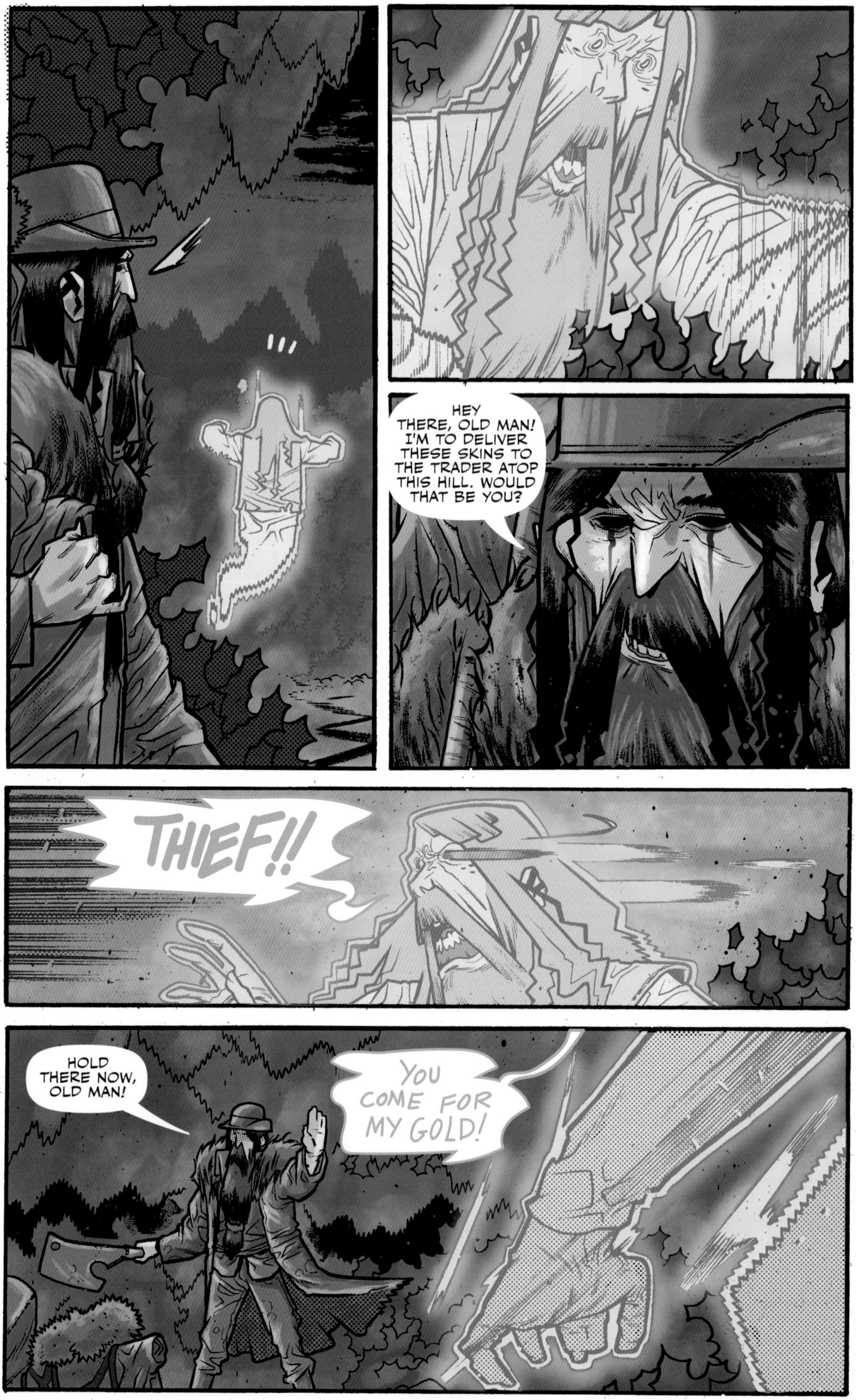
!!!
HEY THERE, OLD MAN! I'M TO DELIVER THESE SKINS TO THE TRADER ATOP THIS HILL. WOULD THAT BE YOU?
THIEF!!
HOLD THERE NOW, OLD MAN!
YOU COME FOR MY GOLD!

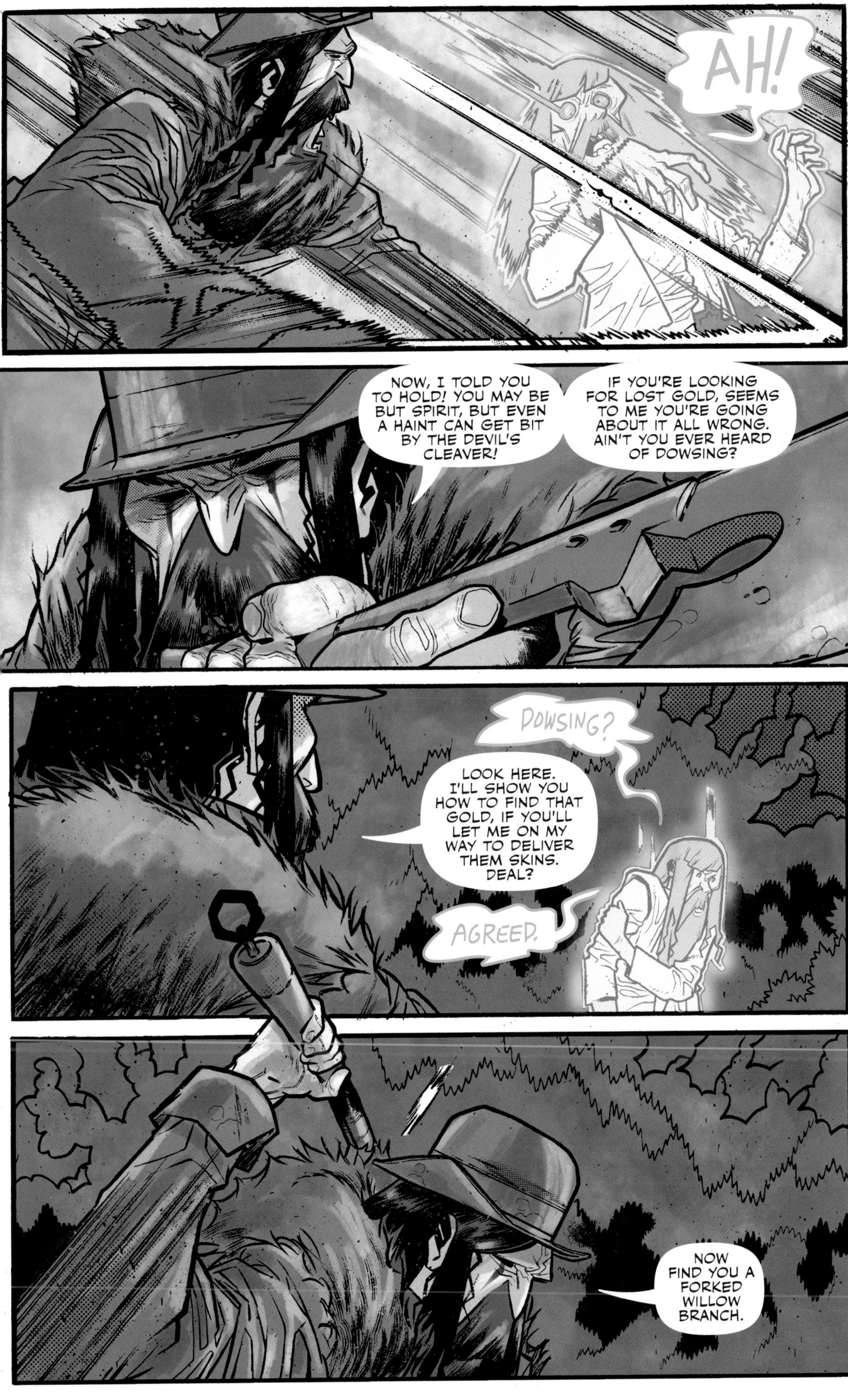
AH!
NOW, I TOLD YOU TO HOLD! YOU MAY BE BUT SPIRIT, BUT EVEN A HAINT CAN GET BIT BY THE DEVIL'S CLEAVER!
IF YOU'RE LOOKING FOR LOST GOLD, SEEMS TO ME YOU'RE GOING ABOUT IT ALL WRONG. AIN'T YOU EVER HEARD OF DOWSING?
DOWSING?
LOOK HERE. I'LL SHOW YOU HOW TO FIND THAT GOLD, IF YOU'LL LET ME ON MY WAY TO DELIVER THEM SKINS. DEAL?
AGREED.
NOW FIND YOU A FORKED WILLOW BRANCH.

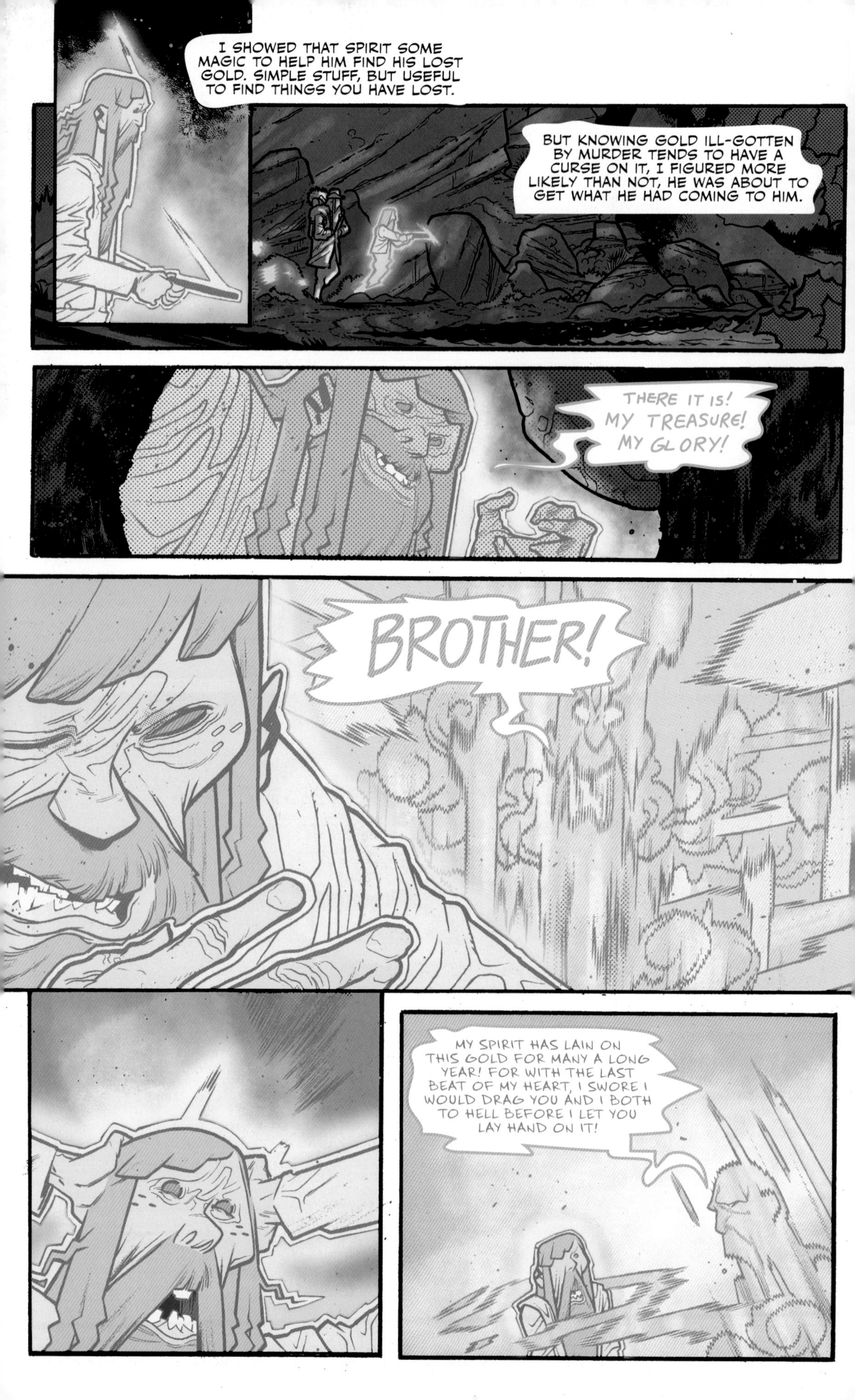
I SHOWED THAT SPIRIT SOME MAGIC TO HELP HIM FIND HIS LOST GOLD. SIMPLE STUFF, BUT USEFUL TO FIND THINGS YOU HAVE LOST.
BUT KNOWING GOLD ILL-GOTTEN BY MURDER TENDS TO HAVE A CURSE ON IT, I FIGURED MORE LIKELY THAN NOT, HE WAS ABOUT TO GET WHAT HE HAD COMING TO HIM.
THERE IT IS! MY TREASURE! MY GLORY!
BROTHER!
MY SPIRIT HAS LAIN ON THIS GOLD FOR MANY A LONG YEAR! FOR WITH THE LAST BEAT OF MY HEART, I SWORE I WOULD DRAG YOU AND I BOTH TO HELL BEFORE I LET YOU LAY HAND ON IT!

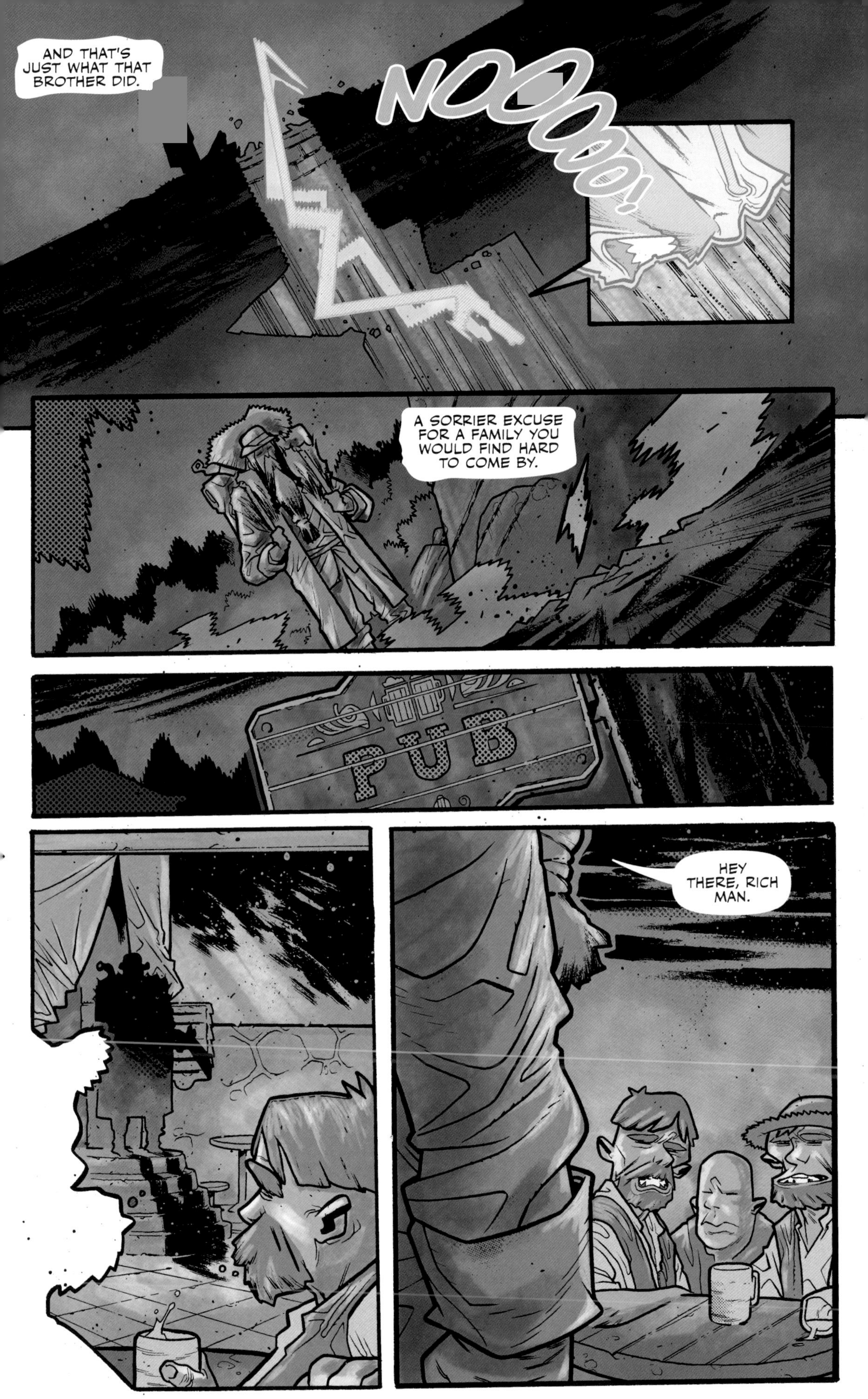
AND THAT'S JUST WHAT THAT BROTHER DID.
NOOOOOO!
A SORRIER EXCUSE FOR A FAMILY YOU WOULD FIND HARD TO COME BY.
PUB
HEY THERE, RICH MAN.

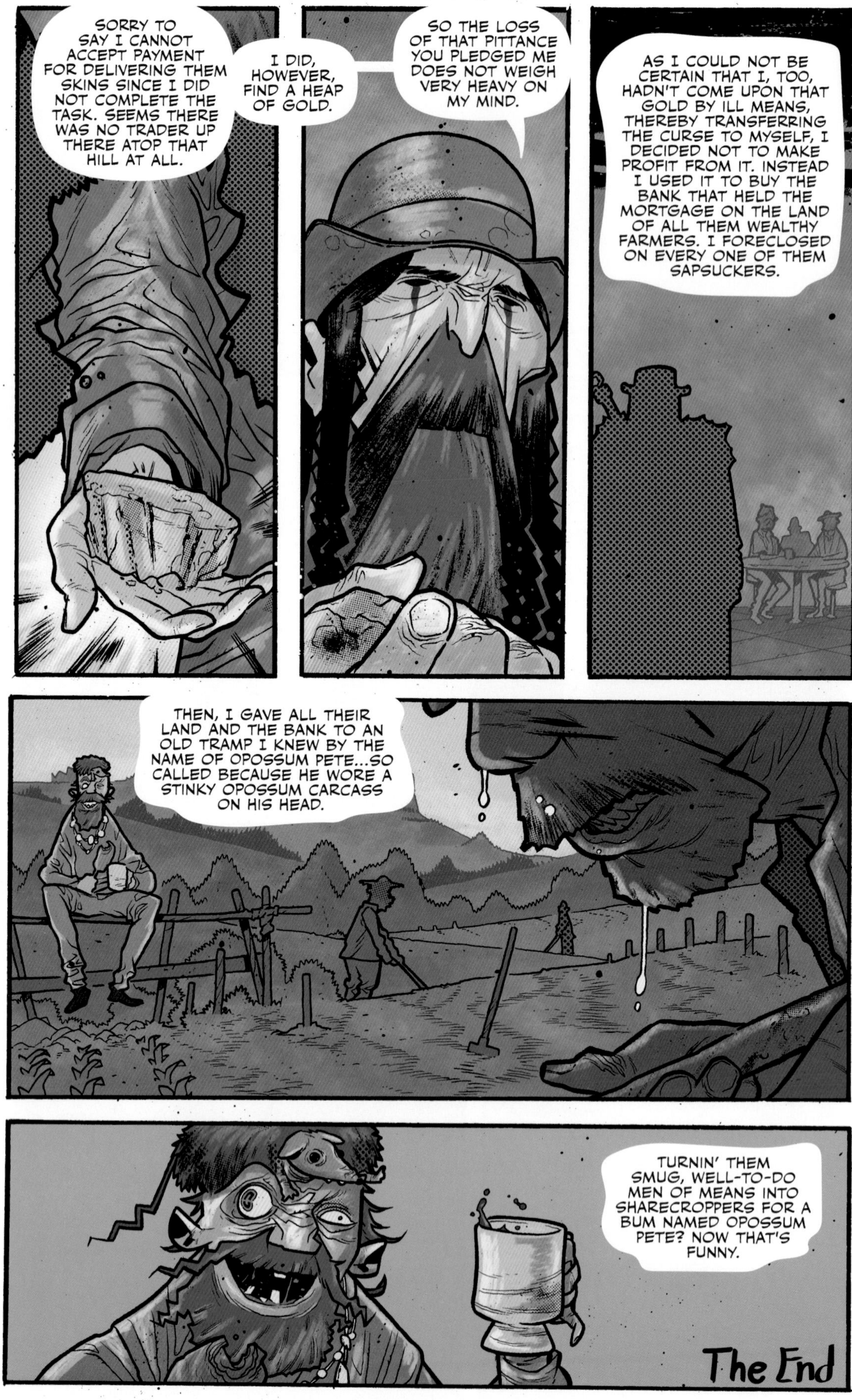
SORRY TO SAY I CANNOT ACCEPT PAYMENT FOR DELIVERING THEM SKINS SINCE I DID NOT COMPLETE THE TASK. SEEMS THERE WAS NO TRADER UP THERE ATOP THAT HILL AT ALL.
I DID, HOWEVER, FIND A HEAP OF GOLD.
SO THE LOSS OF THAT PITTANCE YOU PLEDGED ME DOES NOT WEIGH VERY HEAVY ON MY MIND.
AS I COULD NOT BE CERTAIN THAT I, TOO, HADN'T COME UPON THAT GOLD BY ILL MEANS, THEREBY TRANSFERRING THE CURSE TO MYSELF, I DECIDED NOT TO MAKE PROFIT FROM IT. INSTEAD I USED IT TO BUY THE BANK THAT HELD THE MORTGAGE ON THE LAND OF ALL THEM WEALTHY FARMERS. I FORECLOSED ON EVERY ONE OF THEM SAPSUCKERS.
THEN, I GAVE ALL THEIR LAND AND THE BANK TO AN OLD TRAMP I KNEW BY THE NAME OF OPOSSUM PETE...SO CALLED BECAUSE HE WORE A STINKY OPOSSUM CARCASS ON HIS HEAD.
TURNIN' THEM SMUG, WELL-TO-DO MEN OF MEANS INTO SHARECROPPERS FOR A BUM NAMED OPOSSUM PETE? NOW THAT'S FUNNY.
The End

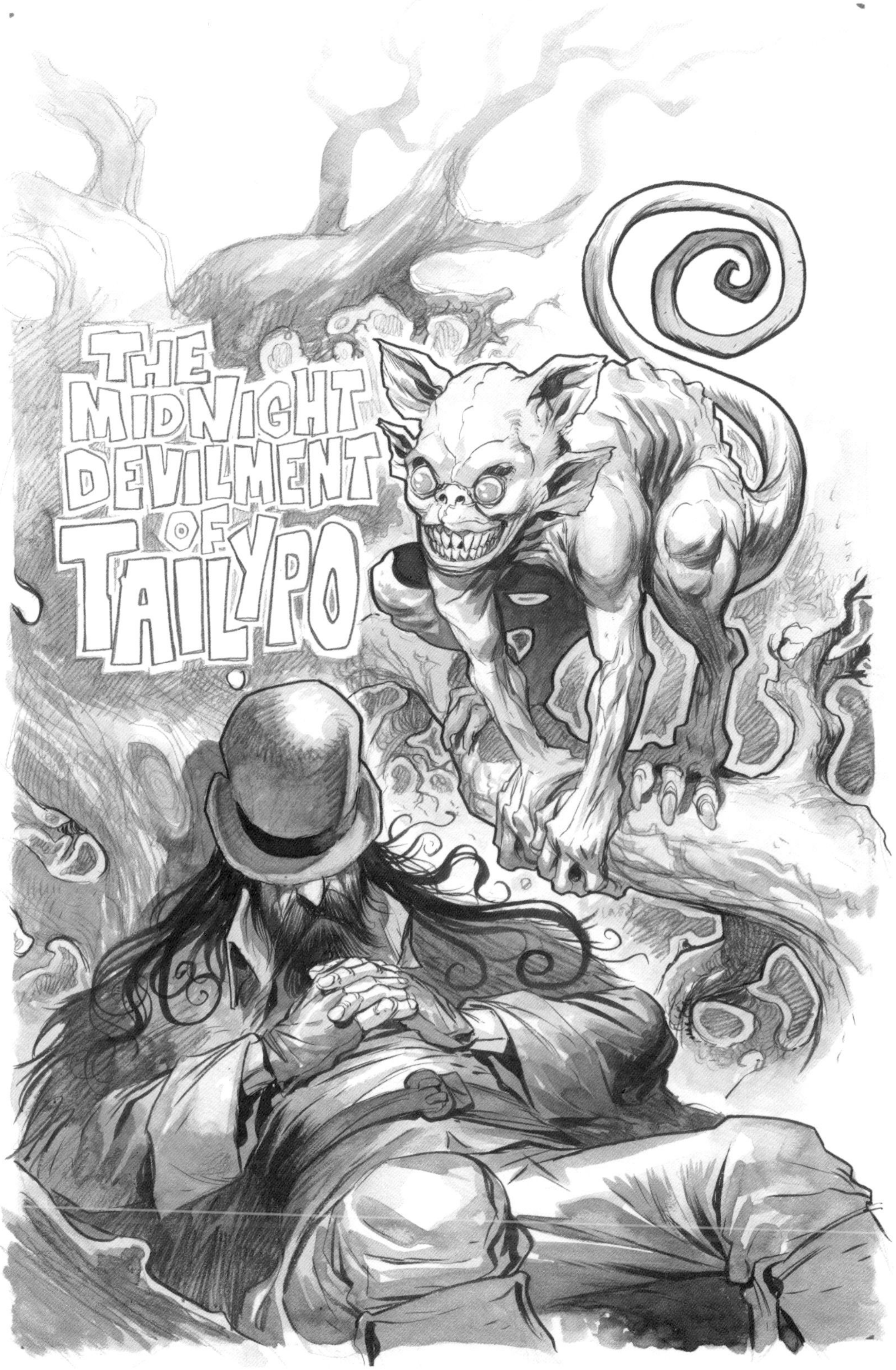
THE
MIDNIGHT
DEVILMENT
OF
TAILYPO

SKETCHBOOK
GALLERY

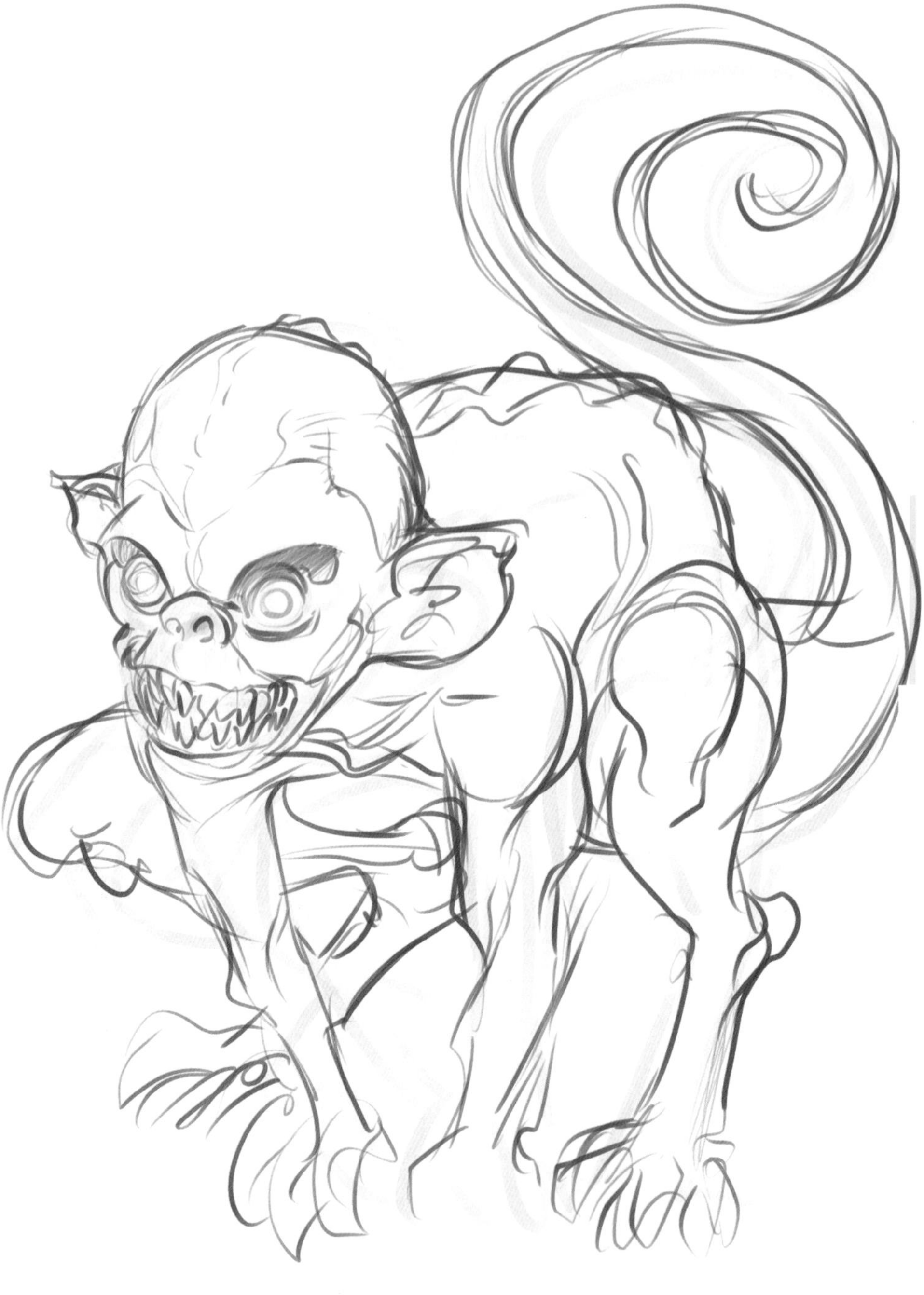

Tailypo is the only character in Hillbilly that comes from an actual Appalachian folktale. I first heard the story of the vengeful monster that loses its tail when I was 9 or 10. As with all things that truly creep you out, it stuck with me over the years. So obviously, when I went to make my overly Southern fantasy mythology, I felt I had to add my own version of Tailypo. He will play a role in the next story ırc for sure.

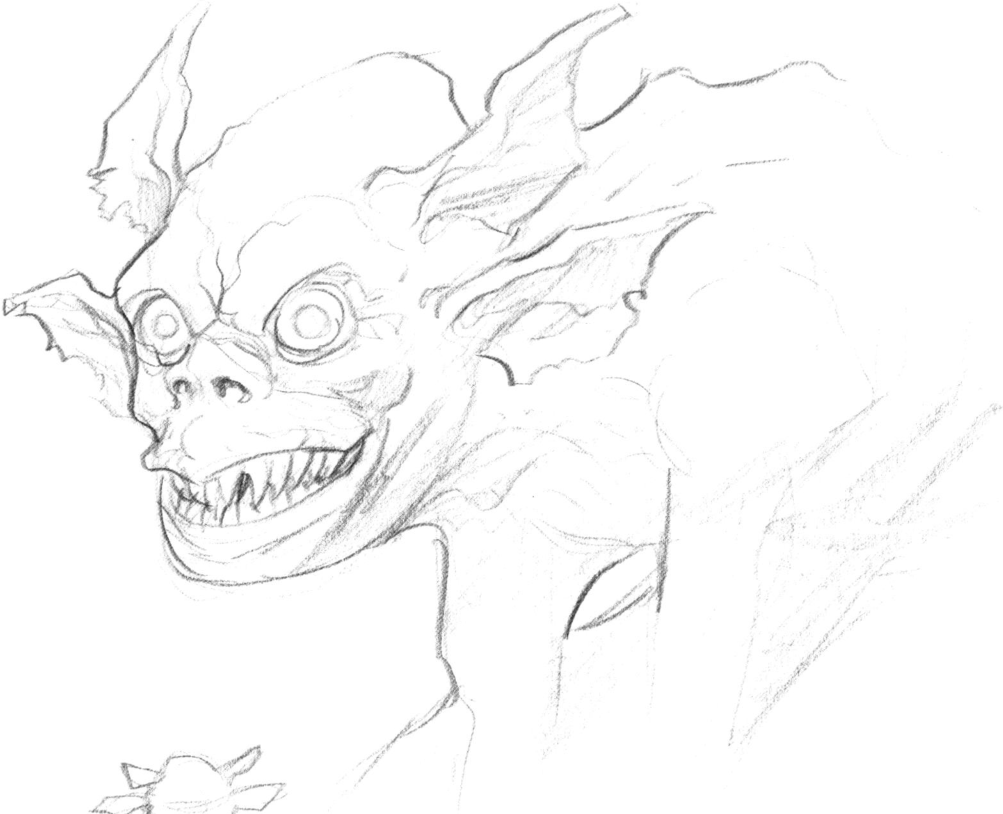

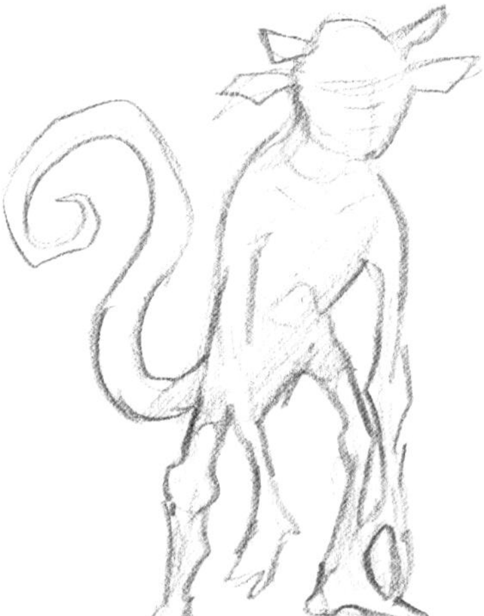

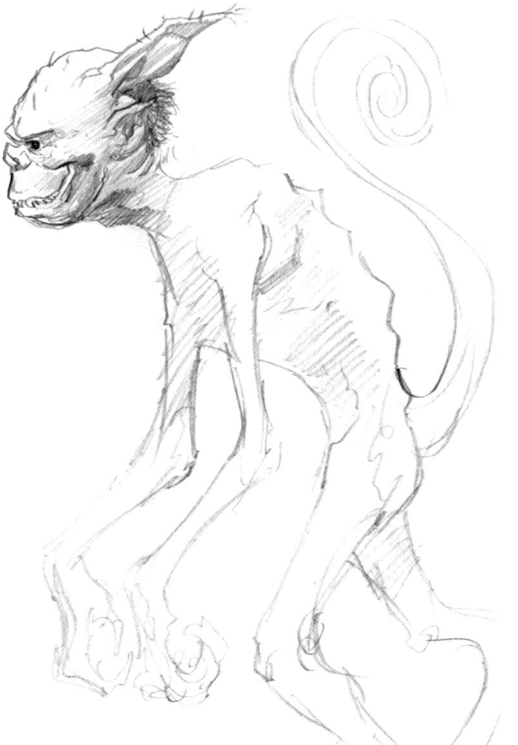

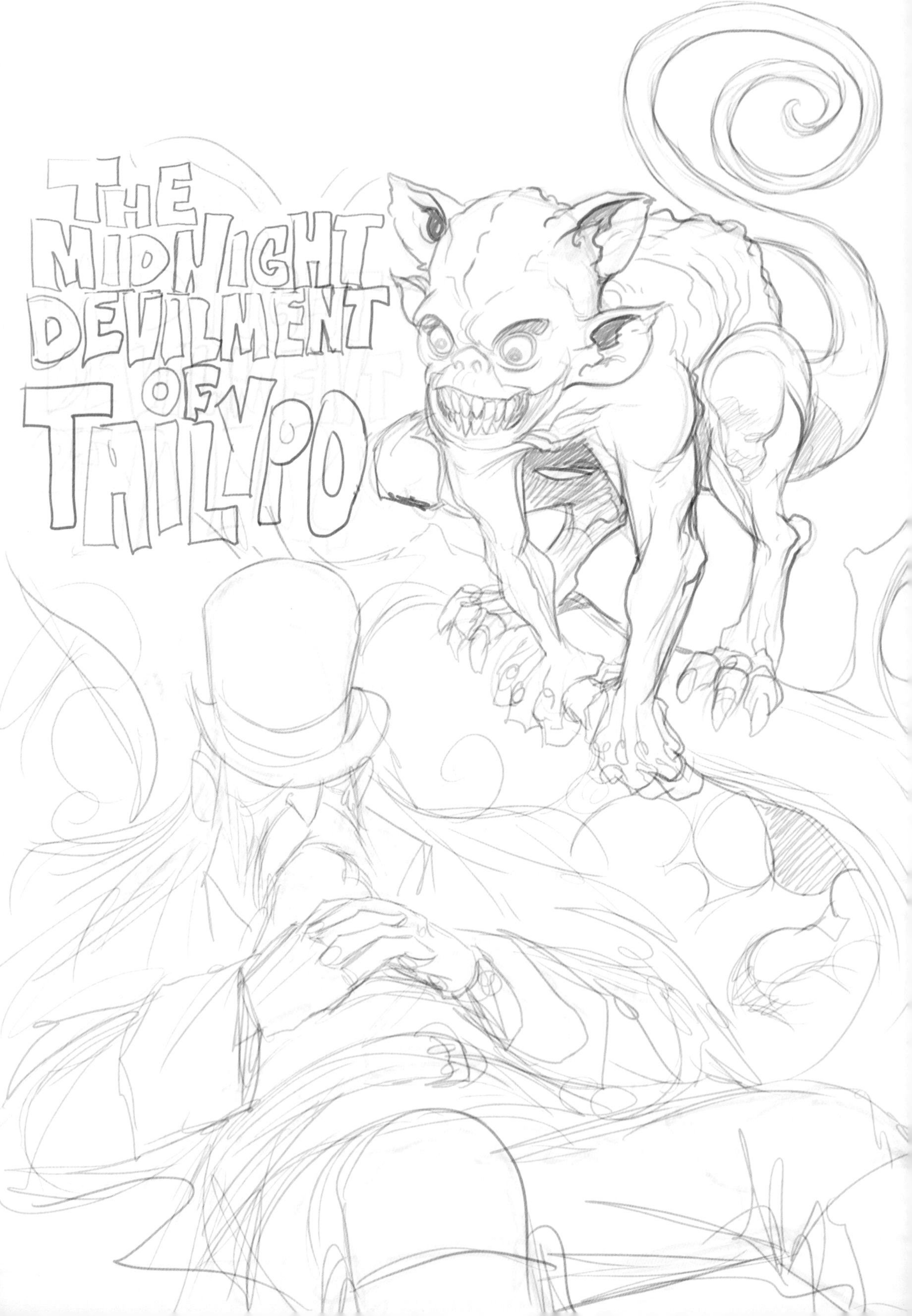
THE
MIDNIGHT
DEVILMENT
OF
TAILYPO

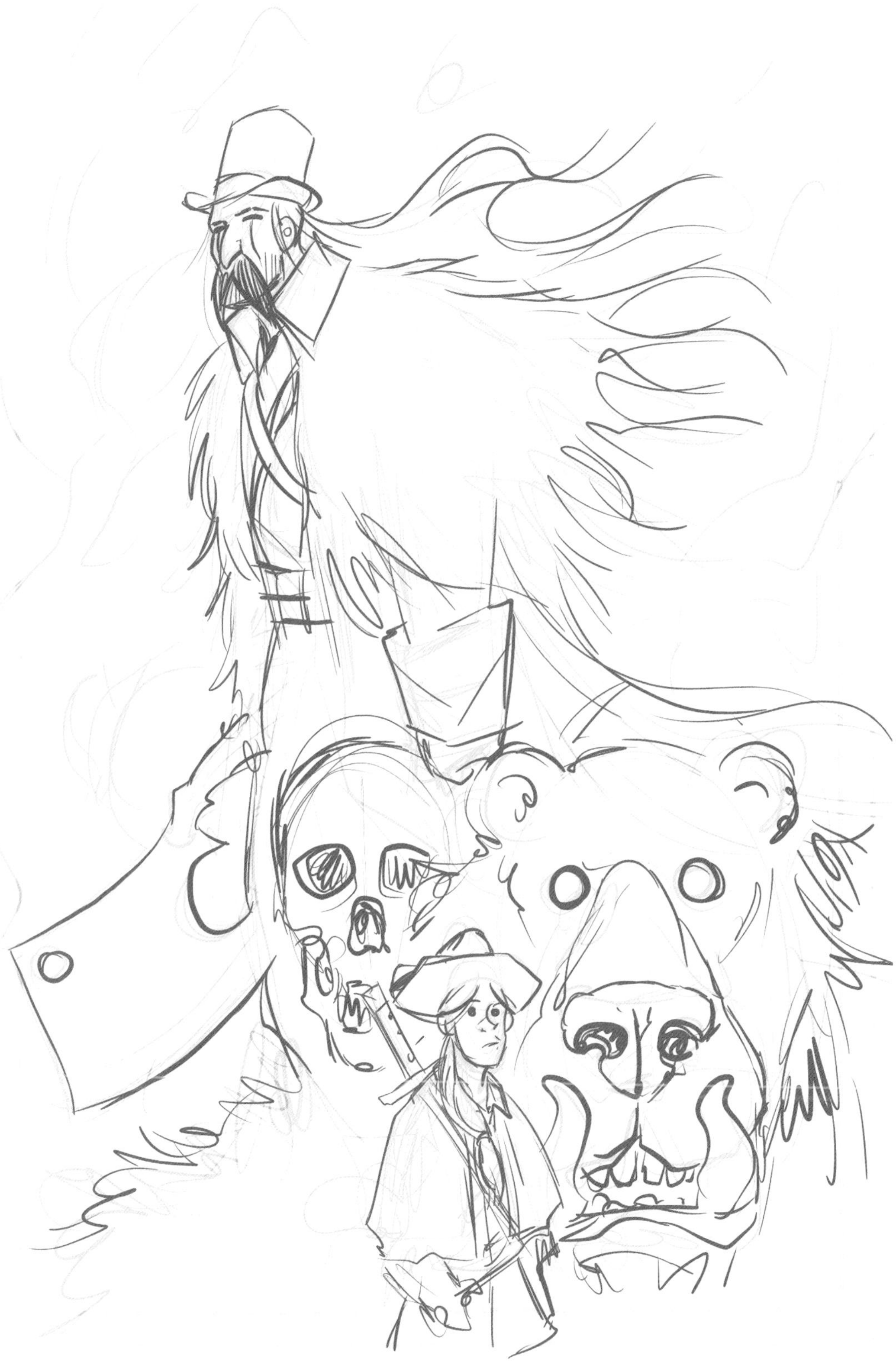

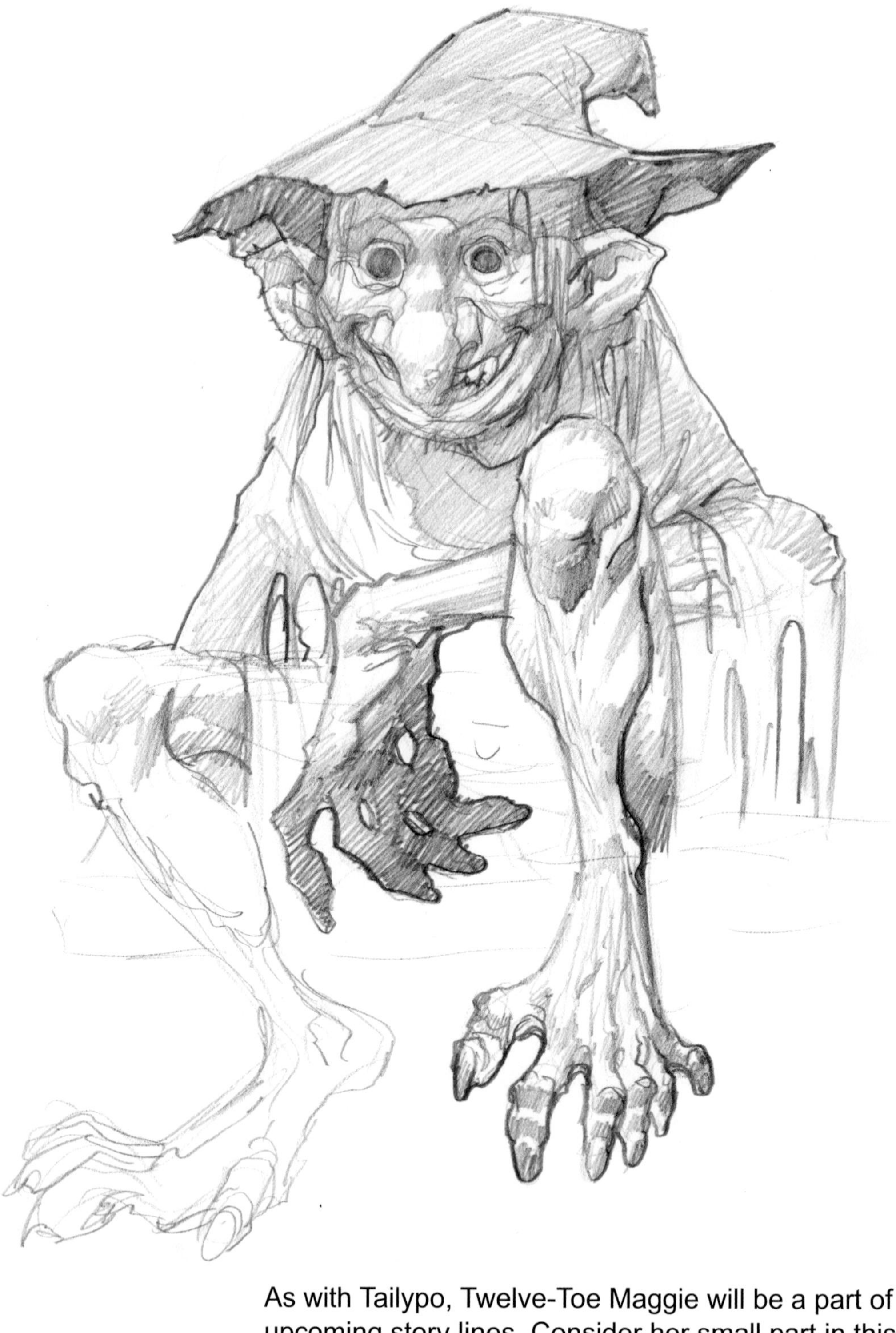

As with Tailypo, Twelve-Toe Maggie will be a part of upcoming story lines. Consider her small part in this collection as an introduction.

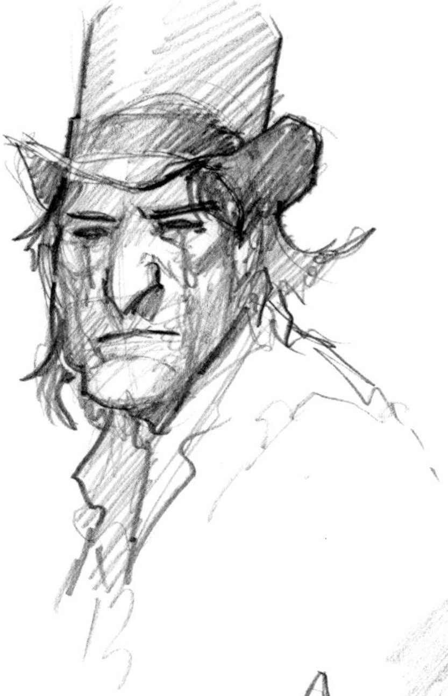

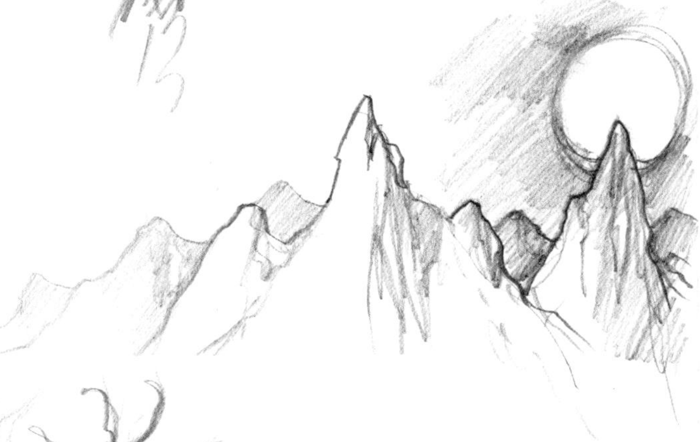

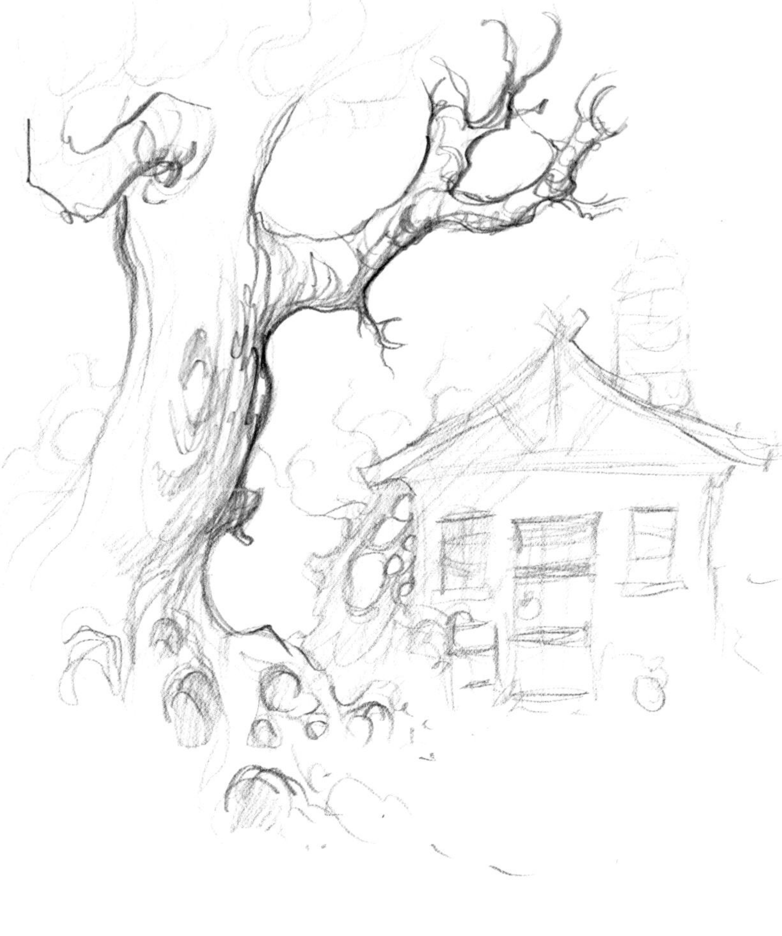

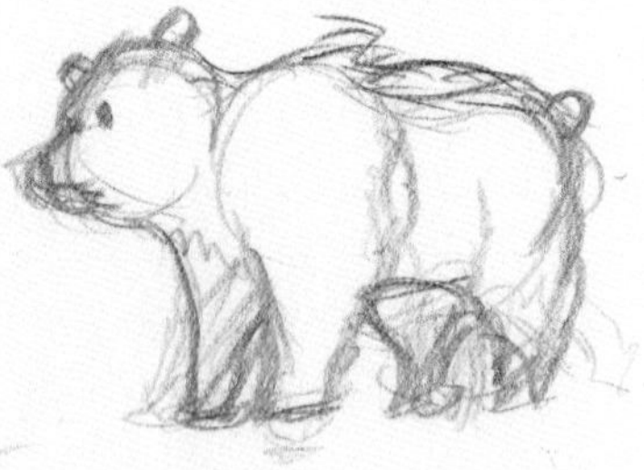

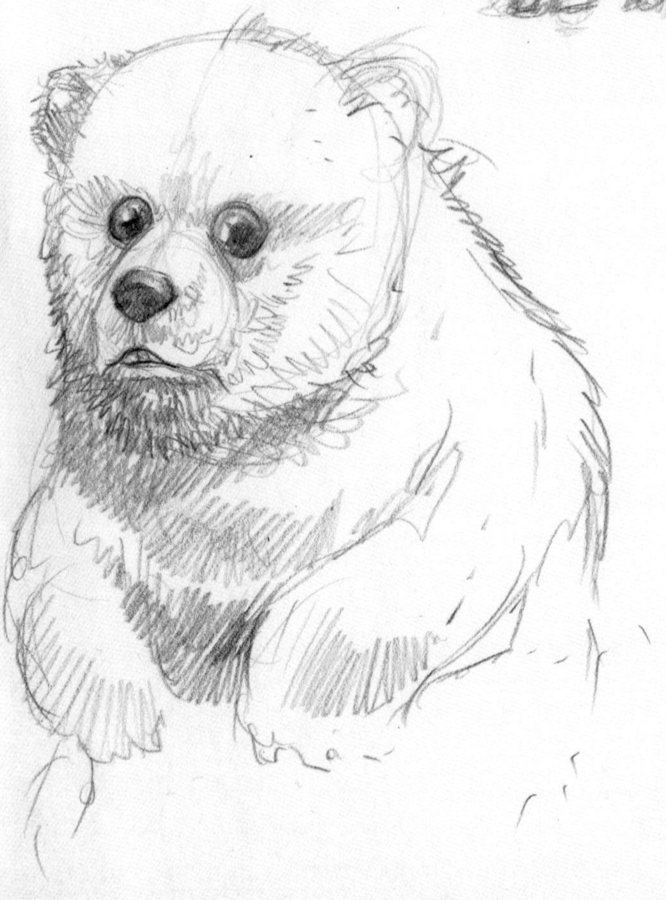

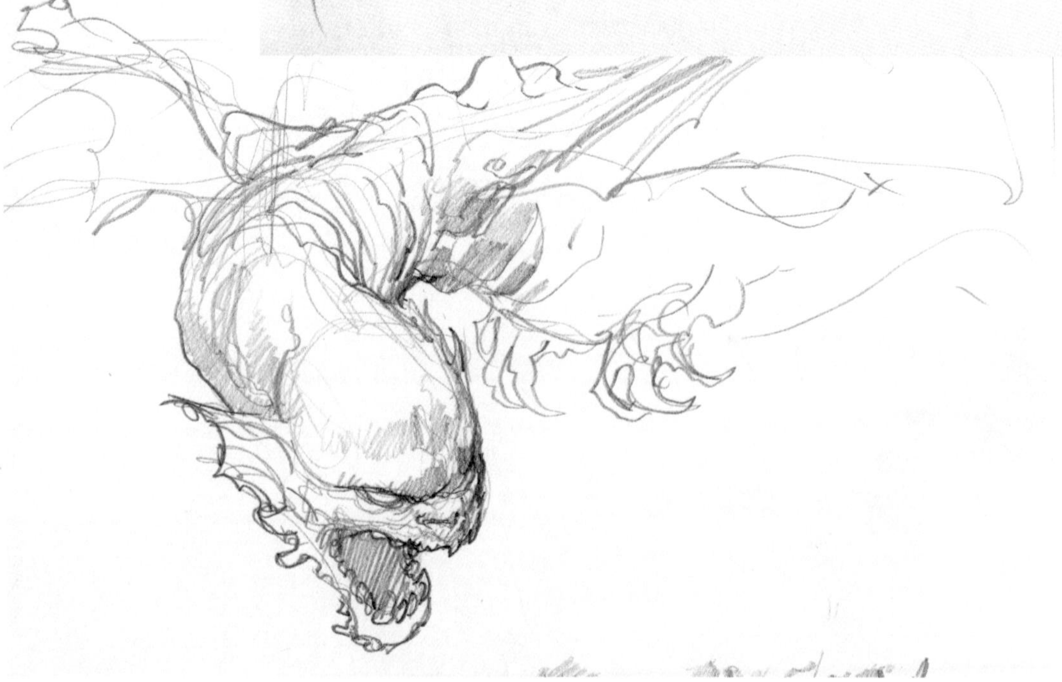

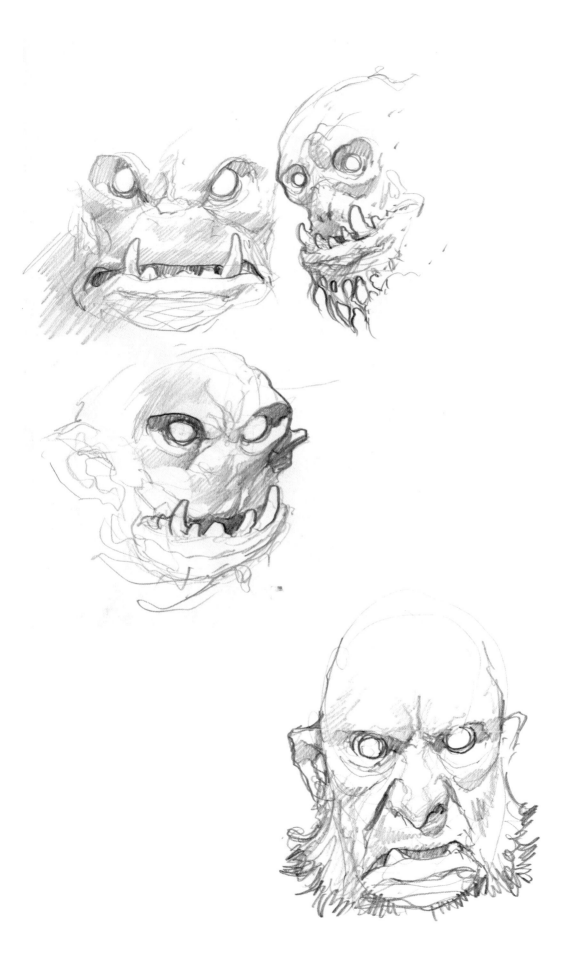

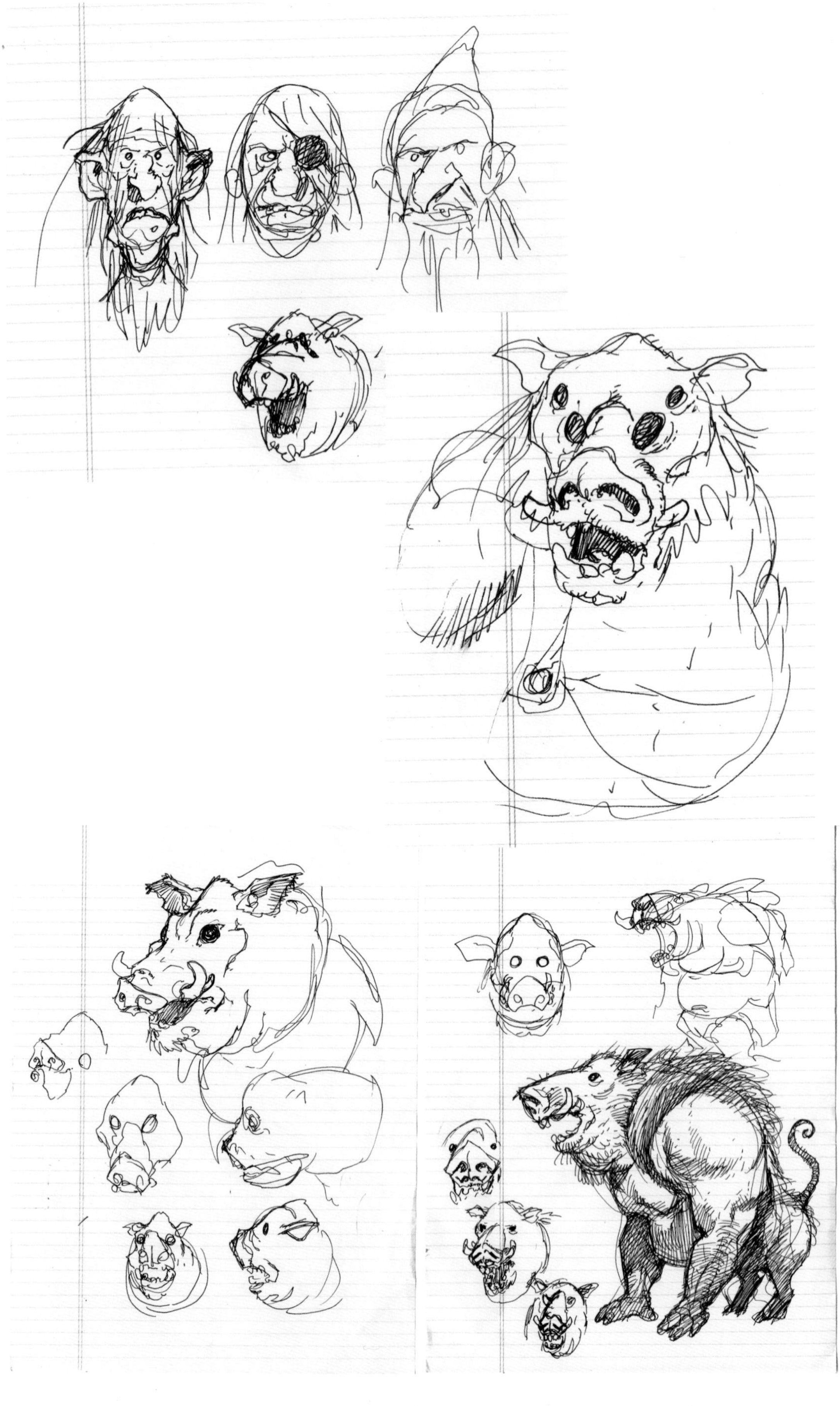